Market Shark

How to be a Big Fish in a Small Pond

Christopher V. Flett

Norsemen Books

Norsemen Books and Ghost CEO™ are registered trademarks

Market Shark, How to be a Big Fish in a Small Pond are registered trademarks of Flett Ventures Inc.

Flett, Christopher V., 1974–
What Men Don't Tell Women About Business, Opening up the Heavily Guarded Alpha Male Playbook (Wiley & Sons).

Also issued in electronic format
ISBN 978–0–9937968–0–7

1.Success in business. 2. Entrepreneurship. 3. Marketing. 4. Sales. 5. Flett, Christopher V. 1974–

Printed and bound in the USA.
Published by Norsemen Books

www.GhostCEO.com

*ATTENTION CORPORATIONS, UNIVERSITIES, COLLEGES, AND PROFESSIONAL ORGANIZATIONS: Quantity discounts are available on bulk purchases of this book for educational, gift purposes, or as premiums for increasing memberships. Special book covers or book excerpts can be created to fit specific needs. For more information, please contact Norsemen Books: info@norsemenbooks.com or 1–206–734–4950

Dedication

In memory of my father H. Vern Flett. From an early age, he instilled in me that if you want to be the leader, you had to step into the position with intention. "You get to write your own story so make it a good one."

And to my children, William and Julia. May you find your own path that is filled with happiness, abundance, and fulfillment.

Introduction

Like many of my readers, I grew up in a small town. Kamloops, B.C, also known as the "Tournament Capital of Canada" (though no one knows why we are known for this, as we never competed for this title) is three hours north of Vancouver. Its previous notoriety came from being where the 'toothbrush' was invented. Had it been invented anywhere else, it would have been called the 'teethbrush' for obvious reasons. The biggest challenge of daily life was ensuring your weren't accidentally dating a cousin, which can have devastating effects on the gene pool. If you have ever been to Arkansas, you know what I mean. Growing up in a town dependent on a paper and pulp mill puts things into perspective. You can work hard in school, get a scholarship (or at least accepted to a university) and get out of town. Second choice is to get a union job at the mill or the mine and fill up your drive way with big 4x4s, snow mobiles (aka 'sleds'), and party every weekend like it's 1999 (remembering the previous comment about tongue kissing cousins). The last and final spot is to find yourself in a mediocre, go nowhere job, praying for a quick death and using both alcohol and the affections of your first cousins (previous rules thrown out the window) to pass the time.

Like my mother and her mother before her, I was born in New Glasgow, Nova Scotia, which holds the title in both 2011 and 2012 as the worst place to live in Canada (Money Sense Magazine). Keep in mind that a big chunk of Canada is Arctic Tundra. It is better to live somewhere you have a good chance of being molested by a horny moose, than in my hometown. My father, from Fort Vermillion, Alberta (an area also well known for cousin marrying) was working on the East Coast, met my mom, had me, and like the Clampetts, moved us west to find fame and fortune. After a decade together, my parents split and I found myself living in Kamloops, B.C. with my mother in a shitty little apartment in the shittiest part of town, stealing cable from the neighbours. The reason I tell you this is not to get you thinking about marrying a cousin (no matter how attractive they are), but rather to illustrate this point: I came from not much, lived in places that might make better penal colonies, and didn't get any 'advantages' through upbringing, other than the fact my parents were smart and could hustle. My mom would drill into me that: I MUST get good grades. I MUST go to college. I MUST strive to make something of myself. And I MUST not be satisfied with being a 'big fish in this small pond'.

Ultimately, she got it wrong. In her desire for me to have a life bigger than hers, she thought that I had to do things on a massive scale, but actually, you have to do important things in smaller, controllable environments. The quickest way to success is to be a big fish in a small pond, not a small fish in a big pond. There are loads of those people; in fact, the word is made up of them. Talk to those of the business elite and you will find out that a majority of them made their money in niche markets with targeted offerings. The problem is we see all the people on television that own airlines, and hockey teams, and have television shows, but when you start to drill down, those that are the most successful did something unique, for a niche market, and owned it. Only later did the reputation of these successes catapult them into the mainstream of business consciousness.

When I ask clients, "Do you want to be rich or do you want to be famous?" about 80% say famous and only 20% say rich. This is disappointing on a variety of levels because our society puts more value on people on television than people of service. Those that want to be rich will not become rich by stretching their resources so thin in an attempt to serve every market. Instead, they target a handful of niche markets and OWN them. I meet mega million dollar entrepreneurs every day. They are not like Donald Trump or the Koch Brothers. They are like you and me. They might specialise in emerging technologies for assisted-living homes, or specialise in selling and installing carpet into hotels, or they have a company that does property management for owners who rent out their ski chalets. Nothing that is going to necessarily blow your skirt up, but they have a niche offering and they OWN it. Every bit of business that comes into that market is theirs to lose, not to win. This book is the tour guide to becoming a Market Shark. The top of the food chain in niche markets where your most valuable clients live. Becoming a Market Shark is a process with which you can determine the markets you want to own, ascend to the position of 'top choice' in that niche, and take the requisite steps to keep your position and profitability in check. I have (and continue) to make a lot of money focusing on niche markets, where we are the unique offering to that market and everything in that market (which we refer to as a 'pond') comes directly to us without any competition.

A client once compared being a Market Shark to being Mafia. She said that the Mafia used to control particular businesses in particular neighbourhoods in Chicago without any competition. They profited enormously and the people that bought from them (or through them) were happy to do so. While I do not agree with the illegal points (or the cement shoes), I do see a resemblance in the models and will happily participate in the best practices of seeing an opportunity, getting in the position to manage it, and making for an environment where competitors realise there is 'easier business to get elsewhere'. If you have ever struggled in building your business model and are not sure how to be 'different' from everyone else, this is the book you have been waiting for. Every one of our Ghost CEO™ business coaches use these tools and all of our clients do as well. It makes business happen quicker, it is easier to focus on what is going to make the most revenue for you, and allows you to avoid the competitive nature of business and only compete with yourself. This is not a book meant to be read once and shelved. It deserves a spot on your desk, to be nearby when you have a question, are feeling stuck, or need reinforcement that you are doing the work required to own your markets. If you find yourself lost or losing market position, come back to the book and look for what you have not been doing consistently, or what you have failed to do. You can quickly implement the strategies and reaffirm your position in your markets. Do not deceive yourself; the Market Shark is the Honey Badger[1] of business. Anyone can do it, but attitude plays a role in whether you can sustain it. The Market Shark, like the Honey Badger, doesn't take shit from anyone. They do what they say and say what they do. They know that it takes work to become a Market Shark, but once they are there, they reap all the spoils of that work.

There are much harder things to do than becoming a Market Shark, namely:

-   Marrying your cousin, having children, and explaining the teeth.

-   Working in a mine and having the "Black Lung."

-   Trying to compete in a heavily competitive market where all your time is spent trying to be (insert adjective), hip, cool, affordable, new, etc.

-   Going to a college named after something that looks like a deer, and is best known for butchery and animal husbandry.

-   Being born in New Glasgow (**Go Bluenosers!**).

-   And most importantly. Living a beige life of being a small fish in a big pond where you and your work do not matter, will not matter, and will not be remembered after you are gone.

---

[1] Do yourself a favour and look up Honey Badger on YouTube. You will quickly see why this must be your mascot when facing adversity.

If you are not burdened by any of the challenges listed above, you are already better positioned than most to be very successful with this content. Practise makes perfect so get reading, make notes on things to come back to (or dog ear the pages, highlight, post it, or the like), and start implementing. The book is written in a sequential fashion so that you can read and implement as you go.

Because small ponds are, well, small, you need to have a handful of them to start. Don't put your eggs all in one basket. Rather than trying to hunt in one big pond and put 100 percent of your time into that, it would be best to target 6, 7, or 8 smaller ponds, get known by them, and be the only vendor in the game. In the bigger ponds, every project is an all or nothing. In the smaller ponds, some will move fast, some will move at a moderate speed, and some will move slowly. It is irrelevant to you because you will be nudging all of them ahead. So the small ones give you immediate cash flow, the medium will give you cash flow down the road, and the long-term plays will take a little more time, but you will still be getting paid.

Building efficiently around this process is focused on getting clear on the system by which you will engage these markets. First, you have to be very clear on what you are offering is to them, how you've customised it specifically for them, and how it will be different from other offerings made by competitors. Against local competition, you are outside expertise. Against larger talent, you are offering a more intimate service. For established competition, you are looking at things in a fresh way. For fresh competitors moving into your market, you are established and have a proven track record. You need to know how you position against everyone else who is, or could be fishing in your ponds.

Because these small ponds are relationship focused, don't rush them. Some people build trust and intimacy quickly but for others it will take time. Some clients are ready to go on the first meeting; others need days, weeks, or even months to trust you. These are the three simple steps we outline heavily in this book: they need to know you, they need to trust, and then they will buy from you.

Once you have systematised your approach on creating relationships by adding value, the rest is just time and attention. When you have this dialled this in correctly, then you can duplicate this system repeatedly and will find your sales cycle shrinking in time. Never be so stuck in your ways that you don't do an adjustment if it is required, but ninety-five percent of your market can be engaged in a similar manner, will follow the same process, and you will get the same type of results from them.

Finally, take the relationship to a slightly deeper level than you might otherwise. In broad markets it is simply a numbers game. You just serve more and more people and there are always more coming behind. In smaller ponds you are required to get to know people on a slightly deeper level. Befriend them. Find out about their lives. Find out about why they do what they do. Above all else, listen. More often than not your markets will tell you what the problem is and what they want the solution to be. Your job, as difficult or simple as it is, is to bridge that gap. Your ability to bridge that gap is the solution that you are selling. Business is not personal, it's transactional, but it is built on personal relationships. Never lose sight of that.

Not sure if you want to be a Market Shark? That's a trick question. Of course you want to be a Market Shark. It's like asking someone if they want bacon on something. If they don't, they are likely evil and you should run away. You picked up this book because somewhere deep inside you know that you can be of a higher value to the markets you serve and create deeper value in your business model by focusing your attention on markets that you can manage. Of course, you get all the benefits – you get the fortune, you get the reputation, and you get to see your work make a difference – but on top of that you can build a sustainable business model that can be grown over time through your efforts and through the conversations those markets have with others. Market Sharks have markets that build themselves for the Shark. You get rewarded from your hard work by spending your time doing things that matter, not competing with those who only want to compete on price. Ask any service provider in a highly competitive market what their Number One Pain is and they'll tell you it is differentiating himself or herself from everyone else in the market. Most businesses can't clearly define what they do so it ends up always coming down to price. Until reputation, it is always a price play. If you're not the lowest price, you don't get the work. Luckily for you, in this book, we also go over the missing differentiation tool that most professionals are missing.

When I bring up the concept of Market Sharks, people often say, "Oooh, sharks. Gee, sharks just go around and kill things." That's not true. Sharks are misunderstood. Yes, they have big teeth and they can be a bit scary but they do what comes naturally. In this book, we will explore some of misconceptions of sharks as a teaching aid.

Somewhere in our psyche we have categorised sharks as monsters. Truthfully, sharks are at the top of the food chain because they are efficient, they conduct themselves with intention, and there is a grace to what they do. It may be difficult to get agreement on this from seals and other munchables in the food chain, but sharks don't start their day looking to make things bad for anyone else. They're simply doing what comes naturally. For Market Sharks, developing profitable niche markets is a natural habit.

My intention with this book is to help you to develop ponds of business and to become the Market Shark in those ponds. Market Sharks don't attack anyone. In their role at the top of the food chain in that pond, Market Sharks get to enjoy a relatively peaceful, benevolent existence.

As we move forward, remember that not all small ponds are small in a geographical sense or from a population standpoint. They are small in the number of people servicing them. I remember when Ghost CEO™ started offering business coaching to professional women in 1999 we were the only ones doing it in the North American market. Now, in 2014, there are dozens of other companies and practitioners but we get to hold the Market Shark position because of years of service, our established track record, and the loyalty of our female clients. We continue to be rewarded because we started servicing a focused female clientele a decade before other companies thought that this market had any value.

Go forward fellow Market Sharks and own the ponds of your choosing. Doing so will deliver you both riches and perhaps some notoriety, but most importantly, will ensure you do not become that suckerfish everyone has in their aquarium, the one that eats poo. That just is not right, and imagine trying to get that taste out of your mouth.

So let's dive into what it is going to take for you to swim upstream into your selected ponds and become the Market Shark that you were meant to be. Cue music from Jaws...

Best,

Chris.

Chapter 1: Market Shark Characteristics

When researching this book, I compiled an inventory of characteristics that seemed common among all Market Sharks in my networks. Then I contacted a diverse group of 40 Market Sharks I know around the globe, and asked them to grade their competency on each of these characteristics. Each individual shark scored high in every single characteristic. They weren't strong in one and weak in others. They were extremely strong in every one of them. Upon additional questioning, I discovered that each of them possessed some characteristics naturally, while others required "practise" with the help of professional development and mentorship from other Sharks. It's not uncommon for Market Sharks to have an inflated opinion of themselves; however, and under scrutiny and from mine and others' interactions with them, I was able to validate that they did possess all the characteristics required to be a true Market Shark.

You might be wondering, what are these characteristics? How many do I possess? Worry not. Through explanation and examples, we will cover each of the eight most prominent characteristics of Market Sharks in this and the following chapter. We will consider how a Market Shark 1) adapts and evolves, 2) is always moving, 3) is consistent, 4) is always hunting, 5) Bumps opportunities, 6) is smooth 7) acts big and 8) can smell "blood".

The common thread across all the characteristics was leadership. Each person in the Market Shark focus group completed this statement: "The Market Shark..." Of the 40 people interviewed, 39 answered the sentence with either: "leads," "is the leader," or "is in the front." The one black sheep answered, "is awesome" which tells us that Market Sharks don't suffer sensitive egos. Because leadership unifies the eight characteristics, we will side with the super majority and begin this chapter with leadership.

The Market Shark Leads

I do not believe in natural born leaders. Most of us might be prepared to lead and once we see the benefits of setting the course, we either stand in that spot, or step back and let someone else take responsibility. I clearly remember arriving home from soccer camp and telling my dad I was tired of the stupid games the other kids wanted to play. I asked for his advice on how I might be able to get them to change their minds and play the games that I thought would be more fun. My father suggested that if I didn't like what the kids were doing, I should step in and lead them to what I wanted them to do. I remember looking at him with confusion, unsure of how I could persuade these kids to make me the leader. I asked, "How am I supposed to get them to follow me?" to which he replied, "Most people are not interested in being a leader, and in fact, they will look around for others who might step up to lead them. In almost every case, to be a leader, all you need to do is assume leadership. More times than not, people will rally behind you as soon as you step forward." This seemed far–fetched to me, but I decided I'd give it a try. The next day at camp when the time came for free play, I said to everyone, "We're going to play 'Kick the Can' now." I didn't pose it as a question – "Can we play Kick the Can?" – And I did not seek consensus – "Would you like to play kick the can?" – I just simply stated that we were now going to begin playing "Kick the Can". To my surprise, all the kids got into a circle, we found the token 'can object' and I split the group up into equal players on each side. The whole time I was doing this, I was shocked that everyone was doing exactly what I instructed them to do. No push back, no complaining, no jockeying to have their game played instead of mine. From that moment on, all the other kids in my soccer camp looked to me to decide the games we were going to play. Talk about feeding the monster! Since then, anytime I have been a member of the group and unhappy with the direction that the group is going in, I simply assumed leadership. I have never had anyone challenge my authority on direction once I assume the leadership position.

The million-dollar question is··· are leadership skills naturally embedded in my DNA or did it take that one situation aided by the advice of my father to convince me of the powerful secret that nobody talks about? Is it possible that all you need to do to get your own way is to assume leadership? Answer: Yes, but you have to back it up.

I'm entering my twenty-fourth year of business and I'm a constant student of leadership. I go to seminars, attend workshops, and I read every book I can on leadership. I read the biographies of powerful business titans, I talk with peers about their methods and techniques of leading, and I think of myself as a repository of leadership information, both style and application. I want to share with you some of the best practices that seem consistent when tested against different cultures, different countries, and different personality types.

The fundamental component, common among all of these contexts, is that a leader must be both willing and able to lead. They must be willing to stand in the front and lead by example. They must also have the mechanics of leadership .This means that they can identify the objective, determine the steps required, complete those steps (or manage others doing so on their behalf), make corrections as required, and take total responsibility for the outcome. That last part is where I think most people feel discomfort in leading. They don't want to take complete responsibility over an outcome.

Leadership gets a bum rap when the person placed in a position of leadership does not possess the leadership fundamentals required to be successful. You either have someone technically sound who isn't interested in leading people (the reluctant leader) or the person that has to be the leader without the technical skills (the incompetent leader). One of the corporate world's favourite quotations is, "Managers get promoted to their highest level of incompetence." In my experience, that sure is true.

A true leader has both parts of the equation. They are technically sound and willing to stand in front and make decisions, knowing that the outcome sits squarely on their shoulders. The technical aspects of leadership can be learned, as can responsibility, but only if the student is willing.

Market Sharks tap into these leadership characteristics and assuming leadership roles becomes a self-fulfilling mandate: the more you lead, the better you get. The more tools, techniques, and skills you pick up as a leader, the more effective a leader you become. Time in the saddle is key for anyone who wants to be a leader, so the time to start leading is immediately.

When we combine leadership with the other characteristics we cover in this chapter, we will see a powerful toolkit start to emerge. Any one of these characteristics is strong on its own. When combined with any or all of the other characteristics they become truly powerful and a multiplier effect starts to take hold. Leaders invoke trust with those who follow them by being consistent, skilled, and dependable. All traits possessed by true Market Sharks.

In the coming pages, after the explanation of each characteristic, I've included questions you should ask yourself which will offer you time for reflection and self-assessment. You can determine how strong or weak the characteristic currently is and how you would like to build on it. I encourage you to write out the questions that you're working on and tape them somewhere where you can see them – maybe on your computer monitor, the mirror in your bathroom, or even on the dash of your car. Put them where you will see them so you are reminded regularly to ask yourself these questions. It might seem weird to do this, but trust me when I tell you it works.

To acquire a new habit, we have to be clear with the intention to practise is and commit to doing so for at least thirty days in a row. After thirty days, that habit should be in place and you can start to add additional habits (characteristics) to fill out your toolkit. Remember... stick with it! Everything worth learning will take time to understand the practice and the components that make up successful application. You have to use them to learn them, much like martial arts or the piano. Theory will only take you so far. These characteristics can be acquired and developed by anyone who commits to their practise and mastery only comes after much practise and application of the characteristics. These are the basic business mechanics; you need no prerequisite skills to become a skilled technician with every one of them. Are leaders born? Who cares? We can build leaders and today is your first day to tighten what will become an impressive leadership capability. Now for the characteristics that will change your business life forever.

The Market Shark Adapts and Evolves

The only thing that is consistent in business is that it changes regularly. Most professionals get into their profit model and then close their eyes, grip on tightly, and hope that everything turns out well. This is short-sighted because professionals who are aware of the shifting sands of markets tend to stay on top. Those who ignore market messages and put their heads in the sand, end up being buried and out of business. Companies that go out of business do so because they were unaware of changing market factors. It could be that they misread market indicators, but in my experience, they simply weren't looking. The ability to adapt and evolve is a cornerstone of having not only a profitable, but sustainable business model that you can count for years to come.

Adaptation and evolution are very tightly related. When you adapt, you find a new place in a changing model. Evolution will actually change you, the services you provide, and how you engage with an existing model. In business we are required to change when the market corrects (adaptation) or when we grow or are forced to grow (evolution).

The Ghost CEO™, which started in 1999, has gone through many adaptation and evolutions since we began. When I started Ghost CEO™ back in 2000, our focus was on offering business coaching to men and women looking to grow their business model. Every man that came in was at least twenty years my senior and would want to fight with me about the success I already had in business (talk about a shitty way to spend an hour). Then well-prepared women would arrive for the meeting with a list of questions and an hour spent coaching them felt like five minutes (an indicator that you are working with the right market). After a month of suffering from asshole-itis, the first evolution that I made in the business model of Ghost CEO™ happened. I made the conscious decision to stop working with men and to focus entirely on professional women. In hindsight, what a fantastic move, but at the time the decision was simple – to focus on working with a market that wanted support, and to stop working with the one that wanted to argue every point.

As the company grew, we continued to adapt our model to service different markets. Initially, we worked with professional women working in jobs but seeking career advancement. Then we moved into start-up entrepreneurs, while still servicing our professional clients. In 2006, we noted a trend of professional women leaving the workforce to have children and wanting to start entrepreneurial pursuits at home, so we continued to adapt our model to service an ever-growing niche population. In 2007, when the financial markets starting showing signs of weaknesses, we predicted that we would have to shift as companies started to lose money and show fatigue on a mass scale. We forecasted that training budgets for business coaching to middle and senior managers would dry up. We pulled back on our efforts aimed at that market about a year before the effect started to happen, and reallocated our focus to entrepreneurs, that had been in business at least a year. We went from having a practice that was about sixty percent working professional, forty percent entrepreneur to about ninety percent entrepreneur and ten percent working professional. In 2008 when the market started to collapse and go into a death spiral, we entered a growth trajectory built on business owners who wanted to survive in an ever challenging market environment. They started to call and hire Ghost CEO™ coaches for their businesses. Our company grew and grew as the markets failed. In the four years to follow, we had double-digit growth when other coaching businesses were closing their doors. In talking later with owners of coaching companies that closed their doors, they knew there was a correction but they just hadn't done anything about it until it was too late. Their business simply dried up.

This is how we adapted on a macro level, but on a micro level, there are different things to consider. I will use our work with female lawyers to illustrate the point. We had always focused on lawyers of 5, 6, 7 years of practice and worked with them on how to bring in clients so that they could work on files that interested them and not just be handed files by a senior partner. In most cases, the files coming from the senior partners involved crappy, "grinder" work. From working with these 'senior associate' lawyers, our name started to get around to female partners in law firms who were "named" partners but not "equity" partners. This meant that their names were on the letterhead but they did not share in the profits of the firm yet. We worked with female partners teaching them how to originate files, for themselves and others, in the firm. A partner that originates files quickly gets on the equity track. After the first full year of working with us, most of those "paper" partners became equity partners due to their ability to originate work and show bottom-line results to the partnership group. We reviewed the success of this model and decided to evolve the way that we worked with senior associates. The conversation went from, "Let's originate files so that you have interesting work to work on" to "Let's start to originate files so that you quickly get on partnership track at the firm if that's something that you want."

In 2007, we undertook a study to determine how quickly our clients were growing within their firms. The average Ghost CEO™ client that was a 5 year call or greater, went onto partnership track within twenty-four months instead of the standard sixty months. This one insight created a massive opportunity and evolution in our model. Rather than saying to the market that we can teach them how to build business, we focused on the elusive partnership track, which most firms keep secret on how it works. For senior associates, we suggested that within twenty-four months they will be partnership track. With named (not equity) partners, we suggest that we can have them in a position to make equity partner within twelve months. These are big boasts to make to a very discerning audience; however, our reputation and our ability to accomplish this time and time again have proven these claims. Now we are inundated with requests from female lawyers, accountants, engineers, and architects, all looking to increase the trajectory of their careers into equity positions.

The question is, "How do I know when to adapt or when to evolve?" The answer is that you need to be watching your markets all the time. This does not mean that you pour over reports, statistics, and market intelligence on an hourly basis; instead, you need to create practices that will give you an insight into what is happening. Here are a couple of points to help you with this process:

1. **Place indicators in your markets.** Think of these like motion-activated lights outside your house. If something happens, the

light goes on and draws your attention. This could be a set of Google Alerts set for your industry, reading trade magazines related to your market or your industry, or attending conferences. Anywhere where you can gather information (aggregated by someone else) that you can consume efficiently.

2. Speak to other professionals in the industries you service and ask them what they are noticing. What's new? What's changing? What's got them excited? What's making them nervous? What are they doing differently next year? These are all great open-ended questions for gathering information. If you talk to four or five people on a regular basis and notice you're hearing the same information from everyone, then you can be confident a shift is coming that will benefit from your attention and possible course correction.

3. Talk with existing clients within those markets and track what is having an effect on them and what they are noticing. For us at Ghost CEO™ we have a strong contingent of clients in financial services. Our coaches were talking among themselves about the nervousness and unease that our financial clients were displaying in 2007. These clients started to show concern about where the market was going, the housing issue was a topic that came up in most coaching sessions, and it seemed there was a common feeling of unease among all financial services clients, from financial planners through to pension managers. We had a clear indication that there was going to be a market shift but we did not know when or how big it would be. As a group, we discussed what the potential impact could be, we laid out every scenario that could happen, and how our company would respond to each. One scenario predicted that many of our competitors also in financial services might be unable to make the shift fast enough, which meant there could be a huge exodus of our

competitors out of business coaching. We formulated a plan around how we would cherry pick the best coaches, get them to join us and then go after their clients once the market corrected and came back. These are strategies that we began to implement in 2008 and continued into late 2012.

4. **Do not put your head in the sand when the shift is happening.** You need to face changes in the market head on and seek to understand where those markets are going and how you can get into position to capitalise on them. With our financial services clients like Bank of America, RBC Dominion Securities, and other brokerages, we knew that their wealth managers were going to take a hit and that many of them would start jumping off the bus. We met with the managers of each branch that we serviced and suggested that their wealth managers have a couple of sessions with us so we could show them how to insulate their book of business from the downward trend. Our business increased on an investment advisor level by over 30 percent each year in 2008, 2009, and 2010.

5. **As these shifts happen, take a moment and look at them objectively.** Is this a true market correction, or is it your evolution (or both), where the true opportunity lies? Most professionals ignore what is required and stay steadfast in thinking that things will come around. Remember that the only thing consistent in business is change and you will gain market advantage by seeing the shifts ahead of time and planning for them. If you are piloting the Titanic and you see the iceberg, change course! Not doing so can have a catastrophic effect on your profit model and your business as a whole.

Here are some questions that I would like you write down and post somewhere so you will see them on a daily basis. You want to practise this habit consistently for at least thirty days so that it is added to your toolbox and you can use it as a navigation tool using forward.

1. In each market that I'm in, which people in my network always seem to have the inside track or inside information on what is about to happen?

2. What information do I need to know about each of my markets to be able to track how they are doing things and when they are changing important details or strategies?

3. What can I track with my existing clientele that will serve as a market indicator for what that niche market is doing?

4. When markets have gotten away from me in the past (and have adapted or evolved without me), what questions do I wish I would have asked ahead of time so that I wasn't caught flat-footed?

These four questions are a great start in placing indicators in your markets as an advanced warning system that a shift is coming. They will keep your eye on the horizon and give you fair warning of changes coming up the pipeline, thereby allowing you the necessary time to adjust course and position yourself for the opportunity. Be vigilant and stay on your toes. Change equals opportunity, if managed properly.

The Market Shark is Always Moving

When you get busy, you will get lucky. For many fish, and sharks in particular, they need to move to survive. Their movement through the water pushes oxygen through their gills, which allows them to breathe. If they stop moving, they die. The same is true for business professionals. Success requires always moving around, looking for opportunities, sourcing deals, and getting information on their markets. They relax occasionally (which means swim a little bit slower), but they never stop. Stopping is dying. Market Sharks feel most comfortable when moving because they know the larger the territory they cover, the greater the number of opportunities.

Once you are in the regular habit of moving, looking, exploring, searching for, and uncovering different information about your market, it becomes intoxicating. You might think you are doing this, but consistency is the key. The common practice of going like a dervish, getting busy, slowing down to do the work, running out of work, whirling out again like a dervish is not the way, and so on. When you see that small consistent steps each day deliver way more than the sprints, you need to step into this new, slower groove. I found that when I go head deep and allow the obsessive compulsive disorder side of business to take control, it seems like I want more and more and more. I want to see more, explore more, hear more, read more, and often I need to back off a bit so I don't burn myself out. I am like the little kid at the Easter egg hunt. I'm turning over tables, knocking people out of the way, and my eyes are darting around like I'm a meth addict. Whenever I go into this manic pattern, I force myself to slow down. Even so, most Friday afternoons, at the end of my work week, I feel like I am stepping off a treadmill. I've been going so hard and so fast for five full days that when the time comes to back it off a bit and sharpen the saw for the weekend, it can mean a four or five hour transition to take it back a notch.

By doing business development on a consistent basis and seeing yourself become that big fish in a small pond (Market Shark), you notice that as you move and search for opportunities consistently, these opportunities appear everywhere. Everyone you talk to is a client or knows a client. Everything you see and anything you hear will start to relate to an opportunity.

When I first started, I thought that there were two paces: a turtle pace and a rabbit pace. The turtle pace was normally the characteristic of those who were uncertain or a bit nervous. The rabbit pace was for those confident entrepreneurs who knew what they were doing. It is like when you watch an artist at work. A new artist considers colours and carefully pencils in the outline of the painting, erases and reworks, ensures the brushes are ready and stands back to have a look before painting. Compare this to the famous Sunday afternoon TV personality Bob Ross. You remember this guy? He had the big curly hair and painted little green trees. Well, Bob did not spend much time planning; he just got down to painting. And it seemed like every painting that he created was magical. No matter what he attempted, it turned out well. This did not happen by chance. His experience in doing hundreds, if not thousands of paintings resulted in his having the confidence to know that the painting he was doing would work out and that if he did get himself into trouble, he would be able to work his way out of it. I remember him saying that to paint a good painting; the first step was to start painting. What I realised is that there is a third animal in the race. It is the goat, an animal that is steadfast and determined. Not dillydallying, but also not running ahead of itself. Bob Ross was the Goat of Painting. He would wade into the canvas; see where it took him, knowing that by doing the work he would get the results. Be the goat. Be Bob Ross, without the big hair, but feel free to have 'friendly little trees' in your work life, whatever that might look like.

As you start to become 'goat-like' in your activities, be mindful to not get stuck. If you find yourself sitting in your office or at your house wondering what to do, that is never going to start the process. If you feel stuck, the first thing you should do is just start moving in the market. When you do start moving, again, be consistent. Remember that the natural process for the entrepreneurs I have met is that they are more like sprinters than marathoners. They do short bursts of activity followed by long periods of inactivity. They do a big burst of activity and nothing happens, so they retreat to their houses or offices and lick their wounds and throw pity parties on why things are not working. They look around at others who are seemingly not doing the same volume of activity, yet lapping and surpassing them in performance. The reason is simple: consistent small efforts always trump irregular grand efforts. If struggling entrepreneurs would just be consistent, they would start to see that the small steps pay off for them in their business model, and sprinting is not required.

Going to one industry group every month (if it is in fact, the right type of group to be going to) is much better than going to ten events a week and then doing nothing for three months. For our clients, if they say they are struggling with filling up their prospects in their Sales Funnel, the first thing their coach will look is their activities. How frequently are they moving in the market compared to periods of inactivity? Most clients start with us and their normal habit is to do their work in sprints. We work with them on changing from this behaviour to doing a handful of small things every day. This is where success begins. As they start to move in a consistent way, they begin to notice a positive impact on their business almost immediately, and are less tired from running all over the place.

The Market Shark is Consistent.

An old saying suggests that if you want something done, you give it to someone busy. This is horse shit. When I first started consulting, I was one of these feast or famine consultants. When I was hungry, I worked like a dervish. I would work the phones. I would be on road trips. I would have any and every meeting possible, all of this at a frantic pace. Once I got a contract, I would cease all that activity and focus on doing my work. When I noticed that I only had a couple more payments coming from that particular contract, I would reignite frenetic development mode (triggering famine mode) until I got another contract (trigging feast mode) and fully stop all business development activities. This is an excellent way to exhaust yourself. I followed this feast/famine process for the first year and nearly killed myself. After twelve months, I came to a common sense realisation: what gets me busy keeps me busy. If I don't have time to do business development, I need to hire someone to do so on my behalf or, better still, because I love business development, I need to hire someone to do the contracted work, so I can continue with the business development (the part that I loved). This was a game changer. As I hired people to do the contract work and I started consistently to do small things on a regular basis, my company grew. No more exhausting famine and feast cycles. I realised that becoming a Market Shark did not take a Herculean effort. It took consistent commitment. As I became a fixture at events within markets, prospective clients started to become more familiar and comfortable with me. They started to trust that I could be depended on and that I would be there delivering my best every time we interacted. It did not take much effort to manage these groups of prospects on a regular basis, but I did have to make the rounds and engage, and for me that was on an easy to follow, monthly timetable.

When you become more consistent, you will notice how many other 'fish' in your markets deploy the feast–famine cycle of engaging with the market. They come in hard, disappear after a few months, and then come in again. They start cold each time they re-enter the market and the markets (and their prospective clients) do not like this. Markets want people and companies that they understand, people that they know, are familiar with, and trust.

Here are some questions to ask yourself (and remember to write these down and post them somewhere you can see them daily.

- What three things can I do consistently (weekly or monthly) that will create visibility and credibility within my markets?

- Can I commit to doing these things at least six times in sequence?

- What activities can I do daily that will increase my visibility in my markets?

- Who else is a consistent player in these markets that I could potentially team up with?

- What do I want the measurable result to be from my activities to prove to myself that I have invested my time wisely? (More clients is not a measurable goal. Number of clients, value of clients, and other quantifiable measurables are what we are looking for).

Above all, remember that consistency is key. Those who are consistent out-perform those who are erratic. If you want to get lucky all you need to do is get busy and be the goat!

The Market Shark is in a Constant State of Hunting

Building on the previous point, you have the safety off your gun and ready to fire. If you want to be successful, you have to be able to go out and get business. To see these opportunities, your default setting needs to be 'hunting mode'. Inside our company, we jokingly refer to people who have this mind-set as truffle sniffing pigs (building on the reference the client used about me). They always have their noses to the ground looking for a scent of the good stuff, and we pride ourselves in having this characteristic as one of our own prized traits.

Incorporating an earlier characteristic, you have to be moving if you want to be hunting. While I was at Hydro, my boss challenged me to put on a children's safety fair at Aberdeen Mall, the main shopping centre in Kamloops. He wanted me to get in front of as many families as possible to promote our energy efficiency programs. I asked him, "What's the budget?" He said, "You don't have a budget." I looked at him and stated, "We're a power company and you're not giving me a budget to build this marketing event?" to which he replied, "No, but I have faith in you." I went back to the office thinking, "How am I going to run a big event at a mall and attract many people with no budget?" I spent the rest of the day thinking, "If I had a budget, who would I invite and what would make the event cool?" My wish list included having the fire department there with some of their rescue trucks, the ambulance service so people could see the inside of an ambulance, the Police Department (R.C.M.P.) K-9 unit, and in addition to other vendors, Hydro bucket trucks on which we could give rides to kids in the buckets. (These are the trucks service the electrical poles.) The whole theme was "children's safety", so I decided to hold the event the weekend before school started. I knew that there would be a lot of traffic to the mall that weekend because parents would be taking their kids shopping for back-to-school clothing and supplies, and that way I would be able to show large numbers without having any advertising dollars. Then I got moving, not sure what to do first, but I knew that in order to hunt, I had to be out and about engaging with people. I called the ambulance service, the fire department, the police department and got them all engaged in participating in the event. I knew that by getting community partners in place, the event would be more attractive to the media to promote and cover. That said, I still had an uphill climb to get 'free' media for my event. Keep in mind that (1) BC Hydro was looking to promote power conservation guised in children's safety, and (2) every media organisation we approached knew how much BC Hydro made so it would be a tough sell to get them to cover us for free. So, I had to go into "beast mode."

I went to the first of two radio stations in the city and asked them to sponsor the event. They asked what the budget was and I said, "Zero." You can imagine how popular that made me with the ad rep. They said, "We don't think we can do it for nothing, especially for a utility company." I let them know that I was talking the other radio station, who was already preparing an offer to be the exclusive sponsor, but I really wanted to partner with this one and was hoping they would reconsider. Then I left their office and walked across the street to their competition. I presented the opportunity to them and said, "My boss just sent me across the street to talk with that station who want to be the sponsor, but I'd really prefer to work with you. As we only have space for one station, I'd really love it to be you but I understand if it can't be. Please think about it and let me know." Then I went back across the street and let that station know that I had just been in touch with the second station and they were preparing their official offer. That day both stations went back and forth competing to give us time to block the other one out. In total, I was able to raise just shy of $13,000 in free advertising, including being onsite for four hours during my event.

I implemented this same strategy again with the local print media. By the time the day was done, I had the Kamloops Daily News offering the front page and a full internal page afterward to thank the event's sponsors. The television station came when they found out we already had radio and newspaper sponsors. Once that was organised, I went out to the private sector and invited people to participate in the event. Most weren't that interested in paying us to be part of the event (remember we were the utility company that they already sent money to on a monthly basis) but, once I shared that we had leveraged over $30,000 in advertising of which they would be part of, I had an avalanche of private sector businesses looking to participate. In total, we received $30,000 in media, got $21,000 in cash and in-kind sponsorship from the private sector, and had just shy of seven thousand people attend the event over the day. It was one of the largest initiatives done that summer and at a total cost to the company of 'zero'.

I use this story to illustrate that you do not necessarily need to know how everything is going to work out or to have the entire game plan laid out before you start hunting. At the outset, I did not think that I was going to play the media off of each other to get a deal; I just went in and had my first conversation. While securing those various media deals, I realised that the opportunities were all around me. The only thing I was sure of in the beginning was that there would be a lot of kids at the mall and we would be sure to grab their attention by having fire trucks, ambulances with the lights flashing, police cars with K-9 units, and bucket truck rides.

I started moving and I started hunting, and these two habits go hand in hand. This habit (characteristic) is one that most business owners get stuck on. They are not sure what to hunt so they don't hunt anything or they are like me, where they get too familiar with the feast and famine scenario and then only hunt when they are not busy and stop hunting when they get busy. If you hunt consistently, you are never 'not busy'. We remind clients when we see them ease off the throttle that the activities that got them busy will keep them busy. If they stop doing the business development work, they will stop having business to do. This statement might be one you write somewhere to remind yourself daily of the necessary 'care and attention' your business development needs. When you get slammed with new work and have phone calls to return that you don't have time for, re-read that statement. It is sad that the easiest thing to do for busy entrepreneurs is to cut out the activities that are keeping their companies alive.

As you hunt more consistently, it will get easier. You will yield more results in less time and you will start drinking your own Kool-Aid. When we start working with clients, consistency in action is more important than the actual action. Like someone losing weight, it is less about the particular exercise and more about 'moving'. Clients balk at first, telling us how busy they are. From a coach's perspective, it can feel like dragging a cat to a bath. Within thirty days, they become like a little kid on a scavenger hunt, running around and looking under everything for opportunities. This is where the magic in their business model begins to appear.

It only takes thirty days before the habit becomes ingrained. Clients start seeing all the opportunities they have previously walked by and they will begin picking up those opportunities. Once you begin picking up and closing opportunities simply through being consistent in your hunting, it is hard to 'un-learn' that. Making this commitment for thirty days will change the trajectory of your business. Afterwards, the hard part is staying out of the feast/famine process that has become so familiar. There are only two times when you stop hunting – when you sell your company or when you die.

The Market Shark Bumps into things Intentionally

Most shark attacks on humans occur because the shark thinks the person is just another source of food. A surfer wearing a black bodysuit while paddling on top of a surf board might look like a seal. A shark ventures in, has a little nibble, realises it's not a seal, spits it out and leaves. If there is something in the water that is moving, alive, and in the vicinity, the shark will bump it to see if it is something worth eating. This is a great trait that Market Sharks readily apply in business.

When you hunt consistently, you will see more and more things that catch your interest. Unsure if they are targets right off the bat, you may dismiss them. Don't do this until you "bump" them a little. Pick up every rock and walk over to every opportunity so you can have a better look. If you find yourself acting biased and that bias is getting in the way of what you are doing, challenge that bias. You will find yourself looking at an opportunity and, if you can remove the bias, you may see things from a different perspective and see that it is a true opportunity. When it comes to exploring your market and hunting for those opportunities, use a system by which you "bump" the opportunity (we'll get to this in a bit).

Years ago I had a client in the Pacific Northwest who had a serious 'hate-on' for realtors. She was a fellow business coach in a different model and her model was an obvious fit (to me) for real estate professionals. When I brought this up as a potential target market, she turned up her nose (like she had stepped in dog shit with bare feet) and told me that she was "adamant about not working with realtors." When I inquired further, she shared that she had had a bad experience with a real estate client in the past and absolutely refused to do business with them, non-negotiable.   Upon deeper consideration, I identified that she was judging an entire market of people through her experience with one shitty realtor, early on in her career when she was still learning the ropes. I was curious if she might be open to re-considering as her experience had happened years ago and could have been an isolated situation. She agreed to give it a try and with a distasteful look on her face, she accepted an offer to speak to a room full of realtors on her area of expertise.

The day of the event I called and reminded her to put the bias aside and to treat the group like she would any other client market. She promised she would do her best and try to get herself in the right state of mind to offer an objective experience to these realtors. I went about my work that day waiting to hear how it went, secretly wishing that she would have a different experience, as I knew that this would be an extremely lucrative market for her. She called at the end of the day and said, "Chris, I'm a little bit surprised at how my event went today. It was literally one of the best audiences I've ever spoken in front of and their questions were unbelievable. From a room of thirty realtors I already have five people who have called me wanting to find out more about my services." I said to her (in a mocking tone), "You have got to be kidding me! Realtors? But we hate realtors! They're not a market for you!" and then I went quiet. She started to laugh and said that she had quite possibly judged an entire group by the actions of one and was now cautiously excited about exploring that market.

This is a prime example of how bias can taint our vision. It would have been easy for her to dismiss the invitation to speak to this group and thus bypass getting known by thirty people in the market and having five engage her to find out more about her practice. Those five clients represent about $25,000 a year in revenue for her. I am happy to say now that not only has she opened up that market within her practice but she is now re-considering other markets that she had already formed an opinion about. She is willing to see if things have changed or if her perception of them has changed.

Here are the steps you can take to "bump" different things in your markets to see if an opportunity is there. Bumping is an action that can only be done when you are hunting, and, as stated before, hunting can only be done when you are constantly moving. You can see how each of these components, even though they can exist independently on their own, have a multiplier effect when you pull them together into your habitual business development.

1. Look at all things that catch your attention regardless of good or bad.

2. Get up on it and have a good look around it (bump it!).

3. Ask some questions to qualify if there is an opportunity there.

4. Do the answers fit your business model? Do not change what you do right away for any particular market. Be discerning with who gets your attention.

5. If there is something that keeps grabbing your attention after bumping it, continue to explore but set a timetable for making a decision about it. You don't want to think about things forever. A good rule is to give something thirty days of consideration and if, at the end of thirty days, you are not prepared to act on it then put it on the back burner.

6. If you bump something (or someone) once and it does not resonate with you do not keep bumping it hoping that you will get a different outcome or a different feeling. Things rarely change. **Diarise to check in on this market in a year to see if things have changed.**

7. If what you bump does resonate and interest you but does not show an opportunity, don't get upset. Just swim on to the next opportunity. If you get pissy, you will stop being curious and miss things that might otherwise bear fruit. Think back to the real estate example. After being disappointed with her initial interaction, the client had to go through the process of letting it go (with a little supportive nudge from her coach) to look at the opportunity in a new light. Remember, twelve months is a good timetable from which to reassess if a market has shifted in a direction that is aligned with your business model.

As you are conducting your yearly assessments, consider these questions.

• What opportunities have I shied away from and why? This could mean individuals, companies, or industries.

• Are there markets that I have formed an opinion about that deserve to be reassessed?

• What questions will I ask during my bump process to see if there is a true opportunity for me now? Keep in mind that not only do markets change but that you change as well. A market that you may not have fit with in the past may now be a custom fit for you.

Note to yourself: Do not get too caught in thinking you understand every market forever moving forward. Things change, people change, you change, your services change, opportunities close, and opportunities open. Be curious, yet discerning. When we have meetings at Ghost CEO™ we say, "Everyone, and we mean everyone, gets the time of day once." If we do not see a fit with a client, a company, or an industry, we diarise for twelve months from that date to have another interaction to see if something has changed (on either side) that could lead to a new opportunity opening up. About 30% of our business comes from these markets that were previously dismissed by us, or that failed to engage with us on the first pass.

A Market Shark is Smooth in its Movement

I want you to visualise fish swimming around in the ocean. Now you see a big fish swimming smoothly, gliding through the water with intentional movements (maybe it's a shark – good if it is, as it fits nicely into this analogy). It is almost hypnotic. Now picture a little fish darting around. It is jittery, jerky and in no way smooth. Imagine that fish on a hook fighting for its life, struggling, pulling, pushing, diving, and surfacing. When you imagine these two images, which fish seems powerful to you and which seems to be in trouble?

When I started Think Tank Communications Inc. in 1999, even though I wanted to be the smoothly moving fish, I admit I most closely resembled the flailing fish. I would race to meetings, work late into the night, send emails at all hours (without spellchecking them), and I made all the rookie mistakes possible. I recall one mentor saying to me, "Chris, you look like someone whose pants are on fire. You are all over the place like a chicken with its head cut off. You need to calm down, slow down, and think about what you're doing. You're sending the wrong message to the market." Although I did listen to the comment, I really thought that I had to be twenty places at once, processing hundreds of different thoughts at any given time, and keep all the balls in the air. It was like being the plate spinner in the circus. I would start getting plates spinning on the poles and right as I get to the end of the line, I would need to run back and restart the first plate. If I didn't rush like a madman, the plates would start falling and I'd look like a fool. This was the story I told myself in my head.

With a year of this jerky movement behind me and being totally burnt out, I took a step back and looked through objective eyes at how the market perceived me. I realised that "be busy" work and "meaningful work" are two very different things. If you frantically jump all over the place, you are telling the market that you are not sure what you are doing, that you're in crisis mode, that you're lost, or that you're simply don't have control. As well, frantic behaviour attracts larger competitors who will step into your markets and eat your lunch. Sharks are drawn to struggling fish, knowing there is a meal to be had. Someone who is calm and collected always presents as much more competent and able than does someone who is frantically racing around. In business, we refer to this as being 'measured'.

If you find yourself acting frantic or you hear people say it looks like you are rushing around all the time, you need to pause and consider what message your actions send to the market. Running around does not impress anyone. It just tells people that you are not that good at what you do. If you are saying to yourself right now, 'Well how do I know?" Let's be honest. You know. You are either in control or managing fires. If you are a firefighter, keep it up! If you are in any other profession, time to get your shit together. You are sending a bad message.

Some behaviour is common to people who operate in frantic mode. They show up only a minute before or are entirely late for meetings. They send emails at ridiculous hours of the night, early mornings, or over the weekend. They are constantly dishevelled and searching for papers they can't find, asking for emails they've lost to be resent, and always asking for extensions on things they've promised. There is help for such people; it's called an intervention from Plate Spinner's Syndrome (PSS).

Here is the process we use with clients when they find themselves in the grip of PSS. It allows us to support them in bringing things to a manageable level. If you find yourself overwhelmed and you are producing underwhelming work, these are the steps you should follow. If you run around looking like you just burnt your privates this is also a great process for you to go through. Regardless of the situation, you will find that using these steps will help to bring everything back into focus.

1. **Stop.** Stop everything that you are doing and go somewhere quiet where you will not be disturbed. Turn off your phone. Turn off any other external stimuli that will knock you off balance. Just be quiet. You will not die if you don't check emails/voice mails ten times per hour.

2. **Assess the situation.** Why are you frantic? Why are you running around like your hair is on fire? What is creating so much distress that you behave this way?

3. **Plot a course, moving slowly, to get you into a professional pace.** A pace in which you can get the work done, you can deliver on your promises, and you don't resemble a chicken with its head cut off. Look at what you are doing that isn't accomplishing anything. Social media, surfing the web, multi-tasking. All lead to Plate Spinner's Syndrome.

4. **Get into a cadence.** Once you get comfortable with that pace, gradually start to speed things up. Only step up the speed once you understand the process that you're in. If you are on rocky terrain, slow things down.

5. **Every move that you make should be a smooth move.** Any mis-step that you make (which will inevitably happen as it happens to all of us) must be taken in stride. Don't let it derail you. Take a pause to regain your composure and then get back on course.

6. **Control your approach.** When you are starting in business or opening up a new market, the nervousness and excitement of it can pull you out of your groove. Temper yourself.

7. **Breath.** It's important to take a breath on a regular basis, to slow down, and to focus on being in the moment and being intentional towards what you wish to accomplish. Going off half-cocked will do nothing but get you into trouble. Make recalibrating your focus a daily practise to ensure that you are properly positioned in the markets that you serve.

My friend David Reeve is a thought leader in the area of corporate culture. He's the founder of Unleash Culture (unleashculture.com) and he shared with me a quotation at a board meeting that has become one of my favourites. It's one that the Blue Angels Drill Team used in their perfect flying:

"Slow is smooth; smooth is fast; fast is lethal."

The lesson of this quotation is that you need to 'understand the movements in their basic components'. You use the movements in a smooth fashion until you are confident; then you can speed up. When you can do each movement both smoothly and quickly, you become lethal. In sport they call this "muscle memory." You continue to do the action in a way that is mechanically sound and once you have that action down then you can speed up and get really good at it.

If you ever get a chance to watch a Market Shark work a room at a networking function, you'll see what I mean. They are precise and fluid, and every move and engagement is intentional and done with a predetermined outcome in mind. Their precision and delivery comes from working their craft over and over and over, until it seems perfect. But perfection is a bit of a fallacy. Perfection can never truly be attained, so we must continue to strive to be better today than we were yesterday, knowing that we won't be as good today as we will be tomorrow. This is why we practise. Every day we should be advancing in our ability to implement our different skill sets.

If you are unsure whether you are smooth or jittery in your motions, consider the following questions:

• Do your palms sweat in business settings?

• Do you have an upset stomach while engaging in business?

• Do you look forward to events or do they stress you out?

• Do you know what you are going to do or do you just wing it?

• Do you feel like you are forgetting something?

• Do you feel like you are going to 'mess up'?

• Is your confidence level high?

• Do you have contingency plans in place for different business settings and situations?

These types of jerky movements by a professional in their interactions with others often come from uncertainty. Their body language, verbal language, and interactions all seem a bit awkward. All of this can be sorted out through being prepared. Prepared can be defined as "to put in the proper state of mind." Here are some questions that you can post in a visible area to prepare yourself to smooth any jerkiness in business. We have clients that have this list on their phone, on a Post It in their car, or taped somewhere on their desk.

1. What do I want to accomplish in this specific situation?

2. What does a positive outcome look like for me?

3. What would contribute to a negative outcome?

4. How can I mitigate anything that would support a negative outcome?

5. How can I practise my process until it is smooth? (Remember, slow is steady; steady is fast; fast is lethal).

6. How will I judge my performance afterwards?

By looking at these things analytically and objectively, you can remove some of the emotion and make your interactions and delivery a bit smoother. People say I'm smooth but I have probably given more than five hundred presentations in business and I practised each of those presentations physically or at least in my mind an average of ten times. If you had done five hundred presentations you would be smooth, too. Be mindful that every interaction you have is an opportunity to practise your craft and the smoothness of its delivery.

The Market Shark acts like a Market Shark.

In every market that you're in, there will be some bigger and some smaller fish. It's best to avoid the bigger fish if you can't be friends with them. They will smash you if you get in the way and it is very difficult to compete with those who are much larger than you. They will eat up your time and resources which are better invested in smaller ponds with less big fish.

On the other end of the spectrum, smaller fish are easier options for lunch, but do so only if they get in your way and are disruptive to your business model. It is better to co-exist with the smaller fish. If you're thinking about teaming up it is always better to scale up rather than down (pun intended). Scaling up means you swim with bigger fish. When you work with those who are bigger, faster, and smarter than you (yes, some people are smarter than you), it ups your game. Ask any real competitor who they would rather play against – someone better than they are or someone worse. If they have one lick of confidence, they will opt to compete against someone who is better. When you play with those who are better than you, you become better.

My dad used to say, "If you want to fly with eagles, don't run with turkeys." This applies in business as well as in life. The smaller guys are skirting around seeking crumbs to nibble on while the big sharks are looking for the full meals. Sharks are discerning about where they invest their energy and time, and they are efficient with how they do things. I have learned a lot from working with people who are decades ahead of me in business. When the opportunity arises to work with them, I am forced to run just to keep up and to pretend that I'm not as winded as I really am when we meet. I have never personally benefited from partnering with someone smaller than me (who I end up dragging along) rather than being challenged by them to move faster. The bigger fish always raise my game. The minnows irritate and frustrate me.

But be prepared! You may need to change your terms of reference from time to time around how you define a big fish. As you become a big fish, those who you considered to be big fish in the past become equals and you need to set your sights higher. When I first started, one of my mentors was instrumental in teaching me how coaching worked and how to engage clients. Over the years of building my practice, I would continue to check in with this mentor, asking advice, and we got to a point about four years into our relationship when she said to me, "It's probably not a good idea for you to call me for advice anymore." At first I thought I may have done something to upset or insult her. When I asked her about it, she shared that, in her opinion, I was at the point of surpassing her and continuing to access her for information would not make either of us feel good nor further develop my skill set. Although this was a bittersweet moment for me, in hindsight I can look back on it and appreciate it for the gift that it was. She wasn't telling me that she didn't want to interact with me. She was telling me that it was time to find a new mentor who I could continue to learn from and who would stretch me.

In my first book, What Men Don't Tell Women About Business (Wiley 2007), I commented about one of my most important mentors, Alvin Con. Alvin was a Market Shark at Intel and every lick of business I did with him forced me to be on my toes and to run just to keep up. I wasn't half as good as him on my best day if he was having a horrible day. This guy was a business machine. I remember talking to him one day about wanting to get more into the technology space to get known, to which he nodded his head in consideration. It was a Thursday afternoon and we were having lunch, which we did on a weekly basis. We were strategising about business models and I was taking more notes than speaking (a rarity for me). Alvin looked at me and said, "You know what? It might be a good idea for you to present how Support Call Centres work at the Intel conference I'm holding in Vancouver." I looked at him, feeling very appreciative for the opportunity, and said, "Absolutely. I would love to. When's the conference?" He replied, "Tomorrow." "Tomorrow!" I exclaimed, "You want me to present at a conference tomorrow? How will I get on the speaker's list?" He said, "I control the speaker's list. I'm going to put you on as the lunch keynote." I looked at him and said, "What the hell do you want me to talk about that's going to be of interest to your different technology resellers?" He replied, "I want you to talk about how call centres can support wireless technologies." Please note: We are talking 2002 here. Wireless wasn't what it is today; it was still an emerging technology. He looked at me and said, "Do you want to refuse?" I said, "Of course not, but I should go. I have some research to do."

I ran to the bookstore and bought every book I could about wireless, which, at that time, resulted in the purchase of two titles. One book was about wireless technology and the other was on Wireless for Dummies. I consumed both books and started to write my keynote which he had given forty-five minutes to be on stage. What the hell was I going to talk about for forty-five minutes? I stayed up all night drafting speech after speech, but coming up with anything that I found particularly engaging or that I thought would be interesting eluded me. On top of that, I was terrified that I would embarrass myself in front of stakeholders that I would benefit from getting to know and doing business with. My greater fear was embarrassing Alvin and having him run me off and denying me future access to him

When I showed up at the conference the next morning in my suit, ready to go on stage, Alvin looked at me and asked, "How much sleep did you get last night?" I answered, "I didn't sleep." He said, "Well, this is how the big dogs do it. You're not always going to get much time to prepare but you have to act as if you did. So, use the time accordingly to promote yourself and to say something interesting to the audience." Minutes before I was to go onstage I was not at all confident about my content, so I decided to call an 'audible' (football reference for when the quarterback changes the play seconds before the ball is released). Rather than talking about wireless technology, I decided to change to conversation to be about how to build intimacy with clients accessing the support in a call centre. Although slightly off topic (but still very much related), it was an area that I knew a lot about, client engagement. For the next forty-five minutes I lectured to these key stakeholders the best practices of client engagement, building loyalty while they were struggling with their gear. This was a serious crowd. I am not talking little hacks who sold modems. Hitachi, Telus, Intel, Hewlett Packard, and Dell were all in the room. At the end of my presentation, I received generous applause and walked off the stage wondering if I had just committed professional suicide. Alvin and his wife, Marion, came up to me and Alvin said, "That was absolutely great. Everybody was taking notes. Really well done." If it was so well done, why did I feel sick to my stomach? So I sheepishly smiled at him and went home to bed.

What I did not know at the time is that I automatically ascended to 'big fish' status by having a Market Shark select me to be the lunchtime keynote. A big part of this whole thing is just assuming the role and either being able to deliver at that level or not. It's too easy to over think how to get there and stay there. It is much easier (albeit a bit more dangerous) to just stand in the place and act as if.

I realised that Alvin had set me up to accomplish something in a twenty-four hour period that most people would have taken at least a month to six weeks to prepare, which is what many of the conference speakers had. He taught me that to be a big fish you have to swim deep and sometimes get thrown into the deep end, which is what he did to me.

This one experience has tailored the way that I now focus on business. While I am always prepared for presentations and meetings, I know that I can call that 'audible' when I need to and change the topic if necessary to position me for capitalising on an opportunity.

Here are some questions to consider when thinking about what type of fish you want to swim with:

1. **Are there some big fish in your life who have characteristics you would like to emulate?** Make a list of all these people and write down the skill or skills they have (their superpowers) that you like to emulate in your own business life.

2. **Who are the small, small fish in your business sphere you need to restrict your access from?** Remember, if you want to fly with eagles, you shouldn't run with turkeys. There will be those in your life that are keeping you from being exceptional. Be truthful with yourself.

3. Of the big fish you know, who might be a viable business alliance? What could you offer them, and what can they offer you? Remember that you need to have value in order for them to want to focus their time (their most valuable asset) on you.

4. Who are some big fish you know about, but who aren't in your immediate circle? Spend some time making a list of these people and think about how you could gain exposure to them. You might need to introduce yourself, ask someone you have in common to make an introduction for you, or use any other strategy that will allow you to start building a relationship with him or her.

To be a big fish, you need to swim with big fish. Make an assessment of who you spend your time with and, if you aren't being challenged, then the fish you're swimming with simply aren't big enough. The fish you swim with should scare you, just a little bit.

A Market Shark can Smell Blood from a Long Way Away

As your business intuition becomes stronger, you will start to identify opportunities farther ahead. Seasoned professionals can spot an opportunity before anyone else in the room. This gives them a notable advantage over competitors. They have seen enough business and situations to immediately forecast what possibilities could be available with any opportunity. Not unlike a Chess Grandmaster who has played thousands of scenarios over and over again, within the first two or three moves, a seasoned professional understands the entire strategy needed to get to check mate. Like a business Grandmaster, you want to explore many opportunities and listen to other business owners about how they find, assess, and close opportunities. It is staggering how much you can learn from your peers, both by listening to their stories and watching them in action.

As you spot opportunities – both those right in front of you or those off in the distance – I want you to ask: "How can I make money with this?" When you are moving, hunting, exploring opportunities, bumping, swimming in the right ponds, swimming with the right fish, and doing so in a smooth and consistent manner, you will be shocked at the amount of opportunities that come your way daily. Your greatest challenge won't be in finding opportunities, but instead will be in processing opportunities and figuring out which are right for you and which need to be dismissed. We refer to this in business as deal flow. You need to determine which are worth investing more time into; and which are just shiny objects that can keep you distracted from the good work.

Every person you meet either "is a client or knows a potential client." Sometimes the opportunities that seem to be a long way out will require you either to move towards them or you to get into position and wait for them to get closer. The farther out you see an opportunity, the more time you'll have to prepare for it. Most opportunities are lost because the person who would benefit from the opportunity isn't in the position to capitalise on it; either because they're out of position or they don't have enough time to address it properly. As you become dialled in with this particular skill set (which like anything has to be practised consistently), you will quickly start to process multiple opportunities and sort them into valuable and distracting.

For all of our business coaches and our clients, they categorise every individual and opportunity they come across within minutes. Every person they meet goes into one or more buckets: prospective client for one of their businesses, prospective client for one of their clients, prospective strategic alliance, someone who has influence over a market they are interested in, someone who can offer them or their clientele a service that they need, someone who obviously doesn't have their shit together (is like the fish in distress we talked about earlier), a huckster (someone who is trying to sell snake oil), or someone who had their attention but won't get any more in the future.

I wasn't born with a talent for categorising people. I have developed this over years of practise through meeting thousands of people. Most of the time I place people into the right bucket. Sometimes I don't get it quite right and I have to move a person out of one bucket and into another. In the beginning of my career, I spent too much time with the wrong people and didn't engage the right people, even though they were right in front of my face. Only over the last five years or so, I have started to make this a strict practise because much of my time was consumed by people who were wasting my time, people who were trying to use me to get access to my markets or clients, or people who I thought were prospects but who were just looking for free advice.

When I first expanded the business coaching practice to Vancouver, I set up shop in Yaletown, one of the trendier business areas in downtown Vancouver. At that time, I would have coffee with anyone who wanted to have coffee with me because I was trying to build visibility for my model. I did forty to fifty coffee meetings per week and my closure rate was extremely low. As someone who prides himself on sourcing and closing new business, this was a hard hit to my ego. However, I started to get wise, and realised that I was spending a lot of time with 'boat anchors' (Definition: A Boat Anchor is someone who makes doing business with them similar to how it would be swimming with a boat anchor tied around your neck).   I immediately implemented a new system. Before I would agree to meet with someone I would say, "What would you like to meet about?" If they could not answer me with something that I found satisfactory, I wouldn't have the meeting. It took getting fed up with people wasting my time, to become more discerning about who got on my schedule. My mantra became, "You can waste your time, but you can't waste my time." As I got more discerning with my time, my closure rate went WAY back up.

Today, I talk to most new people by phone, some by email, and in person only with clients and partners when we happen to find ourselves in the same city and time zone. It is much easier to keep your guard up and empower your gatekeepers to keep people on the outside by using electronic communications. If someone cannot tell me within five minutes why I should be interested in meeting with them, then I don't meet with them. This is the same skill we implement with our clients in their businesses. They personally have five minutes to catch the interest of the markets they're looking to engage with. If they can't do it within five minutes, they don't understand their own offering well enough. This skill is something that we work on at the beginning of the relationship. As you start to tighten this up for yourself, you will start positioning yourself to have a longer view of opportunities and plan for them accordingly. Clients have a difficult time initially saying 'no' to people when being asked for a meeting. They think it is 'rude' or 'off putting', but after a while, they get fed up (as I did) and start to implement rules as well. They end up seeing their closure rate skyrocket as well. I tell to my clients, "I'd rather you lounge on the couch reading magazines than meet with people who aren't going to buy from you."

To know where to start, you should do review your current situation. Write down the following questions on a piece of paper and then answer them. It's not a bad idea to do this weekly in the beginning to see how much time is getting dragged out of you by Boat Anchors.

1. How many meetings do you have in an average week?

2. How many of those meetings are with new clients?

3. How many of those meetings are with qualified prospects?

4. How many of those meetings surround existing business that you are doing?

5. How many of those meetings are with vendors that you already buy from?

6. How many of those meetings accomplish no measurable results?

Remember to include meetings with friends and family during your work hours. GOAL: It is better not to have meetings than to have meetings with people who waste your time. If you are investing time in meetings that have no benefit to you, that's time taken away from exploring new opportunities or seeing them from a distance which allows you time to get into position to capitalise on them.

Here are some best practices to help tighten up your schedule so that you will have the time and vantage points to see opportunities that are way out on the horizon.

1. **Never have a meeting without a clear purpose in mind.** You can use something like, "What would you like to accomplish together in our meeting?" This is a great question to ask people to see if they have their stuff together.

2. **Never have a meeting without an agenda.** "Could you please send me an agenda along with your meeting request?" If they are not prepared to send you an agenda of talking points then you shouldn't be prepared to have a meeting with them. Market Sharks don't meet in the hope that the meeting will be valuable. They know ahead of time before they commit.

3. Never have a meeting if there is no obvious benefit to you. Your time is a valuable commodity. Don't let other people waste it.

4. Your default answer to any meeting request that does not have a clear purpose, agenda, or benefit to you should be, "I'm sorry. My schedule is quite full."

5. Never have a meeting over thirty minutes long unless it's a negotiation. Here's a sample response: "I apologise but I only have thirty minutes to meet. If you want to prepare a concise agenda and send it over to me with your meeting request we can strive to be efficient with our time together."

6. Never have more than one meeting with a prospect unless they have the means and need for what you have (more on this in a moment). A sample response to a prospect, who wants to meet more than once but about whom you're unsure if they're qualified, could be: "I'm sorry. My schedule is quite full right now with clients. If you'd like to share any questions you have I'd be happy to answer them by email as quickly as I can."

7. Never do a favour by having a meeting with someone unless, before you say yes, you know how that favour will be repaid. When a colleague asks you to have a meeting with one their connections you could reply, "I'll have a meeting with your contact but I need to ask you to..." Know how you want the favour returned, before you agree to a meeting.

I previously referenced means and need. I'd like you to write down the following statement which will make your life so much easier as you become a Market Shark: There are three types of clients in the market:

1) Those with means and not need;

2) Those with need and not means;

3) Those with both means and need.

Those with means and not need are people who have money but don't really see the value in what you offer. Those with need and not means absolutely see the value in what you bring to the table but they don't have the resources needed to hire you. The third group is **the group we are looking for**; they are prospects who have means and need. They need what you want and they know it, and they have the money to pay you. Most business owners waste their time chasing people who don't want what they have or selling to people who can't afford what they have. Focus on the third group. This is your market! All the rest will waste your time. If you don't respect your time, no one else will. Time is your most valuable asset and as you grow your business this will become increasingly apparent. Effectively managing your time will allow you to ascend to 'big fishdom'. Being ineffective with time management and accommodating with your schedule will leave you stuck with the small fish. Big fish eat dinner; small fish are dinner.

Now don't go off half-cocked and decide you are going to add all these characteristics at once. You will end up suffering from Plate Spinner's Syndrome. I suggest that you select one or two of these characteristics to focus on and practise. Choose one that you believe you are already strong in, and choose one that take a bit of a stretch for you to get stronger in. I want you to practise each of them twenty minutes a day on a consistent basis, for thirty days. Twenty minutes of practise a day is better than four hours of practise one day a week. These characteristics are all habit based. The more you do them, the easier they get, and the more effective you become using them. Do not get discouraged if you don't get it at first. Learning a new skill is hard, especially at the beginning. Every day you use it will get easier. Every application you use it with will provide insight into how to better tailor your deliver of it. Some people will stop when they get frustrated. Fight this. If you are getting frustrated and take a break and then restart, it's like starting over at day one. I tell my clients to think of it as if you are in Alcoholics Anonymous without the distressed liver. You get a chip for every week, month, and year that you're consistently on the wagon but if you slip up and fall off the wagon just once, you go right back to day one and start the path all over again. Stay focused!

Chapter 2 – Choosing Your Ponds

What Makes a Good Pond?

Choosing the niche markets for your business model into is like selecting a new car. You have to figure out what will fit you, how you will use it, and what it will cost to buy and maintain. When you buy a new car, you probably look under the hood, open up the trunk, sit in the seat to make sure that it is comfortable, take it for a test drive on the highway, and check its handling around corners. You experience the car and then decide if it is something that you want to invest substantial time and money in. Hopefully, you don't just take one car for a test drive and then decide to buy it, as you are much better off trying out a variety of different cars and looking at different options to make sure that you truly get what you are looking for.

When it comes to looking at niche market (ponds), you need to get a good point of reference through exploring many different ponds, like you would cars. We ask our clients at Ghost CEO™ to explore at least twelve markets before whittling that number down to something more manageable, like a target of three. Do not fall in love with markets right away. Do not love them until they love you back. If you find yourself getting excited early on, force yourself to simmer down a bit and give it time to see if it is the 'real deal' or just another shiny object. In order for a pond to be selected, it has to make sense 'objectively', i.e. it holds up well to the tests you are going to put it through. Since 1999, I have watched a lot of businesses fail. They do so for one of these three reasons:

1. The owner is not serious and runs the business like a hobby.

2. The business targets the wrong markets.

3. The business targets the right markets, but offers nothing unique enough to get the attention of those markets.

Here is the plain truth, with no sexy sparkle added: if you target markets that have means and need for your solution and you can educate them on the fact that you have a solution for what they are looking for, you will be successful. Anything else leads to failure. If you do not fit their needs or are not able to communicate your solution, no matter how much you try to romance them or build a relationship with them, they are simply not going to buy. You will be forced out of business and someone with an inferior solution who can target effectively will take your place. Tough? You bet it is, but forewarned is forearmed. Make it easy for yourself and choose low-hanging fruit: markets that have need and means and that you can easily engage with and educate. Business is challenging enough without forcing yourself into an uphill battle with markets that just don't get you.

Many of the initial ponds that you look at will seem promising. You might be tempted to develop them immediately, but take a breath. In reviewing the thousands of business models of our clients, we have noticed that the ponds our clients are most excited about end up being duds (Murphy's Law). And the ponds that are not as exciting end up being the goldmines. Everyone chases the 'sexy' markets and leaves the 'ho-hum' markets alone. Success sits in the 'ho-hum'. Really. Keep your mind open to opportunities and realise that you will not recognise a lot of those opportunities right away; hence the importance of exploring different ponds. It takes a methodical approach to truly determine the viability of a pond and once you are quite sure that that pond is a viable option for your business model, you can start to develop it further.

Sometimes ponds develop like relationships. Sometimes they require you to get familiar them and they have to become familiar with you. You need to go out on a couple of dates and meet each other's parents. Then the love starts to blossom. Rush it and it throws off the rhythm; go too slow and the market might feel you are not that interested. You need to be engaged, but not needy. Interested, but not psychotic. Remember that movie, Fatal Attraction and the bunnies on the stove? Don't be like that. Every once in a while, love at first sight happens. You slip into a pond by chance (right place at the right time), only to realise that it is the perfect pond in which to develop your business. In my experience, slipping into a pond is never a bad thing, especially if there is a market waiting there for you. But, like I said before, if it is the 'real' deal, it is not going anywhere so do not rush it. You accidentally run into it, not expecting it, and find out it is a goldmine. Take your time.

Checking the Temperature of a Pond.

There are hundreds of things you can assess when considering whether to enter a pond (niche market). Rather than driving yourself crazy, you want to choose things to examine that will tell you if a pond will be good for you or if you should keep walking. There are the eight measurements I use when assessing a pond's suitability for a particular business model. These eight have served me very well over the years and have been distilled from dozens I have used. I offer you my Cliff Notes (Coles Notes for my fellow Canucks) version of how to start using them today. First, I will define the eight and then demonstrate how to apply them to your prospective ponds. You might wonder if you have to use all of them or just a few. Use ALL of them. If a market passes the test of all eight, you know you are on to something. If a market scores 6/8 or 7/8, you don't have to dismiss it, but believe me, there are many eights out there so it is worth your time to keep looking.

1. **Measurable.** When looking at a niche market, you have to be able to measure how big the market is. If its size is unknown, do more research to determine the size, or it might be too big.

2. **Manageable.** The niche market has to be large enough for you to sink your teeth into it but not so large that you can never be known as the big fish. If we were hunting electrical engineers, we would not hunt electric engineers in the United States, but you could hunt electrical engineers in Greater Boston or electrical engineers who specialise in marine industries. It has to be pond that can be managed by you and then can get to know you (so they can talk about you among themselves). The market's internal conversation about you is key to being successful.

3. **Definable/Describable:** You have to be able to define what that pond is. You wouldn't say that your market is "Chambers of Commerce" because there are literally thousands. You might say, "One of my niche markets is Chambers of Commerce in Greater Los Angeles." If you cannot define it or describe the market you are targeting, it might not be a niche market. Worse yet, it could be a collection of markets that will send you on a wild goose chase and burn up your resources. If a market is not describable or definable, you will have major issues communicating to it effectively and getting people to support you in penetrating the market. Remember, being unable to describe your market is one of the three reasons companies go out of business. Don't join that group.

4. **Growing.** Target the ponds that constantly replenish the amount of prospective clients inside them. Years ago, I had a client who owned a funeral home and she left New York City to work in the Midwest. When I asked her what led to such a drastic move, she said that she chose a town where she knew

people moved to retire. Every new retiree that came meant she would have prospective customer sometime in the next few years. This seems a bit morbid, but she understood her market and knew that her services would be used to a greater extent with aging communities than with communities comprised of young couple.

5. **No Obvious Market Shark in the Pond.** The pond should have no obvious Market Shark that you need either to bump off or compete against. If you look into a pond and see someone established already, who is taking all the business, and who is a competitor of yours, then it is best to keep looking. Competition eats up a lot of your time and resources and there are many ponds that are under served. The best option is to move on and find something you can enter into as the obvious market leader.

6. **Easy to Claim Dominance as the Market Shark.** You want ponds that have a space waiting for you, where all you need to do is move in and establish yourself. With commitment and consistency, you will soon be seen as the "go to" person for your industry or service area.

7. **Proven Market Demand for What You Offer.** Before you can assess this, you need to know what you will be offering your markets. Then you are in a position to present your solution to see if they bite. Is what you offer something that they obviously want to buy? The best way to determine this is to identify an obvious void in the market for what you do and then test to see if there are any takers.

8. **Market Understands Your Offering (or can understand the offering).** I remember promoting a technology company in the late 1990's and talking with people in their sixties and

seventies about the email function offered in the platform. Email use, although quite widespread, had not been fully integrated into the lives of our ageing population. Halfway through my presentation, while explaining the email function, a woman in the audience asked me, "What's email?" At first I wanted to laugh, believing she was teasing me, but I looked into her eyes and realised that she truly had no idea what I was talking about. So I answered, "Oh, email stands for 'electronic mail'." She smiled and asked, "How much does that cost to send?" I said, "Oh, ma'am, it's free with your service provider." She shook her head, looked at her partner sitting next to her and said, "I don't know how you would get a stamp on something electronic." At that point, I knew that I was in a market that was years away from understanding what I was selling. I tucked tail and ran the other way.

These are the eight factors I look at when assessing a pond. Does doing this type of due diligence seem like a lot of work? It is. But this step, as well as the ones that will follow in this chapter, will save you time, money, and frustration. Any market worth entering is worth doing a bit of prep work around. If it does not hold up under examination, it definitely will not produce should you allocate resources towards it. Put in the time and save yourself some money down the road.

Selecting Ponds that Fit Your Business Model

Here's the thing: If you chase the money, you will never catch it. If you develop markets that you enjoy working with and that you can service the hell out of, you will absolutely develop a profitable and sustainable business model. To find the right markets for yourself, you first have to start with yourself. You have to know enough about yourself to know what is going to fit and what won't. You want to have a business where you can make exceptional money working with great people that you enjoy, doing great work that they appreciate. Business owners tend to think that this is impossible, but I would argue that it is laziness on their part. If they are not prepared to do this foundation work in the beginning, they are forcing themselves to settle for any 'less than optimum' market. Not a good thing.

Developing a market that you hate takes as much effort as developing one you like. Therefore, choose markets that you like (or that you can learn to like). I recommend doing a bit of personal inventory before moving ahead on any one market. Here is a question you have probably thought about but never taken the time to fully answer:

How do you like to engage with clients?

Here is the follow up question: Are you truly curious about who your market could be? Curiosity is a key performance indicator when developing markets. You want to kick tires a little bit and see how they shake out. Do this even with the markets you are unsure about or that you might have a negative bias towards (as previously discussed). When you kick the tires, you are activating the thinking part of your brain. This is a good thing. A lot of our clients get stuck on choosing even one market to serve because they think they can serve almost everyone. But that is not really true, is it? If you find yourself stuck in considering markets that you would like to work with, start with what you already know. It is a bit of a 'cheat' to get you where I need you to be, so let's keep it between us.

I want you to think of your three favourite clients. These are people that you love hearing from, talking to, and doing collaborative work with. Take a clean piece of paper our and draw three columns from top to bottom. Write their name at the top of each column. For each client, think about what things you enjoy the most while working with them. Describe these things in as much detail as you can. We will use some of these characteristics as part of our vetting process in determining what markets to go into. Do they pay on time? Do they respect the work that you produce? Do they return your calls or emails when you have questions? Do they refer you to others? Do they speak highly of you and what you produce? Write down anything and everything you can think of.

Now, on the other side of that piece of paper, make three more columns, and write down the names of three clients that you don't particularly like working with. These do not have to be current clients. They can be people that you have worked with in the past.   I challenge you to make a list of any and all the characteristics about these undesirable clients. We are going to use these two sides as the 'report card' on which we judge markets and prospective clients. Lots of the good side; none of the bad side.   Now it is time to put this into practise in determining which markets will be best for us.

Here are the steps I use and you can use when considering which markets are worthy of your attention.

- Be clear with your definition of 'great clients' for you and your model. Go back to that first side of the sheet and think about what makes a great client for you. Remember that this is a personal decision. It might not be what other people think is ideal and that is okay. We are building a business model that is tailored for you.

- Be clear on how you want clients to buy from you and how often. Take some time and describe with clarity how you want clients to engage with you. What are the steps from their finding out about you, all the way through to the end of the transaction? This is process work and will let you identify what the 'ideal' process would look like for you and the client. Do not think about what you are 'willing to do'; instead think of what you would 'like to do'.

- Be clear on what defines a bad client for you and your model. Flip over your first sheet of paper and look at all the descriptions of naughty clients for you. Look at the things they do to piss you off, describe for each characteristic why their acting that way does not allow you to give them your best.

- What types of clients do you share commonalities with? Commonalities are a key way to build intimacy with your markets. Some areas where you can seek commonalities could be education levels, faith, geography, interests, or even gender. From an education point of view, one of our clients who is a venture capitalist, sources her deals from Harvard grads building their companies. As she is a Harvard grad herself, this opens up a door to a common experience with those who she wants to serve. On a faith basis, we have a lawyer who is Catholic and who specialises in drafting wills and estate planning for Catholic clients. The discussion around faith, and how they want their estate prepared, has a common language that both speak. With geography, we have a client in Alberta who is not only from the Prairies but who is in cattle country and she works primarily with agribusiness. The daughter of a rancher, not only does she provide expertise to her clients but she understands their business model intimately as it was once her family business. With respect to interests, one of our clients is a judo practitioner who sells a line of Judogi (the outfit that judoka wear during practice) and her superior product is introduced every time she takes the mat in a competition. Her business development strategy circles around being a national judo champion. Finally, regarding gender, a colleague of ours is a female lawyer who is divorced and is a divorce attorney. She works with women who are getting divorced to ensure a fair settlement from their husbands. Women flock to her because not only does she have a reputation for taking care of her clients, but she because she knows first-hand the dynamics a woman faces when ending a marriage. These are just some examples. You can brainstorm on your own. Imagine an immigration consultant who was an immigrant themselves, or a menu consultant who had been a chef in a restaurant. If you can share a common language, then you can establish intimacy so much more quickly. Just make sure the shared language is a language that you love. If you are not passionate about it, do not engage it as a market. Here are some commonalities that are easiest for professionals to leverage with their niche markets:

• Education

• Faith

• Geographical Proximity

• Interests/Hobbies

• Gender

• Similar Background

• Marital status

Start to make yourself a list of all the possible or potential markets that you could go after. Write down every group you could go after, even ones that you are not that excited about. The only requirement is that they are likely to be filled with clients (you think). These are groups that you have some type of commonality with, that likely have ideal clients for you, and that you know there are a lot of them in that particular market. I challenge you to come up with at least 40 potential ponds that you could go after if you wanted. You will not go after all of them, but I want you to do a brain dump of all the ones that you could go after if you had to.

Once you've made your list of 40, take a pen and strike through every pond that you would hate working with or that you get a negative reaction to when considering working with them. Trust your intuition here. After all the years of coaching clients the one thing I know is that clients will not engage markets they are not excited about. Save yourself the time and trouble by not going after markets that you are not interested in.

Once you have given your list its haircut, look at the remaining list. From this list make two separate lists. For the first list, on its own page, list in sequential order the markets you think are the most lucrative down to the markets you think will be the least lucrative. Number 1 will be the most lucrative market, and the last one will be the least lucrative. Then on a separate piece of paper set up a second list and take that same group of names. Now list in sequential order the markets that you are most interested in working with down to the markets you are least interested in working with. When you are finished you will have two pieces of paper with the same names listed, but they likely will be ordered slightly differently. Look to see which names make the top five in both lists. If there are none, then expand it to the top ten. So, which names are making the cut in both lists? These are the five names to take to the next stage.

Where to Find your Ideal Ponds

Now that you have your handful of markets to explore, we need to find them. Do not over think this step. In 14 years of working with clients on identifying markets, we have found that even the most elusive market can be discovered using some key strategies outlined below. If after following these steps the market still does not present itself, move onto a different market. Do not beat a dead horse. Here are my quick tricks for turning into a truffle-snorting pig.

Look around yourself. Find people within your existing network that are members of the niche market. If you are hunting accountants, think about who you already know that is an accountant. Your 'accountant' knows a lot about accountants because he/she hangs out with them every day. They hung out with them in university, and have not stopped. People inside a niche market know the mechanics of that market. Asking them will save you hours of research and you get it right from the horse's mouth. Here is another example: If you were hunting artists, ask them: "What events do you go to? Where do you interact with other artists? Where do you buy your materials? Where do you show your art? Do you attend classes or conferences?" The key thing is to be curious, so ask a lot of questions. Talking to members of the niche that you want to engage with is time very well spent. Primary research (you talking directly to members of the markets you want to serve) is hard to beat.

Google the market you are trying to find out about. Give yourself a quick tutorial on "effective search strings." How do you find that out? Google, people! Aren't you listening? It is a mystery to me how few people understand how to use Google effectively when searching. Invest thirty minutes into finding out how Google can search up information on your behalf and you will be well prepared to find the markets you are looking for. If you are hunting female lawyers, you would search "female lawyers" and, for example, "Toronto." If you are not getting hits then you might search "female lawyers" and "associations" and "Toronto." If can't find something right off the bat in your local market, look at national organisations and then see if they have a chapter near you. Using this strategy helped me to book a 90 city speaking tour in less than 48 hours (more on this in a moment).

Use relevant words in your search. When you are searching, use the words "organisation," "association," and the magic word, "conference." Conference is business development speak for where your niche markets get together with one another. We call these 'watering holes'. Remember this term as we are going to reference it a lot in this book.

Do not be afraid of starting wide! Sometimes you need start out quite general and then narrow your focus. There are many organisations run by volunteers that don't have a good website or an up-to-date website. Don't dismiss the fact that they might still be active and so go wide in your approach and then narrow down to find out if the group (niche market) is worth further investment.

To find one, ask one. When you do find groups, ask them about other groups in the space. In most cases, a particular group in a city is well aware of other groups in that same city. Use the insider expertise. Once you find one, on average they will be able to identify three more for you. If I am looking for a woman's group in Tampa, all I need to do is find one and then when I engage them I would say, "What other groups are in Tampa that support women?" The answers might include groups that support female accountants, groups that support female lawyers, groups that support administrative assistants, etc. You will be shocked at what you can find. In Vancouver, BC in 2012, there were over 40 groups that supported professional women – from the Forum of Women Entrepreneurs right through to the E-Women Network, and all the industry groups in between.

If you can't find groups to fit your exact search, consider going deeper. If looking for one-armed wallpaper hangers, look at local renovation groups, schools that teach interior design, or even trade magazines for the construction trades.

On average, each of your niche markets (ponds) will have approximately three-five associations (watering holes) that you will be able to identify. If you are truly stumped, move on to other markets. It shouldn't be that hard to uproot the opportunities.

Case Study: Identifying, Engagement

When I decided to do a speaking tour in 2003 and again in 2007, I used the same process each time. The first tour took me three months to plan; the second just 48 hours. Each tour had over 90 engagements. When planning the first one, I had a lot of help; the second one I planned entirely on my own using the best practices outlined below.

The first thing I did was to make a list of all the types of business women we like to work with at Ghost CEO™. I came up with a list of over 40 organisations, comprised of everything from realtors to lawyers, and all the other groups in between. Then I listed all the cities that I wanted to travel to. Once I had compiled these lists, I started my general search of national organisations, and then narrowed my focus to state organisations and then city organisations. Groups such as CREW (Commercial Real Estate Women) and ASWA (American Society of Women Accountants) have city chapters all over so I used those to fill in most of my cities. With CREW alone I booked 20 engagements just from the contacts on their website. I asked every Executive Director of CREW one question: "What other women's groups are in your city?" On average, they gave me the names of three to five different organisations. Some didn't know of any (but this was rare) and one, in San Francisco, gave me ten names.

After a week of doing research and compiling groups, I had over 250 women's groups spread over the 90 cities. Some were national organisations, some were state, and many were independent groups within the city. Over the following two weeks I booked 114 engagements in 90 cities. Every group that I talked with on the phone was able to tell me about other groups that they partnered with previously. With most of my engagements, two or more organisations came together to share my presentation. In Detroit, four women's groups partnered.

Finding watering holes can be easy, but you need to be clear on who you are looking for. Once on the trail of opportunity, put on your Sherlock Holmes hat and investigate. Find out where they are at. As with any skill, the more you practice "prospecting" the easier it becomes. Choose the ideal client, assign them to a market, find out where their watering holes are, conduct your research to assess the viability of the niche market, and be ready to engage.

How Many Ponds at One Time?

Business owners are broken up into three groups: Those who target everybody; those who target nobody; and those who target a handful of niche markets (ponds). I very much want you to be the third type. The perfect amount of markets for you to develop at any one time is three. Three? You say? That isn't enough! I can easily handle 4, 6, 12, 20! I am business professional, hear me roar! Simmer down tiger. Four is too many, and two is too few. Three has proven to be the perfect number for allocating resources (time and money) and ensuring you are focused. When you start focusing on just three markets, you will discover you become very strategic in your activity. You change from being a generalist to a specialist and those niche markets start to realise and take notice that you are very different from everyone else in the market.

This will prove to be hard for you. You have already spent a large part of this chapter figuring out all the different markets you can go after and as you start to identify markets, it becomes a self-fulfilling prophecy. Markets are everywhere! Yes they are. But just because they are there doesn't mean you have to attack them all simultaneously. You might be going from not knowing how to find a market to seeing them pop up all over the place. Look there's one and another one! This is a common experience and very exciting. But, it can also become dangerous. The more markets you think you can enter; the harder it is to commit to just three. Not only are you going to commit to just three, but you're going to commit to those three and avoid all other markets for a 90 day period. What? Are you crazy Chris? That's blasphemy against the Profit Gods! Choosing and focusing on just three markets will allow you enough time to see which of these markets is going to produce a majority of your opportunities. You will notice which of the three is producing a bit, but could be better. The poorly performing market will show its ugly head, begging for the bullet. That's okay.

Darren Coleman, a well-respected Wealth Manager with Raymond James in Toronto (www.ColemanWealth.com), refers to the three markets as the "Tiger," the "Pony" and the "Dog." His philosophy is that you need to feed the Tiger, ride the Pony, and kill the Dog. Now, don't get all pissy on me and throw red paint on my fur coat, it's just an analogy! The Tiger is a market that right out of the gate starts to produce opportunities for you. The Pony is a market that is kicking along and has potential. It is not as exciting as the Tiger, but you are seeing measurable results from the work. The Dog is normally the one that you are most excited about and it ends up just being a disappointment. After the 90 day mandate, the Dog gets a bullet.

Do not expect to know which is which right off the bat. The reason we put a 90 day mandate in place is because you have to give these markets some time to develop. You don't know until after the 90 days which is which. Some of your markets are going to start off strong and you will get very excited only to watch them sputter out after a month. Others will take a bit of time to warm up but once they are at operating temperature, they are awesome. At the end of 90 days you can look back and identify which ones performed and which one was a failure. Failure is okay as long as you are failing forward. We are looking for the trend.

At the end of your 90-day mandate, you need to have an honest conversation with yourself and classify each of the markets. At that point you need to keep the Tiger happy so keep on feeding it. Do what you do, and don't mess with it. With the Pony, ride it just a little bit harder to get it going a little bit faster. You need to kill the Dog and replace it with the next market that you have warming up in the wings. Make sure that you don't fall in love with your markets or you will end up keeping the Dog longer than you should. You need to euthanise that little bugger and swap it out on Day 91. Our clients fight with us to keep the Dog because they put so much time and effort into developing that market that they don't want to let it go. Until you let it go, it will bog you down with that ugly smell of failure. Let it go. Bullet..NOW!

When swapping out a market, you want to have the next market warming up and that's why it's key to be curious about markets that might fit with your mix always in all ways. You don't want to have a Dog in place and not be able to replace it because you don't have anything on the back burner. This is why I want you to continue to be curious and go through your process of examining markets even when you're working three. As you become more skilled in market identification and practice due diligence on those markets, you'll start having a waiting list of markets that you're ready to engage with should the time come when you need to remove a Dog and replace it with something better.

The greatest concern people have with choosing just three niche markets is that they think other opportunities will pass them by. You have probably heard service providers say, "Geez, I work with everyone. Everyone can be my client." If you say 'everyone', that means 'no one' and because you are a generalist you will sound exactly like everyone else competing for that business. Not making yourself a specialist in three niche markets sentences you to a lifetime of competing on price. Specialising makes a lot of sense in the market. Who do you think makes more money in medicine: A general practitioner, or a heart specialist? Trick question? Yes. Specialist good; generalist bad.

Any clients outside of the three markets that you service do not have to be turned away at the door if they fulfil your ideal client requirement. It is more about focus rather than what you are bringing in for business. The three markets are the ones that you are investing your time and resources in for that 90 day mandate. All other markets will have to wait. For example, if you were focusing on selling to realtors, mortgage brokers, and bankers and an investment advisor happens to come in (one of the markets you're not currently focusing on), you can still work with that investment advisor but you're not going out to actively hunt additional investment advisors right away, just because one came in.   If you like working with that investment advisor, 'investment advisors' could be your backup market for your Dog market. If you decide to focus on more than three markets you will spread yourself too thinly and none of the markets will mature to the level you need them to within 90 days. As well, a panda will die because of your indiscretion and you will have to find a way to live with that.

Having only one or two markets makes me nervous and it should make you nervous too. You need to hedge your bets and diversify your dependence on any one market. We never know which market will hit big and which one will suck, so you want to have three options in place. Here is my step-by-step action set that I use when launching my initial three markets in a new business venture:

When you decide on your initial three markets and have completed the preliminary research on them, it is time to engage them. Go to your calendar (online, on your phone, paper, sun dial) and mark 90 days from today.

When you start, do not invest any time trying to guess which is the Tiger, the Pony, or the Dog. Show them equal love and attention. People are always surprised by which markets perform and which ones don't. This isn't Sophie's Choice. You don't have to pick one over the other...yet.

That said, be mindful of how each of them do by keeping an eye on how they develop (or not). If you can't measure it, you can't manage it so make sure you have some indicators in there to judge their performance. For the ones that aren't working well, keep on pushing. Remember that some markets take longer than others to develop so don't stop working them until the 90 day mandate is up (easier said than done, I know).

I keep a journal to track what I notice about each market's development. You can forget some really interesting things about how markets develop if you don't write them down, so try to keep regular notes on what you are doing, what you are seeing, and things of interest. Down the road, we can review these to see what worked, what didn't, and what we learned from the experience. We will take the best practices and move forward.

If at any time during the 90-day mandate, you see another market that catches your attention, put a pin in it, and start doing your due diligence on it. Do not engage that market until the end of the 90-day mandate. Engaging before the 90 days is up will throw off the formula and will diminish the return on your work. You need to trust me on this. I have seen markets do nothing for 10 weeks and then the last two weeks catch fire and surpass the performance of the other two. Give yourself the best chance of success by staying the course.

As your 90 day mandate ends, prepare to euthanise the Dog immediately and engage with the next market you have done your due diligence on. As you board the new market, do not have a honeymoon. Most take on their new market and forget about the Tiger and the Pony, just because we have something new and shiny to play with. Make sure you are giving your other two markets equal attention. The new market gets 33% of your focus; the Tiger gets 33% of your focus; and the Pony gets 33% of your focus. Keep it even and make it easy on yourself.

After you do the 90-day shuffle a few times, you will find that you have upgraded markets. What used to be awesome, might be 'so-so' now. Maybe you have two Tiger markets and one Pony. When this happens, you can look to 'add' an additional market, rather than replacing one. By this point, you'll be a seasoned veteran, and be able to handle four for a short time. As soon as the new market starts to beat the existing Pony market, drop the Pony market. Get it? You are always up scaling your markets.

Here is a real world example: Let's say I have two markets generating $10,000 a month each and one market generating $5,000 a month. I decide that I want to add a new market into the mix as I think I can do better than the $5,000 market, but I don't want to toss that revenue until I'm certain. I give that new market 90 days to outperform the existing Pony market. If it does, I swap them. If it doesn't, I try a different market for another 90-day mandate. When I have a market that is doing more than the $5,000., I kill the Pony and focus my attention on the new market to grow it even further. Some of you may think I'm contradicting my earlier statement that you should only focus on three niche markets. This is true as you're building the skill of managing markets but later on in this book we will talk about how systems can be implemented to help big fish manage multiple ponds. In the beginning, until you master this skill, limit yourself to three active ponds at any given time. You can start to 'freestyle' a bit when you have mastered this technique. If you start to falter, go back to the basics of three.

Preparing to Engage with Your Chosen Ponds

Oh, baby, you've already come a long way! We know what makes a good market. We know how to decide which markets are going to work for our business model. We know how to find our ideal markets. We know how many ponds we can manage at any given time. Now it's time to discuss the last and most important consideration before you enter and engage with your ponds.

Before we get to that, write down your three markets for the next 90 days:

Market #1 _____

Market #2 _____

Market #3 _____

These are the three markets that are going to get your total attention for next 90 days. Do they look good? Are you excited? Good! Now you need to do your final step in due diligence to make sure you know as much about your three markets as possible. By knowing where the niche markets are and that they have 'watering holes', you can now start to do your research to make sure that they're worthy of your investment. All the work you've done thus far has allowed you to whittle all the options down to the three ponds. This step will set you up for success in these markets and position you as the heir apparent Market Shark.

Here are the questions that need to be answered for each of your three markets to complete due diligence. Remember: Go through these questions for each of your three niche markets. Don't cut corners. How you do one thing is how you do everything so be exact with the information.

1. **What is the size of the market?** This needs to have a numerical value. Big isn't the right answer. You need to define how many target clients are in the niche market. One of the qualities to look for in a market is that it has to be growing and does not have a population that we are going to exhaust quickly. If you cannot produce exact numbers, spend some time making as much of an educated guess as possible.

2. **Watering holes.** You've chosen your market and now you need to figure out where those ideal clients cluster together on a regular basis. Hitting prospects one-by-one is heavy lifting. If you can go to a networking event, an industry group, an association meeting, or a conference, you can see many of your ideal clients in one spot, and over a shorter time. Make a list of the three to five watering holes that your niche market uses to bring its members together.

3. **Buying Traits.** How does your market buy services or products like yours? Do they pay cash? Do they finance? Do they need much time to think about it? Do they buy on impulse? How important is reputation? Do they take the recommendations of others within that pond? You need to have the inside track. If you can find an existing contact who is a representative of the market, you can ask them these questions. If they don't have the answers, they can speak with colleagues to find out the information for you. You can use the same person you used previously in the chapter or someone new.

4. **Loyalties.** Are members of this market normally loyal to a particular brand or does price determine their decision? Are they people who will only buy Coke and not generic Cola? Are they people who look for deals or look for something that is exclusive? How important is service to them? We want to know what will create intimacy in this market so that once we engage them; they feel a loyalty to our offering. Nobody wants a one-time client.

5. **How do they like to be educated on offerings like yours?** Do they like to be presented to? Do they like to have questions answered? Do they like to receive information that they can review by mail, or by email or other electronic formats? Do they like to peruse a website to read up on companies that they do business with? Do they rely heavily on word of mouth? These are all key factors in knowing how to position your offering to the niche market.

6. **What else do they buy?** By understanding who else in the market is selling to your clientele, you can begin formulating how you can make it easy for them to buy from you. Incorporating best practices learned from colleagues is a key way to streamline your business processes to engage with and close clients more quickly. As well, these companies could all become strategic alliances (a topic we cover in depth in later chapters).

7. **How familiar is your niche with your particular solution?** Are they early adapters (those who buy more quickly than do the masses)? Have people in this niche bought products like yours before? If so, did they have a positive experience or do you need to showcase how you are different from other vendors they bought from in the past? What is their education cycle from when they first find out about your business to wanting to buy from you? Days, weeks, months,

years? Do they like to watch other people buy first and then follow? These are all things you can learn by talking to representatives of your niche market.

8. **How open are they to new people entering the pond?** Are they protective? Do they openly welcome new blood? Are the indifferent? It's surprising how many niche markets block new people from entering. If you're not one of them, they don't want to talk to you. Others are very open and inclusive, and anybody who shows interest in servicing them will have a chair at the table. Regardless, there are many strategies that can be put in place to help you quickly become part of that market, and to position yourself as a leader (Market Shark).

9. **How long does it take an outsider to become an insider?** For those vendors coming in from the outside, this is a key point in your development process. When I left Kamloops for Vancouver, I was known as "the guy from the Interior." I made the move to Vancouver and it still took me two years for people there to start seeing me as being from Vancouver (which I didn't immediately correct for selfish reasons). When relocating to Vancouver from Kamloops, we moved directly into the yuppie neighbourhood of Kitsilano. My boxes were barely unpacked when I claimed Vancouver as my new home. Contacts in Vancouver would say, "Where are you from?" and I would say, "I live over in Kitsilano." This would often bypass any feelings that I was an outsider. Granted, I didn't actually answer their question, but it worked. Once they got to know me, it became less of an issue, but it's something to be aware of because it still plays a factor in many markets. They take additional time to trust the 'outsider'. Now that I have a house on Vancouver Island, I've noticed that people are here are referred to as "Islanders" and those in Vancouver as "Mainlanders." The question that I immediately asked my neighbours after moving in (almost all of them from

elsewhere) was, "When does someone become an "Islander?"
They all said that you become an Islander when you decide to
live on the Island. If you ask people born and raised on the
Island the same question, you get a very different answer. I
guess it is the same for everywhere. For anyone who lives in
Manhattan, you know the differentiation that people make
depending on which borough you come from or live in. In
Los Angeles, being from Malibu compared to being from the
Valley will be viewed differently.

10. **Who are the market gate keepers?** Which names seem to
come up repeatedly, and by whom? What do you know
about these gatekeepers? How long have they been in the
market and what role do they play? How much influence do
they truly wield? More on this in the next chapter as well.

11. **Who has offered your service or product before in this pond?**
Are they still there? Where does their offering compare to
yours? Are they more expensive or less? Are they specialists
or generalists? How will you position against others who are
seen as doing the same thing that you do? If there was a
provider in place before you and they left, how long ago did
they leave and why? If no one has been in this pond before,
why? With the female market in the Ghost CEO™ women
were dismissed when it came to professional development
training because there were so many more men in senior
management roles. At the beginning when I told colleagues
that I was focusing on female clientele, those colleagues
scoffed and told me it would never work because women
weren't interested in doing business development. Their
short-sightedness, again, led to a huge opportunity that we
have been enjoying since 1999.

12. **What is the best product or service for you to offer you
market first?** Depending on market dynamics and how they

buy, your most expensive offering may not be what you lead with. Think of Costco: They give you a taste of a chicken wing and you end up buying a fifteen pound box. What will be your 'taster' to offer the market an opportunity to experience your product or service?

13. **Where will your first set of clients come from within the market?** Who are the early adapters? The easiest way to determine this is to watch how certain people buy new services or products coming in. You're not only a vendor but also an observer of your niche markets.

14. **How does the market refer/endorse solution providers?** What causes them to action on this by bringing up a provider's name to another member of the pond? This is a key performance indicator that will lead to your success.

15. **Who are the potential strategic alliances already in the market for your business?** How can you selfishly work with others for mutual gain? Make a list of all the other complementary providers in the market. Consider who they currently have alliances with and how you would fit into that mix, either as an addition or a replacement.

16. **How long do you think it will take before you see profitability trending in the right direction?** This is more a question about financial forecasting. But after you consider who the early adapters are, how likely the market is to receive you warmly and bring you into the fold, and what you're going to lead with as your first offering; you should be able to forecast how long it will take before you start to trend positively on your cash flow. This is key so spend the most time thinking about this.

Ultimately, pond selection is extremely important. Most don't invest enough time and then have to backtrack repeatedly on work they could have accomplished at the beginning. When you truly know your market, you can better understand your market. When you understand your market, you can be efficient in your development of that market. When you are efficient of your development of the market, the market accepts you and rewards you by giving you their business. All of these are the required steps of establishing yourself as the true Market Shark of that market. Talk is cheap. Let's get onto discussing how you can enter and engage your three ponds now with due diligence.

Chapter 3– Entering & Engaging the Pond

I've been throwing around a couple of terms that are best fully defined before we move forward. They are going to be stitched throughout the rest of our conversation, so let's get on the same page. The first one is watering hole and the second one is the pond. Let's define how these two are different from and related to one another.

A watering hole refers to 'a place where groups of ideal clients hang out together.' If you are hunting doctors, a medical association would be a watering hole. If you're hunting lawyers, a bar association luncheon would also be considered a great watering hole for you to attend (if you're allowed). If you know lawyers like I do, bars, taverns, pubs, and places that sell 'grey things' are also good watering holes. Market sharks like watering holes because they allow you to be extremely efficient in how you engage your markets. They are where these ideal clients already get together on a regular basis, and they make it easier for you to have a much larger impact in a shorter amount of time.

A pond, as you may already have guessed, is the slang we use for a niche market. A pond of fish is just like having a favourite fishing hole. It's a place where you feel very confident that every time you go there you will come home with an opportunity. As we explore how to enter and engage your various ponds (three!) in an effective manner, it's best to distinguish between a watering hole and a pond. Every pond you identify will have watering holes, if it doesn't, we'll want to look for a different pond to target. Watering holes get you much farther ahead in a much shorter period. You can connect with a bunch of prospects within a short period, rather than repeat the one-on-one thing over and over again. Watering holes not only give you quicker returns on your time investment (you can vet a lot of prospects before moving them to one-on-one) but also burns your resources (additional time and money) much more slowly.

Reconnaissance of the Pond

Before you prepare to activate and engage any market in person, conduct some 'under the radar' reconnaissance. When you go in a little quieter than you might normally, you can observe dynamics that might shift, or be less obvious when you are inside. When examining your markets, you want to find at least three to five watering holes that will provide opportunity to conduct research on and consider the viability of that pond as a whole. You want to see how these prospective clients attend events, what they talk about, and how they engage with one another.

Our clients go to events regularly, but until they have a strategy, they don't really have any process to follow. They end up missing the obvious entry points because they don't know what to look for. When they get to us, they can be dismissive of the watering holes in their markets. Once we introduce the strategy with them and have them implement it in these same markets, it's like the lights come on. They cannot believe how many opportunities they had previously walked by. Understanding and activating watering holes within niche markets is the one strategy that allows me to build business at least 5 times faster than competitors. I leverage the group that has already formed rather than trying to form groups (heavy lifting). Every business I have built and any business I intend to build in the future will be heavily reliant on watering holes. If there are not a lot of watering holes in a market I am targeting, I move on. Watering holes serve to organise my market, give me information on them, make known what other providers are already in there, and bring them together for me to talk to. Leverage what is already in place; otherwise you make more work for yourself.

Most groups have some type of web presence, like...you guessed it, a website.   These websites normally promote their events, membership benefits, other vendors (normally listed under 'sponsors' or 'partners'), and the leadership of the group (the 'gatekeepers'). If they don't have a website that lists all their different events, they likely have a Facebook page, a Twitter account, or something else that allows you to sign up for newsletters that outline future events. On the Facebook page or the website, you will find photos from their events and the people in the photos are tagged. Research the names and find out who the players are. The individual who appears in a majority of the photos is the gatekeeper (or wants to be an influencer). Knowing this person (or people) is important for you moving forward. They are going to be your entry point into the group. Additional research can lead you to find out who sponsored the event. Often the sponsors end up being the members and their respective companies. Through this research, it's like being a fly on the wall without having to go to the event.

It takes some time to gather this information, as you are often working backwards from one piece of information (a photo or a company name), but once you have done so you will start to get a feel for the group. You start to understand how often they host events. What types of people attend the events and how frequently. What types of companies sponsor the events and on what topics/themes. By getting this picture, opportunities for your engagement start to appear right before your eyes. The one piece of information that I go to immediately if available, is the board or leadership of the group. Normally, but not always, the higher the credentials of the board, the more discerning the group will be. I make a list of all the people who sit on that board and then I Google them individually to learn more about them. LinkedIn can also be a great tool for gathering background on the people who are involved with a particular watering hole. Some groups have a LinkedIn group as well so remember to look for that as well.

When I first expanded into Vancouver, I was curious about the different women's groups in the city. At that time, Vancouver had over 40 women's groups so there were lots of options to explore. Sometimes having too many options is as challenging as not having enough, so I spent much time researching each group to find out their focus, the types of members that they attracted, and the type of board/leadership that was involved in the organisation. In particular, I researched the gatekeeper of each pond, which is something we will explore in depth later on in the chapter.

In looking at each group, I started to whittle down the organisations that seemed to hold the types of clients we were targeting. Being a 6'6" man at a women's event, I tend to stand out. So prior to conducting primary research on each group (i.e. going to see first-hand how things worked), I perused the photos on their websites to make sure that men attended their events. If you are the only guy at a women's event, you tend to stand out like a sore thumb. You can get treated as either an unexpected and honoured guest...or as a creep. I chose to go to events where there were other guys in the photos or they at least had previously had a male speaker. If I thought I was really going to stand out, I would recruit a female friend from that niche market to attend the event and do research on my behalf. I would provide a list of questions for her to find out for me. I continue to use these practices and my cheat sheet of questions is just below.

For the events I did attend, I made mental notes throughout the process. I learned from a young age that 'how someone does something is how they do everything.' You can judge what kind of group you are dealing with by how they run their events. High level attendees do not put up with shit events. I checked to see how registration worked and was managed. How I was received at the door and directed on where to go and what to do. The quality of speaker they had and the topic covered. What type of networking component was involved with the event and if it happened before or after the speaker. The quality of the resources that were shared with the attendees and whether there was a display table where members could put out their information.

Watering Hole Questions – Cheat Sheet

The better you understand the watering hole, the quicker you are to decide if it is somewhere that you want to invest time and resources into, or if you should put that group on the back burner and work on finding one that seems more active in a way that will benefit your profit model. I always make myself a cheat sheet before I (or someone else on my behalf) go to an event that includes all the information that I want to gather. Here are some of the common questions that make my list:

1. **When?** When do the events happen? Is it a morning group, a luncheon group, an afternoon group, or an evening group? I find that the morning and afternoon groups seem to produce better opportunities for me. On occasion, evening groups have been client goldmines, but much more rarity compared to morning and lunchtime groups.

2. **Is the event is held at someone's house?** Does the location rotate each month? (i.e. Chamber event might choose different members to host each month.) Do they host the event at the same place every month (for example, at a well-respected law firm)? That's likely to attract a certain type of attendee as well.

3. **How frequent?** The sweet spot is monthly. Weekly groups tend to be high-maintenance and attract people that need handholding. People who can meet weekly remind me of AA meetings for business. It ends up being a support group rather than a development group. Groups that meet quarterly don't really act as a group so you miss out on some of the watering hole dynamic. Most professionals in control of their work

lives can arrange to be somewhere once a month. They act like a group, and attract the type of people I'm most interested in from a business point of view. Luckily this is the most common you'll come across.

4. **Professional or Bush League?** Is the event well run, well organised, and well managed, or does it look like people are piecing things together at the last minute? If you want to be a professional then you have to work with professional people. Attending patched together meetings hosted by people who don't have their shit together not only looks bad on them but shows poorly on you as being someone prepared be associated with such an rookie event. I always know I'm in the wrong place when the organiser is running around looking for name tags, coffee pots, or wondering where catering is.

5. **Cost?** I tend to stay away from any event that is free. People who go to free events normally have a hard time putting value on things or, even more importantly, have a hard time paying for things. If you are wondering about this, go to a department store when they are offering free cookies and coffee. It looks like a refugee raft about to capsize. I like the cost of an event to be just enough to make sure people are serious but not so much as to be price prohibitive. For your business, think about the types of clients you are looking to attract, determine what price point that market would be most comfortable paying up to. If you're selling Porsches, you probably don't want to go to freebie networking events; if you're selling a real value–based service, you may not want to go something that charges $200 per month to attend. This is why it's important for you to have done the background work to identify and understand the markets you want to serve so you know if your prospective clients are in the room.

6. **Food Service?** Normally the better the food, the better the level of person who attends. Really. People who are value-minded (i.e., cheap) tend not to worry about the food as they just want a good price. Those who can pay will not suffer bad food. I have found that if the food being offered is really good then it's likely that the organisation is targeting people of a more discerning taste. Again, you have to figure out how this fits within your target niche markets. If you see the traditional roast chicken, lasagne, mixed vegetables, Caesar Salad, and hockey-puck buns, look elsewhere.

7. **Quality of Speakers?** Not all organisations have speakers but the quality of speakers from the ones that do, will give further insight to the organisation. If they have government types or policy people, they likely lean towards being a policy organisation looking to peddle influence of the association (i.e. Boards of Trade). If you notice entrepreneurial speakers of great reputation sharing their stories and best practices, that group likely is more focused on professional development of its members. Some groups that are focused on networking will give each of their members a chance to get up and do a presentation (effectively becoming the monthly speaker).

8. **Networking Opportunity?** The sin most organisations commit is not making enough time available for attendees of the event to network. Networking is the key reason for going to these types of events. With options like TED Talks and all the other great resources available online, any event should have a heavy networking component. If it is just hosting speakers, it will end up losing traction against these online resources. When you are building your business and you attend an event with a speaker but don't get an opportunity to meet and talk with other members of the audience, then that's not a good investment of your time unless you are hunting speakers as a

market. If there is no networking component, look for another watering hole.

9. **Printed Name Tags?** It might sound simplistic, but a printed name tag compared to handwritten name tag says a lot about an organisation. Name tags that are printed and set out in alphabetical order suggest that this organisation understands and appreciates the importance of structure and efficiency. Name tags that are handwritten as you check in suggest that the organisation may be doing things at the last minute and is unsure if people are going to attend. I heard one organiser say he did not want to waste a printed name tag on someone who decided not to come. Hope you enjoy that two cents you saved, Jackass. Having printed name tags is a small piece, but it speaks volumes. Trust me, when you have attended as many of these events as I have, you will discover that the smallest things tell the biggest stories about the quality of the group and its organisers.

10. **Organised Seating?** Again, this is a small thing but the way that the organiser decides to seat people is very important. Do they have name placards at each seat designating where each person will sit, or is it a free for all? Sometimes they put table numbers on the name tag which accomplishes the same thing. Do they try to put people together that should know each other? (These are my favourite types of events.) Do they let people seat themselves based on what they are interested in? (Peer mentoring groups do this where they will have an expert in the subject seated at each table and the crowd self-selects what topics they wish to learn.) Is it a mix of any or all the above? I like organised seating; however, I'm not above switching places with someone else if there is someone in particular that I want to talk to.

11. **Any Obvious Leaders?** Are there people in the room that are helping to marshal the event or does it seem like a bunch of church ladies at a bake sale walking around asking who's allergic to peanuts? For my business models, I like to see structure and I like to see different stewards taking responsibility for different parts. Every one of those people giving direction can be considered a potential gatekeeper for that watering hole. I like having multiple options on who I can form relationships with.

12. **Business or Social?** Most business groups are actually social groups that are disguised as having business value. Getting together once a month to drink wine with people you know is not only a waste of time but it has no real impact on your business as a whole. Be discerning with your time and make business events earn your interest in wanting to attend them more than once. Clients often struggle with this because they think, "Well, I know it's social but I'm getting to know people." I ask them, "How much business do you get directly from attending those events?" The inevitable answer is 'zero' so enough said. If you meet somebody at an event and they start referring business and you're doing business back and forth, you may not need to attend that event any more to keep that relationship going. It's for dating, not swinging, people.

13. **Group is Exclusive or Inclusive?** I like to be part of groups where you have to be vetted before you come in. MENSA, Masonic Lodges, Legal Bar Associations, Women Presidents' Organisations, and even Business Improvement Areas have certain criteria that people must meet before permitted to attend events. I like my watering holes to be exclusively inclusive, this means the group carefully decides on who can come in but once you're in, then you're part of the same group. I always like to see groups that have new blood. All of

us have attended events where it's the same people who have been attending for twenty-five years and no new people come. Remember that your markets need to be replenishing all the time, this is one of the criteria for us entering. You want to see a regular influx of new people joining as these are the people you'll be forming relationships with. Groups that are exclusive, but open to new members who meet the requirements are gold.

14. **Head Gatekeeper?** In every organisation, on every team, in every room there is one true gatekeeper – a queen bee, a king – someone who the other leaders look to for direction. If there is only one thing you learn from attending an event (after confirming that it does hold opportunity for you), it is finding out who the true gatekeeper is. You can often determine this just be watching interactions for a few minutes to see who goes to whom to ask questions and who seems to answer most of the questions that come up. This is the name you want to record and keep for the work that is to follow. Be wary, though. Gatekeepers can sometimes be elusive. It can take time to be able to discern the difference between the monkey and the organ grinder. On many occasions I believed I was talking gatekeeper only to realise that they were the monkey and there was an organ grinder playing the tune behind the scenes. So don't jump to conclusions too quickly. Watch carefully and validate your perceptions based on their reactions and the actions of others.

15. **Does the Group Respect Time?** Do they start and finish on time, or are they lackadaisical? I happen to like groups that respect time because their surgical approach to the organisation suggests that the members they serve don't like to have their time wasted.

16. **Membership List?** When you arrive at the event and are collect your name tag, etc., make sure that you scan to see who else is in the room. Most groups that offer pre-printed name tags will include on the membership list the person's first and last name and the name of the company they represent. Look to see the quality and calibre of the names and the companies in the room. If you're hunting small business owners you don't want to see a lot of corporate names and vice versa. This may be the only chance for you to see all the names of the people in the room so make sure you take a few extra minutes to scan for your name on the membership list by saying to the person handling the membership table, "I'm just looking to see who else is here that I know." This is a great opportunity to see who the registrants are.

17. **Reminders?** Did the organisation send you any type of confirmation when you registered or did you receive any reminder about the upcoming event? I find that the level of communication received before an event will often set an expectation about how professional the event will be.

18. **Follow Up?** After the event, does the group do anything to follow up with those who attended? Are any notes or resources sent out? Is a thank you note sent to attendees? Is an invitation put forth for a future event? Let your intuition be strong here. We all know what professionalism is. Determine how they treat people and you'll get some key insight into the type of group and the type of members they attract.

I'm not suggesting that you sit down at the event with your questionnaire. Instead, take in the full experience of the event and then, right after (maybe in your car,) fill out all the questions that you could not answer before. At the end of that first event there is only one question that you need to ask yourself: Does the membership, leadership, and the event itself reflect the ideal clientele I'm looking to work with and want to be associated with? Math doesn't lie. If there are prospects in the room and/or people who can bring you prospects, that's the measurable you seek. Don't fall in love with the group because they serve great food, it's in a great location, at a great time, at a great price, or the people are really nice. You need to determine whether you can get a measurable result from engaging with this watering hole. If yes, continue. If no, look for the next one.

Gatekeeper Reconnaissance

It is time for you to spend a bit more time making a targeted list of all the gatekeepers within that niche market from the various watering holes. Some people stumble on this part because they are not sure who to include as prospective gatekeepers. It's always better to start with a bigger list and then you can remove people when you learn they don't fit certain criteria. All of us have invested time into a person we thought was a gatekeeper only to find out that not only do they lack teeth to get things done and no credibility that you can leverage off of.

When I'm making my initial list of suspected gatekeepers, I start with the association or organisation's executive director. This person may also be called an organiser, a managing director, a CEO – many different titles – but this is the person who oversees the going–ons of any particular watering hole.

After I make my initial list, I expand it to include board members of the different watering holes and highlight members within that pond that people talk about repeatedly. If you're not sure who those people are, consider the names and faces that show up in every picture of events of that organisation or group holds. Look at the sponsors of the events. Is there a certain company or companies that seem always to donate or be involved with particular watering holes or with the market as a whole? Look at alliances that seem to be in place. What other companies are currently offering unique and interesting services to your niche markets?

Think about the speakers. Every watering hole within that niche market seems to bring in certain names as a speaker at one time or another. These are the people already dialled into that niche market and, if they are not competition, could be fantastic entry points for you. They already have the trust of the gatekeepers of the watering holes and thus getting an endorsement from them will simplify the conversation around you potentially doing something with that particular watering hole, especially if you wanted to be a speaker yourself.

This prep work will take a fair amount of time to complete, but it is time well spent and you will make it up by not struggling to figure out things after you are already fully activated in your markets. I always set myself the goal of having at least 20 prospective gatekeepers for each niche market I am involved with. Smaller markets might have less; larger have more. Once I have my master list made for each niche, I invest time to understand who each gatekeeper is. I want to know: How long they have been in the market? Why are they there? What their interest is being a gatekeeper? Who are they likely connected with? And most importantly, what could I offer them that would fulfil a selfish need they have? The better I understand these people before I engage them, the more successful I'm likely to be in the first meeting. I think of it as starting to put together a puzzle and figuring out what goes with what and who goes with whom.

Always consider there could be a political component to these relationships. Some people like to be gatekeepers so that they can support and encourage others; others like to be gatekeepers to protect what is in place so that nothing changes. There are hundreds of other reasons why gatekeepers choose that role. It is important to consider any political edge that a person might have in choosing to be in a particular market. Some gatekeepers can be extremely territorial. Beware.

Once I have my list developed and feel that I have an understanding of everyone on the list (making assumptions based on limited exposure and observation), I start to categorise who I think to be the most powerful gatekeeper in the market down to the least powerful gatekeeper. Once done, I have my hierarchy developed.   Next, I begin to prepare for one-on-one engagement. Start with the assumption that all of these groups talk. Don't start with the top dog on the list or those at the bottom. Enter somewhere near the top. You want to confirm that the top gatekeeper in fact holds that spot. Then you want to get extra intelligence on that person from their underlings. Those near the top will have the best information for you. If you start near the bottom, you are going to be hearing from those 'far removed' how they think things work. You'll visit them later, but stick near the top if you want to enter at a high level, which you want to do, right? (Trick question: yes, of course, you want to enter at the high level with those in control).

Back in the early days of my work in Vancouver I had one of our female coaches attend a Forum for Women Entrepreneurs meeting. I had done research on the different women's groups and had already met a bunch of the executive directors at other meetings but the Forum for Women Entrepreneurs seemed to be a group that everyone talked about but that we as a company didn't know much about. I did some preliminary research and did not see anything that evidenced men attending their events so I provided my list of questions to the female Ghost CEO™ coach who went to the meeting and conducted research on our behalf.

The day after the event, we did a debrief and she had collected a lot of really powerful intelligence about how the organisation was formed, who was on the board, the calibre of members that they served, and the enormous skill and reputation of Jill Earthy, the Executive Director at the time. I asked some contacts Jill and I had in common about her, and the reviews were stellar. Once I knew that Jill was the real deal, I asked a colleague we had in common to make an introduction and Jill and I decided to meet breakfast a week later. You never know how these meetings are going to go because a lot of people in senior positions can fall in love with their title. Jill is one of the most skilled and humble people that I know and about ten minutes into breakfast; we were having belly laughs and talking about how to further support professional women in Vancouver. Right after the breakfast she made an introduction to some of her key staff and we reciprocated by introducing some of our coaches to her team. The relationship started to form over the next few months in a powerful and magical way. It led to our coaches speaking at one of their private events for a vetted group of established women building their businesses. We started to support charitable ventures that they took part in (including me being auctioned off at one of their fundraisers). As the relationship grew, Jill and I started introducing each other to people we had personally vetted and that we knew could support each other's organisations. Ghost CEO™ became a member of the Forum for Women Entrepreneurs. On average we received 15–30 new clients from their membership each year and we are committed to supporting the graduates of their different programs in any way that we can as those graduates move forward in their businesses. In most of their programming, there is some type of Ghost CEO™ engagement if requested. Of all the gatekeepers in Vancouver in professional women's watering holes, Jill Earthy stands out to me as someone who is truly amazing, inclusive, and focused on the best interests of her members.

On the other side of the coin, back in 2007 I looked to connect with the managing director (gatekeeper) of a national women's organisation. I had heard about a women's group in Seattle doing great work that was in line with our work. On numerous occasions when trying to connect with this managing director, I was blown off. I would hear through the grapevine that she had decided that I was not worthy of having a coffee with, even though we would have been a great referral source of new members for her. Rather than trying to break through the barricade and convince her that we were on the same side when it came to supporting professional women, I moved on and connected with other women's groups and engaged with that niche market regardless. Many of her association members became clients of Ghost CEO™ through other groups they were associated with. Three years after my initial attempt to connect with that gatekeeper, the organisation changed their managing director and the new woman was brilliant, a community builder in every sense of the word, and she built an impressive organisation to which other chapters across the nation compared themselves. The bond became so close between our two organisations that she is now a Ghost CEO™ coach along with her duties in the women's organisation.

If you find that one gatekeeper sucks, just put them on the back burner and wait for that watering hole to have a changing of the guard. Focus on other watering holes in your niche market. Just because an organisation has a bad steward does not mean that it's a bad watering hole. It just might not be time for you to enter. That's how it goes...move on.

Gatekeeper Preparations

This chapter is probably starting to feel like a lot of work, and it is. I appreciate that. As we drill down deeper, remember that this is a strategic play, not a tactical play. I am not interested in you going out, working hard, and throwing things against the wall with the hope that they will stick. I want you to employ strategy with which you will find the right gatekeepers who will understand what you do, why what you are offering matters, and why their market cares. When we get this sorted, these gatekeepers will be in position to hand deliver you to a prospective client base. So, stay the course as we continue to drill down looking for the good stuff. Trust me when I tell you all of this will pay off, and sooner than you think it will.

Now we are going to prepare for gatekeeper interaction. All of us have heard the stories of people preparing for a job interview by learning about the company, where it's going, the different alliances it has, etc. That's great, but this does not work for entrepreneurs. Instead, we will steal those great ideas about preparation but use them to begin developing bullet-proof relationships with gatekeepers that we can strategically benefit and who can deliver a strategic benefit back to us.

Take out your research and prioritised list of prospective gatekeepers. Look at them as people, aside from the organisation they are a part of. Human relationships are built on creating a common story, sharing a common past, or a mix of the two. It's shocking how much you can learn about people using the Internet these days. We will use the internet to find out more about these gatekeepers as people. I was doing some business with a Women Presidents' Organisation (WPO) chapter on the East Coast and there was one particular client in that chapter who I wanted to work with. I had spoken with her briefly at a presentation I made months before, but realised I needed the endorsement of the chapter's gatekeeper to position our company to do business with her company. After finding the name of the current gatekeeper of that particular chapter of the WPO, I started to dig. I learned she was a forty-five year old woman with both a law degree and an MBA from a very notable school in Boston. I learned she was Catholic, from 'Southie' (south Boston), married with five kids, had some type of connection with breast cancer, had worked with two law firms previous to starting her own, sat as a PAC president for her kids' school, raised money for her alumni association, was a Patriot's fan, and had testimonials from people in the defence industry. I know you're thinking. I was a stalker going through her trash, but between Facebook, LinkedIn, and Google I was able to get all this information.

Many find it weird to research background information on others. I feel that when you know who you're talking to, you know particular things to share with them and certain topics that you want to avoid. This is not bad and this is not manipulative. It is you investing time to figure out how you can engage with someone in a way that is most likely to support the formation of a relationship. I have teased friends who have used online dating websites and spent hours poring over the questions that try to figure out compatibility. They don't ask questions that different from the ones I was asking as I was doing research on this gatekeeper.

Once I felt I knew this gatekeeper, I reached out to her and we had a great conversation. I brought up key things that she was surprised we had in common. How did I know that she was a Patriot's fan? Well, apart from her living in New England and that being the closest football team to her, her Facebook page had Patriot's artwork on the banner and a photo of her wearing a Patriots' jersey was a pretty easy giveaway. Never underestimate the power of being prepared on who you are talking to. It's where the magic lies. I didn't tell her I was a Patriots' fan (because I'm not; go Seahawks!), but I did tease her by saying, "I know you are a good lawyer, probably Catholic seeing as you are from Boston and likely very analytical. Please tell me you aren't a Patriots' fan?" She got right into it, defending their honour and we had a good laugh over team loyalty. The Seahawks hadn't won a Super Bowl yet so she was beating me up pretty good.

What follows are some of the questions I ask myself before I engage with a gatekeeper to set up a meeting. Don't worry about what will happen in the meeting, as I'll share that with you in the next section. This is you figuring out for yourself who is this person that will be sitting across the table. It can also lead to some discussion points should the meeting stall.   Having the answers to the following questions can only help the situation so put in some time and get on your detective hat.

Individual Gatekeeper Cheat Sheet

1. **Age.** How old is this gatekeeper, and what generation are they likely going to reflect?

2. **Background.** What can you find out about them that will give you a bit of a colour commentary? I always share with clients that the background is like when you're watching a football game and the commentator talks about a particular player growing up in a single-parent family, or working from the age of 14, or coming from a rural or city area – all the colourful stuff that makes that person unique.

3. **Time in the pond.** How long have they been active in the market that they are now a gatekeeper of? Are they fresh out of the oven, or are they an established pillar?

4. **Time in this particular watering hole.** Not only their time in the overall pond, but how long have they been attached to this particular watering hole? It will not surprise you to see many gatekeepers move from watering hole to watering hole, but stay within the same market.

5. **Other interests.** Use the gatekeeper example from the beginning of this section. The gatekeeper was an observant Catholic, entrepreneurial (she started her own firm), involved in the community (was a PAC president, raised money for her alumni association, and supported breast cancer charities), and wanted to know both law and business (had a law degree and an MBA degree). These were other interests of hers that I thought were noteworthy, especially given my openly critical

viewpoint about most MBA programs, something that was better left unsaid at our initial meeting.

6. **Who do they hang out with?** Birds of a feather flock together. Look to identify those they seem to spend time with and you will start to get a better picture of that person. If any of us look at the five people we spend the most amount of time with in a given week, this will reflect upon the person that we are. Try to figure out, by looking at their associations, what type of person they may be. You can also go through their LinkedIn and search their contacts by the city they live in. You'll see who is in their local network. Depending on your level of membership with LinkedIn, sometimes you can only do this if you have the person named as a LinkedIn contact already.

7. **Education.** Are they highly educated? Did they learn on the job? How did they gain the expertise and experience that they use today in the markets they serve?

8. **Previous positions?** I love LinkedIn for this, can you tell? Most people make available their public resume for everyone to have a look at. Where do they come from? What led them to where they are now? Look at their timeline and you'll get some insight into how they progressed as a professional.

9. **Why are they in the pond?** Was it a calling, or a change of profession half way through their career? What can you discover about the reason they are in this pond now? Keep in mind that when you sit down with this person, you will be able to validate any information you have collected beforehand and fill in the gaps with great questions during that first meeting. Don't allow yourself to get derailed or stalled if you have difficulty in answering any one of these

questions. These are just guidelines. You will learn a lot in the meeting as well.

10. **Selfless or selfish.** Are they in it for themselves or are they in it to serve others? Neither is right nor wrong, but if they are in for selfish reasons (this is good!); find out what those reasons are. This is where you could be of service to them.

11. **Superhero power.** What is it about this particular person that makes them exceptional? Are they a great leader, good at raising money, able to leverage connections for others, or are they a knowledge base? What makes them unique compared to everyone else?

12. **What would they want from you?** Ask yourself what would make their life easier and think about what you have to offer, and then try to draw a line between the two. Knowing that you may have something that might be of interest to them gives you an extra card to play if the meeting is going well.

13. **Which of your connections would they want?** Peddling influence is about using people as currency. Who do you currently know that they might want to meet, and vice versa?

14. **Political spin.** Are they right-leaning, left-leaning, or in the middle and, more importantly, how does that relate to your political leanings? Do you see things through a similar political lens, or are you on opposite sides? It is very dangerous to discuss politics or religion so it's good to try to figure this out before the meeting so you don't put a foot (or both) in your mouth.

15. **Family dynamic.** Are they married, single, gay, divorced, widowed, etc. Understanding a person's family dynamic will

give you some interesting insight into what may or may not be important to them.

16. **Who do they report to?** Every gatekeeper has to report to someone. It could be a board, stakeholders, or the government. Find out who they report to so you can understand how you might be able to help them do their work more easily and get the acknowledgement for it.

17. **Who reports to them?** Figure out the hierarchy leading down from them and who does what for them. You will be surprised at how many unbelievable people do unbelievable things with an unbelievably small staff. Often a bit of leverage on your part can make everyone's life easier and endear you to them.

18. **How do they think about themselves?** Do they think they are awesome and buy their own PR? Are they humble? Are they self-deprecating to the point where it gets in the way of things? You want to have strong, confident people who like being around other strong, confident people. If you find yourself having to pick them up, dust them off, and tell them how great they are on a regular basis, it's probably best to invest in another gatekeeper.

19. **What will be interesting about you to them?** This can be difficult for many us who take for granted our accomplishments. Spend some time thinking about all the things that make you unique that you might want to drop into conversation. One of my colleagues has an impressive work history including financial services and NASCAR, but the one thing that is a game changer in meeting her, was that she was in the circus for a number of years as an aerialist. That's classic and not something you hear every day. When

she told me, I immediately demanded photo proof of which she provided and I can validate.

20. **What Do You Have in Common?** The last important list you need to make is one of all the things you have in common. People like people they trust. People trust people they think they know. People 'feel' they know people who they have something in common with. That's why alumni groups at universities are so strong, or people who attend the same church, or even people within the same industry. If you are a Mason, you have over 6,000,000 brothers around the globe. Take some time to connect the dots and see what you have in common with each of the gatekeepers you are going to engage.

These twenty questions will aid you in understanding the gatekeeper as an individual, before your initial meeting. This will serve you throughout the duration of your relationship with them. If you do this for someone who doesn't meet with you, it still gives you valuable insight into the type of gatekeepers that are in your pond. Do the work and you will get the results. Of this, I am absolutely certain.

Chapter 4 – Meeting the Gatekeepers

You have done your research, you have found the watering holes, you know how they work and you know who the gatekeepers are. It's dance time. Get ready to tango! Bust some moves! And shake your money maker!

Engagement should feel very comfortable for you because not only do you understand the market with more clarity and the watering holes within it, but you also understand who the key players are and some dynamics about them. It's like playing poker when you know what's in the other person's hand. You are ready.

The one thing I want you to have in your mind is selfishness. Selfishness is everywhere in business, but we are all too polite to talk about it...well everyone except me. You have a selfish interest in becoming part of the market. You want to sell them something to make money. You know that the gatekeepers can expedite this process. Their doing this has a selfish benefit for you, which you want to exploit. That's the one side of the coin. Now the other side is why someone would want to serve their selfish needs by enabling you to do what you want in the market they have control over. Different gatekeepers will be interested in different things, so you need to be well prepared to identify what that is right away.   Executive Directors, sponsors, speakers, service providers, and members of a pond are all going to have different selfish reasons for wanting to meet with you. Don't make them guess the reasons. You want to outline it explicitly to make it easier for them to say yes to meet with you. Then you can work your charm (and strategy) to ensure they want to further engage you and endorse you to members and prospective clients in that market.

Executive Directors

With **Executive Directors** of watering holes, I like to play it a bit cool and make the meeting more about them than about me. Let's use a well-respected, national organisation to illustrate the strategy. One in particular that comes to mind has chapters across North America. It's a group I like because there are some ideal clients in there for us and I have a strong understanding of their industry so I can talk their lingo.   When I would engage these geographical chapters, the first thing I would do is connect with the Executive Director of a particular chapter and let her know that we were currently working with commercial real estate women in the area. Many of our clients were not currently members of her association and I'd like and would like to meet with her and find out a bit more about the organisation and the benefits of membership. Since Ghost CEO™ is a strong proponent of women networking with the right types of opportunities, we wanted to hear more about their organisation prior to recommending it to our clients. I know that the Executive Director is charged with increasing membership and showing them value. It was fair to surmise that they would have a selfish interest in having a conversation with me should I become a referral source for new members (which is likely if they don't blow the meeting with me). I have NEVER had this strategy not work. I get my meeting 100% of the time.

Sponsors and advertisers

For **sponsors**, their reason for donating money to cover events is they want further exposure in that market. If I represent members who could also be clients of theirs, then they will be interested. To get a meeting with them, I say something like:

> "Hey, Bob. I saw that you're sponsoring many different events for commercial real estate women. This is a market in which we also have an established

clientele. I'd be interested in getting together for a coffee when schedules allow to find out a bit more about what you're doing, should it be a fit for some of the clients we are servicing."

As this script illustrates, I am making it about him and the benefit to him (his selfish interest of selling more), not about the benefit to me. He will think there's some benefit to me but I've dangled the carrot in front of him. If he doesn't follow through, the sponsorship might just be a token activity. If he follows up quickly, he's likely is in business development beast mode (which I like). The one consideration in this is that you will meet with many professionals who don't know how to do business development and your invitation will be a godsend to them. They will then want to know how many clients you can send to them. Approach these meetings as if you were interviewing a potential job candidate. Find out a lot about them and play your cards a bit more conservatively than normal. From a success point of view, this strategy hits about 70% of the time. Of those you meet with, half are pikers (not someone you want to do business with), but the other half are quality people that you can do some business with, maybe even form a strategic alliance with.

Other Speakers

When I am approaching **speakers** in this market, I know that they are promoting what they are talking about for a variety of selfish reasons. They could be exposing the services of their business, selling a book, selling a training program, or perhaps they make their living as a paid speaker. Here's a sample script I might send them:

"Hi, Tom. I see that you're speaking at the Commercial Real Estate Women (Austin) session in February. Our company works with many female organisations and I'd like to hear a bit more about the different content that you deliver, the different markets you're currently involved in, and any markets that we currently have influence in that you might be interested in ."

Can you see how receiving an email like this would peak the interest of this type of speaker? This strategy hits 100% of the time as well, especially if their business is professional speaking.

Service Providers

For **service providers**, you will treat them similarly to sponsors. Do a bit more research on them to see how what they do in that niche market could complement what you are doing. You might not necessarily reach out to direct competitors, but with anyone who is servicing a clientele that you'd like to service, there should be a conversation between the two of you. A script you could use with them could go something like:

"Hi Jenny. I see that you're working with the 'Professional Real Estate Women' in Austin. We have a portfolio of clients in Austin who are also in commercial real estate and I'm curious if there might be some crossover between our two companies. Let's have a coffee sometime soon and we can explore if it makes sense to explore doing something together."

What I'm not doing, and what I truly dislike, is saying, "Hey, I'd really like to meet with you to tell you about what I do, should it be helpful to your clients." Jenny is not in the business of selling my stuff; she's in the business of selling her stuff. My job is to figure out how I can use her to the benefit of my clients and how she, in turn, could use us to the benefit of her clients. To get, you have to give, so you want to model the behaviour of being a fantastic business developer (Market Shark) who understands the pond you are both swimming. As you emerge as a Market Shark, you'll find that a lot of people want to engage with you and have these conversations. You go from being the hunter to being the hunted.

Members of the market

The last group to focus on (and the most important) is the members of the market. These are people already in the market who are either active prospects for you or know active prospects. Ghost CEO™ has more than a dozen strategies we use to engage active members in a market in both sourcing new clients for us and being evangelists for our work. One of my favourites is the 'Sit'. This is where we sit down with a business owner and the only goal we have for our time together is to 'leave them better than we found them'. This is completely 'service-based' and allows us to both selflessly help a fellow business owner (which they are selfishly interested in) and also selfishly give them a taste of what we do so that it is in their head both for their own businesses and those of the people they know. We believe that when someone knows you know how to make more money for their business, they cannot 'un-know' this. Anytime they or any of their contacts struggle with business development or their bottom line, they will think of us.

Another favourite strategy is called "Coaches' Corner." Once a month we invite up to twenty business owners to come together for a facilitated conversation about a business topic of interest. It's a way for us to showcase our expertise on business topics within our discipline. These are always sold out and create a great buzz in the market.

The final strategy we use to engage members of a market is called "A Taste of Success." This is where a coach selects a market within their trade area that they are already servicing or want to be servicing, and make themselves available to members of this market for a complimentary 45-minute business coaching session. We engage various gatekeepers and offer them 1-2 of the spots to use with people in their circle they want to show some love to. Coaches cap the number of sessions to 40 during that week. Then they don't offer it again to that market for one calendar year. It is open to any professional, at any level. The only catch is they have to get one of the tickets provided by a gatekeeper. It isn't open to the general public. It is exclusively inclusive. Much like the 'sit', this is about us leaving these people better than we find them. Clients do emerge out of this sometimes, but our focus is more on having 40 evangelists out there after the week is done.

When doing thing like this, you are going to attract a lot of attention outside of your 'ideal client type' so it is important to let people know that offering a complimentary session in no way means ongoing support or a spot on the roster. Some people in our markets think that by participating in a Taste of Success, they can jump the queue on the coach's waiting list. This is not the case.

Starting the conversation by email

Once you have written the script you want to use, it's email time. Here are my preferred times to send out emails.

First choice: Tuesday Afternoons (130PM–330PM)

Second choice: Thursday mornings (9–1130AM)

Third choice: Fridays between (1PM–3PM)

On Tuesday afternoons people are finally caught up on the work they did not finish the week before and spent Monday and Tuesday morning catching up on. On Thursday mornings, people are thinking about how close they are to the weekend and in a great mood. It is hard to find someone unhappy on a Friday.

Most are happy to book a meeting for the following week or the weeks following. If I send out an email and don't receive a response within 48 hours, I give it a week and then I do a phone call follow up. Billions of dollars of business are lost because someone sends an email, doesn't get a response, and assumes the person isn't interested. On almost every occasion that I call to follow up the person either 1) Didn't get the email or 2) Lost the email and is thankful I called to follow up. Most of the email that doesn't get delivered is eaten by some type of filter. If I were to guess, 50% of my email gets responded to. When I call to follow up, I book a meeting 9 out of 10 times. That 10th person is either uninterested or not someone I want to meet with after engaging on the phone.

NOTE: When you are connecting with people by phone the same time suggestions apply. Tuesday afternoon, Thursday morning and all day Friday are great times to connect by phone. I would avoid at all costs any time Monday and Wednesday which seems to find people who are working a 9-5, in some level of depression.

With all of your engagements, remember to be the "hot girl at the dance." The 'hot girl at the dance' is not chasing after people to dance with. She's cool, calm, collected, and confident. She knows she's hot so she looks to see what's happening and decides who gets on her dance card and who doesn't. She isn't leg humping and neither should you. You are not there trying to chase anyone down; rather, you are showing up, knowing that you will have lots to bring to the table, and that you are discerning with who will be added to your dance card. If someone is being difficult, don't let them in. Keep an eye on that particular watering hole and circle back when the gatekeeper changes. Difficult people equal a wall you have climb, which leads to a situation where you feel like you're being interviewed by someone who feels self-important but who likely has little actual importance.

When booking the meeting, I prefer to set it for a maximum time of one hour. You always want to leave them wanting a little bit more. When preparing for the meeting, review everything you know about them currently, and start to formulate some questions that you will ask at in the meeting. This first meeting is like a first date; you're looking to establish a bond and the initial phases of intimacy with the gatekeeper.

I make a list of all the questions that I want to ask. The more questions I ask, the less I look like I'm selling. Most people's favourite topic is themselves, so if you spend 55 minutes finding out all about them then they will enjoy their time with you. If this is done right, as the meeting is coming to a close they will start to pull you in saying things like, "I'd like to know a little more about..." or "You really should meet...", or my favourite, "You really should come to our next mixer which is on..." These all let you know that you followed a good process with them. So prepare for this by working backwards from this outcome.

Engaging with the Gatekeeper

The gatekeeper relationship is like any other relationship you will have in business. You want to create visibility (they know you exist), credibility (they see that you know what you're talking about), and profitability (they feel comfortable enough to refer you or create opportunities for you). The first meeting IS the first date. You are not talking about anything serious; you are just getting to know each other a bit better and trying to identify commonalities that would warrant a future date. You need to earn credibility with them and vice versa. There are lot of people in high positions who are total boat anchors. The reason we are asking a lot of questions is to see if they are the real deal or a boat anchor. Make them prove to you that they are worthy of a second date with you. And make sure that you are acting like yourself right from the beginning. Trying to be too proper, or funny if it's not your style and isn't comfortable for you will become clear at some point and it will look like you were faking it at the beginning. Any weirdness that you have (and let's be honest, we all have a bit weirdness) will show up at some point. You might as well get it out of the way right at the beginning. For example, with me, I'm relatively liberal with my language. I use profanity in a conscientious way. This tends to shock some people but I talk to friends the same way that I talk to business partners, prospects, and champions. Because my personality is one of being real with everybody, I don't mince words or speak in a way that would surprise those who know me. What you see is what you get. If I try to be untrue to myself and be on "best behaviour" in our first meeting, at some point it's likely that I will let an 'f-bomb' slip, and end up offending them down the line. While I don't scream FUCK in a restaurant, I will say it low so only they can hear. I have found that doing so actually expedites intimacy because it shows that you are being real to them immediately. I am not going to say that this always works out for me, but the people I want to do business with are not going to be derailed by the odd potty word dropping out of my mouth.

On your first date, don't rush it. Relationships take time. Some will develop more quickly than others, but some will take months and many meetings. Back in the early days of Think Tank Communications I met with various Executive Directors of the Science and Innovation Councils around the province. I immediately got along with the lady who ran the Kamloops Science and Innovation Council and we started doing business together within three months. A colleague of hers in a nearby community was slightly more conservative in her style and it took over ten years for us to get to a point where we appreciated each other. She thought I was a jackass (deserved) and I thought she was little too conservative (also deserved). It took time for both of us to realise that we'd put each other on the back burners and after years of watching each other's careers unfold, we were finally able to find a place where we appreciated tour different styles. From this point we were able to explore the synergies of working together. I'm happy to say that just months before I started writing this book, she reached out to me with one of her colleagues to gather some information about my area of expertise which I was more than happy to share with her. She is one of the more brilliant people I have met in business, but our personalities were not an immediate match.

The reason I could let this relationship warm on the back burner is that I had lots of meetings to have, people to see, and places to go. I wasn't putting all my eggs in this relationship working out. You can't force a square peg into a round hole. If, for whatever reason, things just aren't grooving, don't try to force it. Accept that it's not working, and move on. There are too many people out there to do business with, too many conversations to have, and too many first dates waiting to happen for you to try to become something that you're not or for you to expect others to change their approach to better fit your expectations. In business we do best when we work with people who appreciate our weirdness and whose weirdness we can appreciate.

On your first date with a gatekeeper do not act like they are doing you a favour. It's okay to be humble but you and they are equals so act accordingly. If you've done your research properly and you understand your value (you do have value, right?), they should benefit from the meeting as much as you do. You want to keep the relationship on an even keel and every once and a while, if the opportunity arises, flex your superpower in front of them to let them know that you are a serious player. This doesn't mean being dominant with them or bragging. Instead, once you've discovered the thing they need that you can provide, offer to provide it and do so immediately. Show them that you mean business and that you can get business done.

Avoiding the common mistakes

While researching my notes for this chapter, I began making a list of the ways I have watched myself, colleagues, and clients mess up that important first date. Within minutes of starting this list, I had twelve ways this happens, and then this list increased by an additional five once I had thought about it a bit more. I want you to have this list so that you can prepare yourself to avoid the pitfalls that await you. All of which I suffered early on in my career and I hope that they serve a greater purpose of preventing you from doing the same.

Being nervous. The only reason you would be nervous is if you believe the person is more important and powerful than you. Everyone gets out of bed the same way (unless they do a flying somersault like me). They have breakfast, wash, brush teeth, brush hair, get dressed, walk out the door, and try to do their best every day. Don't put people on a pedestal. You're there to assess whether there is a fit and hopefully they're doing the same thing. You're not auditioning and you're not interviewing; you're looking to see if the puzzle pieces fit together. That's it!

Name dropping. People who are insecure like to drop the names of other people, trying to establish credibility on the backs of people they know. This is a rookie mistake. Be confident in the network that you have and keep your network close to your chest, almost like you're playing poker. You don't have to show everyone who you have in your network. Listen to see if there's an opportunity to connect that gatekeeper with a particular person in your network and, if so, do it. Don't brag about hanging out at people's houses for dinner or travelling with certain people. You may think it impresses people but it turns them off.

Being unsure of what you do. There are three questions that every business owner has to be able to answer proficiently to be taken seriously in business: What do I do? Why does it matter? and Who cares? Take a minute to write those down and, if you can't answer them in a way that not only speaks to your niche markets but that makes you sound different from anyone you consider to be a competitor, then you've got some housekeeping to do. Before you start engaging your ponds and their gatekeepers, you need to be very clear about how you're different and why that difference is absolutely awesome.

Overcomplicating things. Business should be simple. If you're making it hard, it's because you don't understand it well enough. Don't use meetings with your gatekeepers to practise how to keep things simple. They will see you as confused, unable to articulate clearly what you do, and they will get the message that you're a person who is difficult to do business with. This is not a brand you want to establish. When you can make things simple for people, they will want to keep you around and use you.

Talking about your many connections. Trying to share how popular you are with a new contact is like sitting down with your friends and discussing sexual conquests. If it was really that impressive you wouldn't need to talk about it. You want people to take for granted that you have a powerful network and, as they bring your name up, it seems that everybody knows you. That's real power. When your meeting is done, if it has gone well, use LinkedIn to connect with them. Then they can see what type of connections you have behind you.

Being too focused on telling your story. Remember that this first date should be all about making the gatekeeper feel important and finding out how you can leverage something you have for something they want. You won't discover this by telling them your life story. When I'm asked about my background while in a meeting, I usually say, "Let me give you the two minute version" and I quickly do so then turn the conversation back to them. This meeting isn't about me evangelising about how great I think I am; it's about me figuring out how I can serve that gatekeeper so they can, in turn, serve me. It is selfish, and it is selfless.

Trying to close on the first meeting. Trying to close a gatekeeper in promoting your business is similar to going on that first date and expecting to sleep with your date. Anyone who is willing to sleep with you on the first date is not likely somebody you want to spend your time with. Real gatekeepers, who have control, will take the time to figure you out and decide whether it is worthwhile to put their reputation on the line in endorsing yours. It is a fact-finding mission for both of you. Don't rush it

Asking for something before delivering something. The old model of business was to get people to commit to something and if they took care of you, then you'd look to take care of them later. People became tired of this because too many favours were going out and not enough favours were being returned. You can completely shift this paradigm through finding out what you can do for that person and, even if they offer to do something for you right off the bat (which happens from time to time), you serve them first. If someone offers me something in a first meeting, I say to them, "Listen, here's what I want but before you do anything for me. I want to do my part for you. Once I've done my part for you, then you can do your part for me. But let's just hold off on your part until then, okay?" People are usually a bit shocked when I say this because they are so used to people taking, taking, taking and never giving. When you change this conversation you stand out as someone who does business very differently, and in a great way.

Talking trash about other people. Don't. Although you will have hilarious anecdotes from your experiences with others, do not share them. While this might be fun within some circles, it is inappropriate in a business setting, especially when you do not know who that gatekeeper knows. You could be making a comment about their best friend and have now stuck your foot so far into your mouth, that there is no recovery. Rather than building an evangelist, you've developed an enemy. They say that 'tact is knowing when to shut your mouth so that somebody else doesn't have to do it for you.'

Making political comments. A simple rule: Don't talk politics. If they press you on who you support, say "I support whichever government is in power. In my business, it pays to stay apolitical in my business affairs."

Making religious comments. See previous rule and substitute "religious" for "political."

Checking your phone. There is nothing ruder than meeting someone and looking at your phone to see who called, who texted, or what email came in. It screams, "You're important, but not as important as whoever else might be trying to get a hold of me." It's rude and, in my opinion, the person sitting across from you should put their coat on and walk out. Turn off your ringer, beeper, tweeter, blinker, and anything else that your phone might do. I put mine on 'flight mode' as a precaution. And I don't care if you think you need to keep it on in case your kid's school calls; it looks brutal. If you have enough of a reason to keep your phone on, cancel the meeting.

Being late for the meeting. First impressions are key. Don't even consider being late for the first meeting with a gatekeeper. If you've booked a meeting for 8:00 a.m. then you should take into account everything that could happen, figure out a contingency plan, and leave enough time for that to happen. If it normally takes half an hour to get from your house to the meeting site, don't leave your house at 7:30 a.m. Leave your house at 7:00 a.m. as it's better for you to get there half an hour early and sit in your car than to have something happen and end up getting there late. Being late tells people that they are not as important as other things in your life and that you have difficulties 'getting your shit together'. No one wants 'that person' in their circle.

Suffering lateness from others. You are equal to the person you're meeting with so you shouldn't sit there subserviently, waiting for them to show up. Here's my rule: If they text or call anytime up until the start of the meeting to let me know they are running late, as long as they can arrive no more than twenty minutes late, then I wait for them. If they will be more than twenty minutes late, I suggest that we reschedule and set it to a location that's more convenient for me next time. If you find that you have been sitting and waiting for more than fifteen minutes without them notifying you they will be late (no voice mail, email, text), do yourself a favour and leave. If you're meeting at their office, it is okay to leave a business card with reception and leave. Do not follow up. I repeat: Do not follow up. This is a great opportunity for you to reinforce that you do business at a certain level and the person you were going to meet was unable to meet that level. Don't rub it in their face, chastise them, or even bring it up with them. Generally, they will feel horrible (if they are a good person) and they will look for a way to make it up to you (we like this). Let them circle back around to you, make their excuses and, when they suggest rescheduling, tell them the time, date, and location you will be available. The ball is now in your court so use it.

Not having an agenda. You have to have an agenda worked out around what you want to cover in the meeting. Don't show up, smile, and say, "Hi. I just thought we should meet." You should have questions prepared and in your head that you want to go over with that person, and then you can explore what it is you can do for them. Everybody gets the time of day once. This is their chance to sit in front of you, tell you what they want, and for you to deliver. We're looking to model what it looks like to make things happen for people. Always have an outcome in mind before you sit down at the table.

Not having a reason to meet again. This should be predetermined prior to the meeting. You should have an actionable that gives both of you a reason to reconnect either in person or otherwise. You need to ask for that second date (if the fit is there) and have a reason ready as to why you should have it.

Not Matching Their Tempo and Energy. Don't bowl them over if you're feeling high energy and they seem low energy, and vice versa. Try to match their energy level so they feel comfortable spending time with you.

By the end of the meeting, you should have validated everything you think you knew about them and their insight on the market that you're looking to engage. Knowledge is power. You need to have discovered by the end of the meeting, one thing that you can do for them. This is the key to endearing them to you. As soon as the meeting is done, do that one thing for them that you identified (immediately) and follow up with a handwritten thank-you note. Many of the gatekeepers I first encountered years ago say that they still have that handwritten note that I sent to them. There is something old-school classy about sending a handwritten note after a well-prepared meeting with someone. Sending an email or a text just does not have the same impact.

Chapter 5 – Chumming the waters

Now that you have your first gatekeeper meeting under your belt, you need to repeat this process with different gatekeepers in each of your markets. I like to have at least 3 to 5 active and engaged gatekeepers for each market that I'm involved in. However, keep in mind that people you may think are gatekeepers don't always turn out to be, so use your first date (meeting) as a way to determine who your all-star team will be in each pond. You may have to meet 18–20 prospective gatekeepers to find your 3–5 active ones.

I want to share with you how to use networking events (watering hole events) effectively and efficiently to develop business opportunities for yourself. Before we get there, however, I want to talk a bit about influence peddling. Peddling your influence is the currency that is derived from and traded within networking events. It's the 'juice' that increases/decreases your value to others in the networking situation.

Everyone likes to know someone who has the inside track. You need tickets to a sold out concert? No problem. You need a Christmas toy that no one can get their hands on? You'll have it tomorrow. You need some media attention? Let me make a call. The person who has the best network of contacts that they can activate, wins. That's it! Everyone you know in business is a client, knows a client, or has some type of purpose for you that can be used for a selfish benefit. To leverage this, however, you need to become valuable enough to them for them to want to do favours for you. I like people to think of me as a "fixer" so that they call me first if there's a problem they can't find a solution for. While this can bite into a chunk of my day, every person who calls me is now on the hook to return the favour when I ask. Influence is a key piece of this however. I get a lot of people calling me for shit every day: introduction requests, inside information on deals, how-to information, etc. Anyone who has met me and has my contact information theoretically has me in their network, but they don't have the ability to have me do something for them. They have to have previously done something for me, to which I'm now indebted, or they have to have an obvious value to me that I can leverage later. If I don't know their value to me, I don't activate. It isn't being mean; it's being discerning.

If you want to understand how to peddle influence, all you need to do is watch the television series, 'The Sopranos' and the movie, 'The Godfather'. When it comes to influence peddling or doing favours, I think of the character of Bonasera going to see Don Corleone (The Godfather) asking for a favour from the Godfather. The Godfather considers the request and quickly agrees to take care of it, but then says to Bonasera, "Someday, and that day may never come, I'll call upon you to do a service for me. But until that day accept this as a gift." In a very similar (but non-murderous) way, you can play this role with the people you do business with. Hopefully you won't cap someone if they don't return a favour, but you do want to be positioned as the 'go-to person' when someone needs something done and they can't find a solution on their own. They get to do this 'once' before needing to return the favour in some way. When you occupy this position in people's lives, you become very important to them. Because that relationship is important to them they will want to showcase to you (by supporting your endeavours) that they want to keep your relationship as a two-way street. If they don't, they are a taker and someone to exorcise from your circle of influence.

Networking's sole value is giving you an opportunity to increase the size of your professional network of contacts. The Market Shark knows everyone and everyone knows the Market Shark. I dislike most networking events because I see the same people hanging out together; standing and drinking glasses of wine like it's a social party. I believe that a networking event is for building a network and that's it. If there's no one in the room that will benefit your business that you don't already know, you should leave (more on this later).

In order to be successful with your networking activities, you need clarity on what type of network you are looking to build and what types of contacts you need before you go to any event in your market. I list all the types of people I need to have in my existing network. I categorise them under these different headings: Prospective Clients, Gatekeepers, Prospective Champions, Prospective Alliances, Service Providers that I need, Service Providers that my clients need, People in Strategic Positions that I can leverage, People Who are Connectors, Cheerleaders, Tagalongs, and Barkers.

NOTE: Connectors are people who can amplify a message. They have an established network and when you put the message to them, they amplify the message by sending it through their networks. Cheerleaders are people who think you are just 'great' and cannot speak nicely enough about you. Your mom is likely the model of Cheerleader you have in your head. Tagalongs are your 'wingmen' at events. They run interception for you and you can pawn off boat anchors onto them. They are very important to have at any and all events. Barkers are the voice boxes. I think back to the circus days where someone would stand up on the soapbox and get the attention of the market attracting them to a particular tent. Both the Barkers and Connectors are your communication line to a mass audience.

After I have developed my list with types of people categorised accordingly, I fill in the names of the people I already have in my network. When I was a kid I collected hockey cards and in every pack of hockey cards, you would get eight to ten players but there was always one card that had a checklist of every player in the set. I would keep one of the checklist cards and I would place a check beside each player's name to show which ones I had and which ones I still had to collect. I carried that checklist in my pocket until it disintegrated. As it got ratty, I would transfer the information on to a new card and continue my search. I use this same proven process as I'm building a network within my niche markets and 'collecting' the right people for it.

I know one thing about building networks. My network will grow exponentially from month to month in direct relation to the quality of people I have in the network. I encourage my people to use me as a 'favour' they are leveraging for others. Since I position myself as a fixer, when someone in my network has a colleague who needs something that they can't help them with, I will leverage it for that third party as a favour to my contact. They are indebted to me; the third party to my contact. The favour becomes a currency between the three of us. As well, the third party regularly finds out that I'm the fixer of their problem and they are selfishly interested in getting to know me better. I am valuable to them; now they have to become valuable to me.

I use LinkedIn, Facebook, and other sites where people list who they know, to try to figure out who within their networks could fill in the gaps of my network. I keep a current 'shopping list' of who I'm looking to add to my collection. My goal is to pick up two or three new contacts that I've been looking for at every networking event I attend. I use the same three questions to find out if they're the right type of person for me:

What do you do?

Who do you do it for?

What makes you different from others who do what you do?

If they are unable to answer these questions then it will be difficult for me to place them.

Every contact I make, either at a networking event or elsewhere is moving me towards trying to fill up my list and check all the boxes. I regularly swap people out of a list. There may be some people who look really good as prospective

Champions for what I do but if they don't deliver they get replaced with someone else I meet. I'm on a constant hunt to find better talent to replace those who are currently in my network. While this might seem a bit cold, time is short. I need to surround myself with the best people and, in turn, be the absolute best version of myself when producing for them so that they will want to keep the mutually beneficial relationship going.

The Power of a Network

This is for the fellow math nerds out there. Remember 'if we can't measure it we can't manage it'? People say it is impossible to measure the power of a network. This is false. It can be measured by looking at the multiplier effect on how networks form. Here is an old equation I found in a marketing book from the 1930's (apologies to the author in that I cannot remember his or her name, nor the title of their book) that relates to the power of a network.

This equation is the power of relationships within a niche market.

$$(x^2 - x) / 2 =$$

the number of relationships in a business network

For those who hate math, hold on. This is the good stuff that your math teacher promised you. For our reference we'll call this equation the "power of the pond." The X relates to the number of people in a niche market. The answer gives the number of unique relationships within that niche market.

Now let's do a couple of sample equations. Let's say that two people are in that market together, and only two people. Remember that 'x' is the number of people in the market. If we fill in our equation, it would be $(2^2 - 2) / 2 = 1$ relationship. That means two people in a pond have one relationship, a relationship that they share.

Let's say that there are three people in the pond. Using the equation, that makes $(3^2 - 3) / 2 = 3$ relationships. Two people have one relationship; three people have three relationships because each of them has a relationship with each other: A to B, A to C, and B to C. Very exciting, although slightly nerdy. Draw this out using stick men if you need to.

Now let's scale this up one more time. Let's say that there are ten people in the market that are connected. The math would be $(10^2 - 10) / 2 = 45$. 10 people sitting together in a room, have 45 unique relationships among the group. This is the power of building a network of contacts, especially a network with the right people in it. Come on! Tell me this isn't exciting stuff!

Getting three hundred business contacts in just 12 months

Before we get into how to use networking events to fill up your networks and establish yourself within them, let me give you my three-step cheat sheet of how I plan prior my networking events so that when we move into the next section about working watering holes and establishing that network, you will know what the goals are.

1. Inventory who I already have.

2. Make a list of all the people or types of people I am missing/ need.

3. Start establishing the network (filling in the holes on my list).

The goal I set for myself is to build my network gradually in any new market in a sustainable and scalable way. I know that every person I talk to, if they're the right fit, will introduce me to a few more people. This is my standard 12-month goal for size of a network within a niche market, assuming I'm starting from scratch:

Month	Total number of contacts within the market
Month 1:	10
Month 2:	20
Month 3:	35
Month 4:	50
Month 5:	75
Month 6:	100
Month 7:	130
Month 8:	160
Month 9:	190
Month 10:	220
Month 11:	260
Month 12:	300

That isn't all the additional people each month; that's a cumulative total, from Month 1 to Month 12. You may wonder why the sequence jumps in numbers that are not equal. It's because the people you are meeting are now introducing you to new people, hence a multiplier effect begins. Depending on the level of people you meet in any given month, some months you may have a huge spike in new introductions. Be less attached to the monthly numbers and more focused on the trend upwards. In Month 1 expect to meet and connect with 10 people. By the end of Month 12, expect to have 300 people in your network. If this happens earlier than 12 months, it's a good thing. Remember quality of quantity.

Not all of those 300 will be met at networking events. Some will be introductions from existing contacts, and through other means, but my focus is being out there and collecting people that have value to me or my clients. Yes, it takes time and you have to be dedicated to the cost, but I've yet to meet anyone with 300 people in a network that don't wield the title and benefits of being a Market Shark.

To do the math and nerd-out one more time (sorry, this shit is too exciting not to share), let's use 300 people to assess the "the power of the pond". Equation: $(300^2 - 300) / 2 = 89,850$ unique relationships in that group. A market of that size has the ability to generate millions of dollars in business benefit for those involved. Now let's get to the where the rubber meets the road and start attending watering hole events with the intention of building a world-class network for your business.

Loud and Proud

You are ready. You have done all prerequisite prep, you have connected with some of your gatekeepers, you understand how to manage your influence, and you have a shopping list for building your network. Now it's time to shake your booty and get in the deep end. Every group is looking for leadership. It's your time to step into the spotlight and shine.

I didn't always do networking events right. Before I started implementing an actual strategy, I would just show up, hoping that I might meet somebody cool, and often leave disappointed. I would get stuck with boat anchors or not be sure where to stand, who to talk to, or how to break into conversations. I was like an epileptic in a fist fight. I was all over the place, achieving nothing. Those days are far behind me. Now that I have a system that produces opportunities every time, I'll never look back. I'm lethal in networking situations. I work the crowd like a Great White works a group of seals.

I get teased by clients when we are at the same networking events together. It's not uncommon for me to work the room hard for 15 to 20 minutes and leave before the speaker even takes the stage. If I'm in a room and I don't see anyone who can fill out my network, I leave. My intention in going to every event is that I will check something off my shopping list and leave with a stronger network than I arrived with. If it seems like that won't be the case at an event, then I head home. I don't care if my admission covered a free drink or appetisers. If there isn't business in the room, I'm out in the car on the way home. I've got enough friends.

Working a Networking Event like a Market Shark

I wasted thousands of dollars on events before I knew what to do. Now every admission I pay gets me at least a multiplier of 10x the admission fee if not greater. It is extremely rare that I get skunked and don't get anything, but remember I'm discerning with the types of events I go to. Here are my 20 best tips for making the most out of a networking event within your pond:

1. **Don't arrive first.** Showing up when the catering staff is still setting out the glasses suggests that (1) you're not busy, (2) this is the highlight of your week and (3) goddamn are you excited to be there! . Being five or ten minutes fashionably late works very well here. The one rule breaker of this is if you are at a seated event and there are people in the room you want to meet, show up right on time, scan the names to which tables your targets are sitting at so you can go and see them later on in the event. It's hard to walk around looking at

name tags to figure this out during an event. At least if you know what table they are at, you can target your approach.

2. **Make a mental list of who you want to meet.** Some organisations don't provide the name of registrants prior to the event. Like I said earlier, I like to have a good look at the other name badges on the registration table when I pick up mine and then I make a mental note of the names or companies that I want to connect with. I circle back around the membership table a couple of times to see if those names have been picked up. If the badges are still on the registration table then I know that person likely isn't attending and remove them from my list.

3. **Get your drink, but no booze.** I know that your admission ticket includes the first drink but that doesn't mean you have to try to squeeze every bit of value out of your registration fee. Soda water is a good alternative. People won't know what you're mixing it with so you don't look like a party pooper. Benefits, aside from not getting hammered or having booze breath, is you take in everything and see any and all opportunities. We have all seen that guy or gal who imbibes the libations a little too seriously and makes everyone uncomfortable.

4. **Walk the room and introduce yourself.** Introduce yourself to everyone, including the support team at the event. If someone is doing registration at the front door, shake their hand and introduce yourself. Many times the support staff are the people who make things happen within the watering hole, so do not take these people for granted. Get to know them, as they are brilliant market indicators for you on what's going on, plus many of them are gatekeepers that people take for granted. While you walk the room, remind yourself that you are there to meet many people. I walk around like it's my

party and I'm hosting. "Are you having a nice time? You need to meet so and so."

5. **Note where people 'fit' into your network.** As you find out about people, make a mental note of where they fit into your network. Some of them will be Clients, Prospective Clients, Gatekeepers, Champions, Alliances, and so on, so quickly try to determine where that individual will fit. This gets easier the more you do it. Interesting people get five minutes maximum; pikers get less than 90 seconds.

6. **Get business cards.** Don't be concerned about giving out your business cards; focus on getting other people's cards. You are collecting people; you're not looking to be collected. If you find somebody valuable, ask for their card which you will then use to follow up with them after the event. I take four or five of my business cards to an event and intentionally run out so that when people ask me for a business card I can say, "Sorry. I've already given them all out, if you can believe that." Not only does this show that you're popular (you are popular, right?), but it gives you a reason not to give a business card to a Debbie Downer who wants to know if you want to have lunch sometime to commiserate about how business is hard and look at pictures from her cat's last birthday party. It seems Mr. Whiskers is her 'fur baby'. (True story!)

7. **Be Nice to all service staff.** 'Please' and 'thank you' goes a long way. I watch to see how people treat service staff. Some people will be nice and courteous to you, and then be dismissive and rude to the event staff. This is telling to me and it should be to you as well. Do not do business with these people.

8. Introduce yourself to gatekeepers you have yet to meet. If you recognise someone's name but you haven't met them yet, go up to them and say something like:

> "Hey, Joan. I've been hearing your name all around. I wanted to come and introduce myself. My name is ... I'm really glad to finally meet you."

Leave it at that. You're not there to pitch to them or to give them the details about your business; you're just putting a face to the name. Remember: Visibility, credibility, profitability. Your job at networking events is to create visibility. Your job in the one-on-one meetings to follow is to create credibility and, if done properly, that will create profitability. So don't jump the gun by trying to spew out all of your information. Just go up and be cordial.

9. Engage the gatekeepers you know immediately. As soon as you get to the event, register, get your name tag and then engage the gatekeepers you know. You want to let them know that you enjoyed your first date together (first meeting) and that you're happy to be supporting events like this within the market. You're following through on your interest in being part of the market and once they know you're in the room, they will think about who you need to meet. It's a win-win for you.

10. Actively introduce people to each other. Since you are working the room like a dervish, you will be meeting many people. As you meet new people, think about others those new people should meet in that room, either your existing contacts, or people you have just met yourself. You want to position yourself up as a connector of professionals. What better way to start than by introducing two brand new

contacts to one another. Everyone likes a mover and a shaker, so be that person. Remember, it's all about influence peddling. Introductions fall underneath this.

11. **Think of yourself as a politician.** Shake hands with a good firm grip. Make eye contact. Give them your full name, and find out about them. Be interested. If you're not naturally interested in people then networking is much harder. Try to figure out what it is that interests you about people and go there. If you want to see master networkers – people who rely on the ability to build networks of people who will give money and vote for them – watch how politicians work a room. I'm always curious on how people introduce what they do. That's my focus when meeting people.

12. **Approach groups of two, not singles.** If you approach a group of two people who are talking to each other, you can introduce yourself to them, find out what they do, and then it's very easy to move away from the two–person group, leaving them to talk with each other. When you approach a person who is standing alone (1) they're likely uncomfortable being at the event, and (2) it's hard to ditch them. You're always looking for another person to come into the conversation so that you can excuse yourself and leave them with each other. When I do find myself stuck in the 'single person' situation I look for someone to palm them off to by saying, "Hey, Ted, have you met Ramona yet? Come on over and let me introduce you." Then I walk over and introduce Ted to Ramona and then excuse myself so I can keep on hunting. This is why it's important to bring a 'tagalong' or 'wingman' with you who can run interference.

13. **Make notes (in the bathroom).** I don't have Irritable Bowel Syndrome, but I do spend a lot a time in the bathroom at a networking event. I hide out in a stall, making notes on the

back of business cards I get from people I want to follow up with. Due to the sheer amount of people I meet at events like this, I may hit the restroom two or three times to quickly jot down notes about things they said. I find that if I leave this until I get home, I have a hard time putting a face to a name. If I have notes on their business card, I'm much better equipped to remember them.

14. **Toss the piker's business cards at home.** There are some people who desperately want you to take their business card. They are like Hare Krishnas selling apples; they will not let you leave without one. It is hard to say to these types of people, "Keep your business card. My leg doesn't need humping today." I just smile, take the card, and appreciate that even though I'm going to be adding to the landfill, paper is compostable. I put my 'keeper cards' in my inside breast pocket; the piker cards go in either of the side pockets of my jacket. Do not empty the piker cards into the garbage at the event. You will get caught! You never know who could see you throwing their business card into the garbage, and that's really hard to recover from. As an aside, years ago I gave a speech in Florida to a terrible group. I mean totally horrible. It was like I woke up and found myself at a piker convention. The group that booked me handed me the cheque and then they gave me the token pen with their emblem laser cut into it. If you've spoken at as many events as I have, you'll find there are two things that are always being given – branded pens and branded day timers. I don't use a day timer because it's not 1980, and the branded pens always seem to be the most horrible pens in the world; they run out of ink just seconds after you test to see if they work. To make a long story short, rather than just putting the pen and all the business cards given to me into my briefcase to dispose of back at the hotel, as I was walking out of that event, I emptied the big stack of business cards into the bin. Then I

thought I'd make the load a bit lighter, turned around and tossed the pen and its case in a perfect arc into the dumpster from about ten feet away. I was admiring the spin I got on the pen and its case, when I looked over and saw the organiser and the woman who presented the pen had been watching me throw their gift into the dumpster. Granted I had done so with some panache, I may have even kicked out a leg during the process, but I can't imagine that played very well. I pretended that I didn't see them, walked away, and reminded myself that any future opportunities it might be better to dispose of things in a more private setting. Not one of my best moments.

15. **Meet ten people who have value.** It's great to glad hand a lot of people, or to quickly work the room and meet everybody, but you want to challenge yourself to find and meet at least ten people who have value. Remember that value doesn't necessarily just mean a prospective client. This could also be a service provider to you, a potential strategic alliance, or a potential client for one of your clients. Everyone has a place a in your network and sometimes you have to work a bit harder to figure out where they fit, but it's your job to figure out how. Don't forget the support staff. Their value can be more than you imagine.

16. **Be the hot girl at the dance.** Don't jump all over people. Let people know you've arrived, gracefully make your way through the room, and don't be too excited to see anyone. Be cool, confident, and curious to see who in that room might fill up the network that you are building.

17. **Have an exit strategy for when you find yourself trapped.** When you're trapped by Debbie Downer, say to her:

"It's so nice chatting with you but I have lots of people I need to say hello to because I'm not here for very long."

Shake her hand, and then keep going. It's very hard for people to say, "No, I don't want you to say hello to other people. I want you to listen to some more stories about Mr. Whiskers!"

18. **Influence peddle.** This is an opportunity for you to demonstrate your ability to wield influence. If you're talking to someone and they have a problem that you can solve then make a suggestion about how you can solve it. I'm not talking about them buying services from you, but about you pointing them in the right direction to find their own solution. You want them to know that you know how to make things happen.

19. **Don't be the last to leave.** We have all had that person come for dinner who just won't go home. You are in your pyjamas, dishwasher loaded, and making the kids' lunches for school the next day. Awkward!   Being the last to leave reeks of desperation. Go find something more important to do, even if it's organising your sock drawer, petting your many cats, or catching up on episodes of 'Hoarders' on your PVR.

20. **Immediately after leaving, conduct a post-mortem.** Sitting in your car or on your walk back to your office, consider how the event went. Was it worth your time and money? Did it have the right type of people in the room? Is it something you will go back to? Is it the type of event you need to be 'seen at' in order to ascend to the position of Market Shark? Do you need to adjust any part of your strategy to gain greater benefit from attending in the future?

All in all, networking events are the most efficient way for you to engage your market and expedite your ascension to the position of Market Shark. You get to rub elbows, be seen, meet new people, connect with old contacts, and further the relationship you have with the gatekeepers. It normally takes three events for you to both get comfortable, and start to be seen as a fixture of the events. If you start missing them, you start to lose the traction you have made. If an event sucks, don't go back. If it is great, make it part of your regular business development routine. Now let's discuss playing the role of Market Shark in all aspects of your business.

Chapter 6 – Becoming the 'Market Shark'

Acting the 'Role'

We've all been at a business event and noticed an individual enter who possesses the charisma, the confidence, and the posture that immediately says "I'm someone worth watching." Market Sharks behave in a unique way that is noticeably different from their peers. Everything they do is intentional and no matter the situation, they feel comfortable because they are swimming in their pond. Market Sharks are absolute in their actions. They act the way others would expect. They are the measure to which others compare themselves. They are not the exception to the rule; they are the rule. The Market Shark always has his or her shit together when out in public.

From the first moment you enter your markets, people will watch you and track your behaviour and actions. If you come in meekly and then overnight become overly confident, they will think you are putting on a show. If you come in too strong and too fast, they will think you are a bull in a china shop and that you lack class and courtesy. You need to be very clear on what your role and responsibilities will be within that market as the Market Shark, before you enter the market, and then you need to play to that role perfectly. The trick to pulling this off seamlessly is to learn how to be two-faced; to have a private face and a public face. The private face is for those people in your life that you love, love you, and that you can be honest with. This is who you are when you are at home, with your feet up watching television. The public face is the face you put forward to the market. It's the face of professionalism, of non-judgement, and that of someone who gets it done each and every time. No one in business really wants to hear your sad story, your struggles, or the crisis of confidence you might have to overcome every day. They want their Market Sharks to be strong, confident, powerful, and assertive. They rest assured that the Market Shark is getting things done. How would you feel if you watched the President of the United States come on TV and tell everybody that he was concerned about whether he was making the right decisions and was hopeful that things would work out for him? This is such a ridiculous scenario because the President is an Automatic Market Shark in the political arena.   On the occasions when we have watched Presidents and other political leaders stumble or act unsure, the public eats them alive. When your market accepts that you are the right person to hold the spot of Market Shark, you must not disappoint them by faltering. Everyone makes mistakes, even Market Sharks, but they never take their hand off the wheel. They keep control of the situation and right the ship or they are out.

This is not about you faking it or being someone that you are not; rather, it is about highlighting the things that that market most wants to see in its leaders. When you play the right role, your market will trust you. If you are fake and inconsistent, they will roast you and then eat you for dinner.

There are six strategies that I suggest you adopt to assume the role of Market Shark in your markets. Print these out and tape them to your computer monitor so you can review them each day. Take them down when you know them forwards and backwards. The work is worth it. Each of these strategies can be measured and managed. By effectively implementing and managing these strategies, your markets will get what they expect from you and you will enjoy the spoils.

1. **Look at other professionals who are already in the pond and who are held in high regard by others.** What are they doing that is so revered by the pond? Analyse everything they do that is engaging the market in a positive way which you can emulate. After documenting all the characteristics, identify those ones that most closely match who you are already and

begin to highlight these characteristics when you work in those markets.

2. **Have a look in the mirror right before you walk out the door.** Be clear about who you are as you engage your markets. Your market is expecting a particular person to show up and if you aren't that person, you need to do a mental adjustment and step into the role that they expect of you. Market Sharks don't get days off in front of their markets. If they are on, you are on.

3. **Watch your tongue when talking about anyone else.** Many people will criticise others (in particular, competitors) to position themselves more advantageously to their market. True Market Sharks don't have to do this because they are confident that they know what they do, why it matters, and who cares, and that they can serve those markets much better than any other competitors. Their work speaks for itself. Reputation plays a massive role in this, but you have to earn that. When I hear somebody criticising competition, all I hear is insecurity. Market Sharks do not have time to criticise their competition because they are too busy dominating them.

4. **Increase your Emotional Intelligence.** Emotional intelligence has been covered in many books so it's best just to give you a quick overview and then you can go look at other books to get more detailed information about how to develop those tools as you ascend to the level of Market Shark. Essentially, Emotional Intelligence is composed of four main components:

   (a) perceiving emotions,

   (b) using emotions,

(c) understanding emotions, and

(d) managing emotions.

Let me give you a quick example of each.

Perceiving emotions. This is your ability to know if the person you're talking to is having a positive or negative response to what you are saying. When I was a kid, my dad used to love to sit at the mall when my mom went shopping and he would just people watch. I remember him saying to me, "Just watch people and look at how they interact with each other. See the people in love, the people who are fighting, or the couples where one of them is having a lot of fun shopping and the other one can't wait to get home." In university I honed this skill further while I worked as a bouncer in a night club. Because the music is booming and you can't hear conversations, you're constantly watching for body language and looking to see who's too drunk, who's getting aggressive, or who doesn't really want to be there. The better you can perceive the emotions of others and their response to what's happening, the better you can manage situations.

Using emotions. This relates to your ability to engage people on an emotional level. Most sales in business are done for emotional reasons. Volvo likes to remind people that they were the first car company to have side-impact airbags. This was a feature that did not seem particularly exciting until Volvo mentioned the fact that children are 800 times more likely to survive a side-impact crash in a Volvo than in any other car. This moved the conversation away from the cool engineering feat of having side-impact airbags to mom and dad looking at little Tommy and thinking that they want him to survive to see another birthday should they be unfortunate enough to be in a car accident. Using emotions is a key piece in a successful Market Shark's toolbox.

Understanding emotions. This takes things one step further by understanding how emotions drive people. You understand how someone you're working with acts when angry, under stress, depressed, fatigued, when they feel like they're being ripped off, and when they feel like they're winning a negotiation. The better you can ascertain how emotions affect each person; the better you will be able to engage them, whether they are a client, a colleague, or even a partner. Emotions can drive people and they can cripple people. It can cause them to strike out or turtle. As you tune this skill you can make adjustments in the moment.

Managing emotions. This is the cherry on the top of the first three. When you can identify the emotional response someone is having, you will know how that emotion can be used in a business setting. You will understand how that emotion is having an impact on them and then you can then decide how to manage that emotion to your mutual benefit. Many customers who get angry while at a retail store would happily never shop there again if they felt that their concerns have not been heard. However, if a manager comes out from behind the till and says, "Listen, I can see that you're really angry. I want to take a few minutes to hear what you have to say and then explore every option with you to make you happy." This is a manager who has high Emotional Intelligence and knows that an angry customer is an opportunity to develop a lifelong customer. Market Sharks shine in these situations.

5. **Highlight the best of you for your business.** Develop a persona for your business that is not fake, but highlights characteristics that you know are most attractive to your market. One of my mentors referred to this public personal as "applying eyeliner." Draw attention to the assets you already have by accentuating them.

6. **You are not Madonna (as in rock goddess, not Mother of God).** Don't try to recreate yourself repeatedly. Consumers like things that they are used to. That's why McDonalds

stands the test of time. A hamburger is a hamburger and French fries are French fries. They're not trying to make curly fries or home fries; they're giving customers what they expect. Market Sharks (McDonalds being one of them) know that when something is working in the market they shouldn't tweak it just to see what will happen. Any time you try to shake things up without good reason you will end up confusing your market and pissing them off. Anyone remember New Coke? It nearly destroyed the company. Don't scratch if there isn't an itch.

Above all else, if you're going to be a Market Shark, don't play small. Here are things for you to think about on a daily basis as you look in that mirror and decide if you have a Market Shark looking back at you before you walk out the door.

- Never publicly criticise yourself.

- Don't ever doubt your abilities in public.

- Don't talk about things being "hard" or "outside of your control".

- Don't sit on your tail when opportunities are in front of you. Market Sharks always swim over and nudge the opportunity to see what's there.

- Be hungry. Go after everything that fits within your business model. Markets like to see their Market Sharks swimming around doing what they do. No one is impressed with a lazy fat cat. Even if you have enough, continue for the sport of it. The only person you are competing with is yourself...right?

- **Tired is for losers.** Suck it up or tell the market that you're busy in meetings and go home and have a nap. Never tell people that you're too tired, exhausted, or run down because Market Sharks love action. I'm not going to say that I don't get tired sometimes, but it's not something that I advertise. If you need a nap, go have a nap.

- **Remember that when someone asks how you're doing, they don't really care.** Don't emotionally dump on them. This isn't Dr. Phil. If mommy didn't love you, your market doesn't care. Excuses are for losers and sad stories are for the therapist.

I remember when the recession was happening in 2008 everyone was running around like chickens with their heads cut off. They were watching the financial markets plummet and businesses were frantic and thinking that it was just a matter of time before they were forced out of business. We sent out messaging to our clients saying that this was going to be quick and possibly the most exciting and opportunistic time in their businesses' lives. While everybody was running away from the market fearing the unknown, we were going to pilot our business models and those of our clients into the fire because we knew that opportunity lies in difficulty. The hobbyists in business (those people who are not serious about growing a true business) would be running for the hills and looking to secure corporate jobs. We knew that those hobbyists, who had been competition both for ourselves and our clients, would leave behind a client list that could easily be picked up. The traffic jam was about to open up.

I am proud to say that from 2008 to 2012, not only did we not have one single client who lost their business, but the average growth for those clients during those four years was 30 percent, per year. We were doing anything magical; it was just that their competition left the market and it was open for us and our clients to go in and dominate. I am still surprised at how many coaching companies told their clients to batten down the hatches and ride out the storm. On behalf of the Ghost CEO™ and its clients, we thank those other coaching models for that advice.

The Ghost CEO™ model practices the five stages of business development:

1. Visibility
2. Credibility
3. Profitability
4. Sustainability
5. Scalability.

Visibility means letting people know that you exist. **Credibility** means letting people know that you're good at what you do. **Profitability** means that they pay you. **Sustainability** means that your business continues to grow. **Scalability** means that your company can grow exponentially larger without you having to do more work. This all sounds exciting but it has to happen in sequential order and the hardest work is required at the beginning.

When we talk about visibility being the process of you letting your market know that you exist, we mean just that. People can't buy from you if they don't know about you. However, before you can tell the market about you, you have to have all your shit together. You need to know what your Market Shark persona is and how you are going to manage it. You need to be clear on the three questions:

What do I do?

Why does it matter?

Who cares?

Take a moment and write down these three questions on a blank piece of paper. These questions are a game changer for your business model and they will likely the three questions you hate more than any other three questions in the world. You will hate them more than being pulled over by a police officer. You will hate them more than hearing a doctor say, "We need to talk about your test results." These three questions are going to drive you bat shit crazy, but they drive everyone crazy. Most businesses bail when it comes to this work because it just feels too hard. However, when we do the hard work, the market doesn't have to and when you make it easy for the market, they will buy from you. Look at these three questions with hatred in your eyes knowing that one day (and that day will be very soon) these three questions will be what separates you from everyone else. Being able to answer these questions effectively is what separates the Market Sharks from those little fish that eat fish shit off the sides of fish tanks. I refer to them as "sucker fish", and that name fits very nicely.

Since 1999, I've been using the three questions as a major foundation piece of the Ghost CEO™ model. In that time, I have talked to literally tens of thousands of entrepreneurs around the globe and you know how many have been able to answer the three questions well on the first or fourth try? Zero. Not one. Nobody. Nada. They spew out the generic shit. I'm a landscaper. I'm a financial planner. I'm a personal trainer. Barf, boring, and lazy. If they can't answer the questions well, they will only ever compete in the market on price and they will NEVER be Market Sharks.

Market Sharks answer the three questions (What do I do? Why does it matter? Who cares?) in a way that is customised to each of the markets that they are in. When you are able to share with each market what you offer them and the solution sounds customised and credible, it will be worth it for them to talk with you about what you can do for them. Once they know about you, they cannot un-know about you. The only thing worse than having a bad reputation is having no one know about you at all. When you don't answer the questions well, you become beige. You fade into the background and aren't worth talking about (a bad thing).

With each of the three questions, your answers must be delivered in one concise sentence. I'm not talking about a run-on sentence with half a dozen semicolons. I'm talking about a nice, clear sentence. As Albert Einstein once said, "If you can't explain it simply enough, you don't understand it well enough." Here are some questions to prime you for your practise in answering the 'three questions' for each of your markets:

- What is it that you're offering that is unique to your markets?

- Is there a reason why you are the best to serve this market?

- What benefits are you offering this market? (Remember that we market on features, but we sell on benefits. Benefits are the emotional connection that clients have to a service or product).

- What solutions do you provide that have been customised for your particular markets?

As you start to consider what makes you different from other providers and how your solution is unique to those you're looking to serve, you should see a unique picture emerging that shows you as something very different from others in your market offering a similar service. In each of your one-sentence answers there should be enough customisation that your market will understand that you are the ideal candidate for them to work with. Do not worry; I will give you an example at the end of this section to illustrate how this happens. In the meantime, remember that this is requires practise. You're not going to get it right the first time, or even the tenth time. Not unlike a potter or a sculptor, you're going to put things together and then whittle it away until the point where you get it to bare bones. This is when the responses perfectly answer the three questions and create an emotional connection with the markets you are looking to serve.

Once you are satisfied with your answers to the three questions for each of your three niche markets, it's time to practise them. I want you to write down the three questions on a piece of paper and post it where you'll see them every day. Every time you look at them, determine which of your niche markets you want to practise with, and recite your answers to the three questions. You know you are prepared when answering them is as easy as reciting your phone number. Once you have them reasonably well memorised, recruit the help of someone else (partner, spouse, neighbour, family member, kid, etc)., who will ask you the three questions at unexpected times so you become used to answering them anywhere and everywhere.

When I'm working on the answers to my three questions, I take it a step further by finding a practise partner that is a representative of one of those niche markets. If I'm hunting female physicians, I'll find somebody within my network that I already know who is a female doctor and ask her if I could run my answers by her to see how they fit and sound to her ear. Do not underestimate the importance of getting peer review from a niche market representative. Once you can impress them, you're ready to go.

This homework always sounds easier than it is. It is repetitive, can be boring, and you will want to stop before you should. You will overestimate your comfort with the answers only to find yourself in the perfect situation to deliver the answers and stumble, reverting back to your old script. I want to share with you a story to show you how one client worked with this diligently and the exceptional results she got. If she can do it, so can you.

A few years ago we had a young and talented graphic designer come in. She had an impressive portfolio of work but she found that she kept being beat out by younger designers who were able to underbid her price substantially. As you can imagine, this caused her great frustration because anyone who has invested time in learning their craft through going to school for classic training wants to be paid fair market value. However, this massive influx of new designers entered the market and they competed solely on price. To further frustrate the point, many in her industry were self-taught and not particularly good, but clients did not fully understand how to buy design so they got away with it. Aside from breadth of training, there one key point that proves to be a challenge for all products and services: if you are unable to distinguish how you are different from others who do what you do (in this case, graphic design), the only thing you can compete on is price because most customers do not know how to buy. If you don't teach them how to buy, they'll look at the lowest price first because they don't know how to assess quality. There are many prospects we meet in our practice, who have found substantially cheaper business coaching options and ask why we cost more than some online competitors. We say, "You can find cheaper, but you won't find better. Ask those models if they will forgo locking you into a contract and if they can guarantee results. If they can, then you are comparing apples to apples." This strategy is something I encourage you to steal if you're able to back it up.

Let us return to our example of the graphic designer client. We sat down with this young graphic designer and went through the three questions. Here's how she answered them:

Question #1:   "What do you do?"

Her answer: "I'm a graphic designer."

Question #2:   "Why does it matter?"

Her answer: "Well, because serious business owners need to have nice looking design."

Question #3:   "Who cares?"

Her answer: "Everybody should care, but they don't."

You can probably guess from her responses, she was frustrated. Being extremely talented compared to the peers who were beating her out on work, it's a frustrating position to be in; not knowing how to tell your clients that they aren't comparing apples to apples, they're comparing apples to rocks. So we dug down, asking her again about what was unique about her offering, why was she the best to serve the market, what benefits was she offering, and so on. She really struggled with this. So we changed tack and said to her, "If you could work with one particular market, which would you like to work with?" She responded, "I'd love to work with golf courses, but that's just not reasonable."

Whenever we hear something like this, it usually is a story that a client has told themselves that has no root in truth. She may have broached the subject with a golf course once before and they didn't show interest, so in her mind it became, "Golf courses won't buy my design." If you've ever been to a golf course, you'll know that many them have beautiful design so we know that they hire designers, but they are probably like the majority of businesses, and don't really know how to buy design or how to compare designers effectively.   After a bit of time working together, and some gentle nudging, we decided with the client, that her two main markets were going to be golf courses going through a rebrand and home developers building around golf courses. (Note: we encouraged her to have a third market, which ended up being law firms. Best for you to know we are consistent in our advice regarding three niche markets).

As we started to work through the questions with her, it started to feel like we were sifting for gold. Pick up a pan of dirt, shake, shake, shake, and look something shiny. Nothing? Throw it away and start again. Together we were able dig down to the answers to her three questions that would pinpoint golf courses as being a viable market for her. Today, she answers the questions like this:

Question #1:   **What do you do?**

Answer: I own a design firm that specialises in rebranding world-class golf courses.

Question #2   **Why does it matter?**

Answer: World-class golf courses need to have world-class collateral to fulfil the expectations of golfers visiting their website. No matter how beautiful your course is, if your collateral looks bad then the expectation will be that the course is crappy.

Question #3:   Who cares?

Answer: World-class golf courses that want to deliver a consistent experience to their clients from the clients' first experience hearing about the golf course right through to putting into the 18th hole.

If she were competing with 99 other firms, and they answered the questions the generic way and she answered them the custom way, she would have an enormous advantage over them. This is the power of the questions and answering them properly. Every business should put time into working through these questions, but most either don't know to or don't think it is that important. They are stuck with the '30-second elevator pitch' mind-set and thus will always compete on price.

As an aside, the designer went from struggling to make a living to making six figures and being a role model for others within her market. She has truly become a Market Shark from her own efforts.

Creating Credibility

Credibility means letting people know that you are good at what you do. It's walking the walk. It is what separates the marketers from the technicians. Marketers talk about what they're going to do; technicians do it. Credibility for your business is the pivot point in which prospects with 'means' and 'need' transition from research mode to transaction mode.

For product companies, this might mean you letting someone test something during a demonstration. For service companies this can mean giving people a little taste of what it looks like to work with you. It's about getting your service or product into the hands of prospective clients. This is why demonstrations work so well in department stores.

Market Sharks know how they do business, they know the value they bring to the table, and they are exceptional at building visibility. The only thing they are better at than creating visibility is showcasing their credibility to prospective markets. They are never afraid to let someone see behind the curtain, but they don't let them live there. They give them a quick peek and then move back into the discussion.

Credibility, as you ascend to becoming a Market Shark is all about knowing that you are good at what you do and are proud to talk about it and share it with others. People have a lot of choices. They need to experience you and what it would be like to do business with your company in order to feel confident in buying from you. It is about you removing the obstacles that get in the way of people buying from you. Think of the shoe company Zappos. It is a challenging premise to sell people shoes online, when they can't try them on. Zappos decided to offer free shipping both ways to their customers and to rely heavily on feedback from other customers on how shoes fit (too big, too small, just right). That way, customers can buy a pair of shoes online at 3AM. Have them shipped to their house. Try them on and if they don't like them, send them back at Zappos' cost, not their own. Zappos is a phenomenal example at removing the obstacles that get in the way of customers buying from you by creating a 'noteworthy client experience' for them.

When developing credibility, you have one chance to make a good impression. You either establish credibility or you don't. The best way to increase your chances of establishing credibility successfully is to know what you do and be able to communicate that effectively to your markets. This is why so much focus is placed on answering the three questions properly. Winging it is for amateurs. Your client interactions should be so well-rehearsed that they seem natural. When doing this heavy lifting, remember that once you've created visibility and have established credibility you'll be rewarded with business. The markets (your ponds) see you as a real player – as the Market Shark. Other Market Sharks in complementary areas will hear about you and start to think about how they can use you to advance themselves and their businesses selfishly (a good thing as long as it is reciprocal).

Credibility, like charity, starts in the home. You should be fully practised before you step out the door. Here are some daily exercises that will help support your credibility in being seen and known as a leader in you markets:

Read daily about what is going on in your industry so that you are current around advancements. You never want someone in the market to ask you a question about your industry that you don't have the answer for. Markets shift on a monthly, weekly and, sometimes, daily basis so you need to be on top of what is going on. Market Sharks always have their eye on the market and where it is going so they know how to adjust their plans. Imagine going into a camera store and asking about a new model of Nikon and the camera store owner telling you that he'd never heard of it. How comfortable would you feel about him being an expert on cameras? Imagine you are going in for surgery and read about an innovative technique in the NY Times. You bring up this technique with the surgeon only to have him say to you, "Geez, I haven't heard of that technique yet. That sounds interesting." How confident would you feel about having that surgeon work on you? In both cases, that's the point where credibility starts to erode.

Practise answering your three questions until they are easy to share naturally. As you are working on your three responses for each of your three markets, remember that each market has unique needs for what they need to hear from you to see you as credible vendor. Going back to the example of the graphic designer, her three markets were law firms, housing developments around golf courses, and golf courses doing rebranding. She doesn't want to tell golf courses about the type of work she does with law firms. She doesn't want to tell the law firms about her work with housing developments around golf courses because they don't care. Your messaging needs to match the person you are talking to. This is why the three questions far surpass the old school system of having a 30 second elevator pitch. In its basic form, it was 'taking shit and throwing it against the wall hoping it stuck on to something.' A few years ago I went to the zoo with a colleague and at the monkey cage we saw these little monkeys throwing their shit at each other. It almost looked like a game of dodge ball with the monkeys throwing turds. I looked over to my colleague and said, "Doesn't that remind you of a networking event where people are throwing their shit at each other, hoping that it sticks?" We both had a good chuckle, but there is truth to this. Any time that you go to a networking event in the future and you watch someone deliver their 30 second elevator pitch, I want you to think of those monkeys.

The elevator pitch is the 'shotgun' approach; the three questions are the 'sniper' approach. With the three questions, if you are targeting the right market (those with means and need), you will hit your target every time.

Ask friends and family to think of objections prospects might have and then spend some time addressing how you would respond to those objections so that you become confident with your answers. Again, it is great if you can find people who represent your niche markets, as they will give you the best objections. Professionals are nervous or even fearful of objections coming up, but objections give us an excellent opportunity to further develop why we are a credible option for our prospects.

Here is an example of preparing for objections. We work with an accounting firm that is not one of the big four, but is sizeable, with over 20 offices and 2,000 employees. Because they service clients that are large multinationals through to small localised companies, they need to consider objections that they are either too big or too small, depending on the client and the expectations.

For the large clients that might be concerned they are too small, they could say things like: "We have all the bandwidth of a big four without all the overhead, therefore we can give you the same level of expertise without gouging you on price." Since they know an objection will come up that they are not as big as the big four, they have a great opportunity to affirm that they are a viable option. For smaller clients, who might worry they are too big of a firm to work with, they could say, "I understand you're used to working with a solo accountant. With our firm we can scale with your growth. Because our services expand and contract with the client's needs, we can be with your company as long as you are operating and you won't have to shop firms. You'll get big firm resources at affordable rates."

You can see how positioning is key and how objections give us a great opportunity for reaffirming our market position to the prospect. Never run away from objections; instead invite them from friends and family to brainstorm all the questions and concerns that a prospective client could put forward so that you can be prepared to answer them. Being forewarned is being forearmed. Market Sharks see objections as a way to extend the value of working with them, not as a reason not to.

As you are working on how you educate a prospect, role play as much as you can with someone else so that you are comfortable both with content and the tempo of the conversation. Figure out what is important to bring up and what is not. Work out what to do if a prospect has a lot of questions, or if they have almost no questions. You want to get used to talking about your business intelligently and confidently. I have a handful of role playing partners that I work with in business and I always set the scene for them to let them know how I want them to act. I might say, "Okay, I want to practise my pitch and I want you to be disinterested," or "I want to practise my pitch and I want you to hammer me on budget questions." I invite them to be the best and worst versions of a prospect so that I can get a 'feel' for what's important to bring up in the presentation, depending on how the prospect acts. I want to know how to move things along and how to slow them down. How to deal with tough personalities. How to address objections before they come up as a pre-emptive strike for credibility. I want to experience every scenario in my head so that when alone, I can run through scenarios myself and practise key messaging. When you are dialled in and in front of a prospect with means and need, you should be golden. Once you have established visibility and credibility, and answered (proactively or reactively) any objections, you are positioned to close.

The last point, and maybe the most important, is to remember to always walk your walk. Market Sharks aren't tentative or unsure. They know what they do, they know how they do it, and they know how it benefits those they work with. There is not one doubt in their minds that they can get it done each and every time for a client. You are in a business practice for a reason. You are constantly adjusting and tweaking your approach for the optimum outcome (new business). Self-analysis is key. You know if it sounds smooth; you know if it sounds comfortable; you know if your pitch is addressing objections. Any part that you skimp on or breeze over will come back to bite you in the ass, so put in the time now. Experience is a cruel teacher and watching viable prospects walk down the road without buying from you is hard. Credibility takes months or years to develop and seconds to destroy, so act accordingly. The more preparation you do at the beginning, the quicker you realise the benefits.

Closing Pond Business

Business is for the brave. If you have a solution and a prospect has a problem that that your solution addresses, ask them if they'd like to work together with you. When suggesting this to struggling entrepreneurs, the excuse is, "I can't just ask them for the work!" That's exactly what you need to do, because asking is the easy part. The hard part is establishing visibility and credibility to the point where the prospect is ready to be asked if they want to work with you. Business owners and professionals mentally convince themselves of hundreds of reasons why people won't buy from them. If they repurposed that time and acknowledged why people should and would want to buy from them, they would have twice the business and half the stress. The Market Shark is his or her own biggest fan. You must know what you're good at, why it matters, and why people care. As soon as you share that information with intention, don't be surprised by people showing interest in working with you. Then all you have to do is ask to complete the process.

Early on in my coaching career I had created a lot of visibility and had established credibility but, for some reason, many people I considered ideal prospects didn't become clients. Back then, I was in the practise of providing prospective clients with information and giving them a taste of what coaching looked like, then inviting them to come back when they were ready. Because I was fortunate enough always to have lots of clients it was never really an issue since I always had a full client roster, full sales funnel, and a waiting list of people looking to get into my practice. Time would go by (sometimes upwards of a year or two) and I'd run into some of these past prospects who hadn't closed and hear that they were still struggling with their business models. I'd say to them, "Why didn't you ever call me?", and they'd say, "I thought you didn't think I was ready to work with you or that you weren't interested in working with me. If you were, I thought you would have suggested we do something together." This came as a surprise to me because I felt that people who wanted support in their business would simply ask for it. Upon reflection, I realised that the market has been conditioned to be 'sold to' and not directly selling to the market can be perceived a lack of interest on your part. Furthermore, they think that you do not feel that they are ready to work with you. I have a little Catholic guilt around this because I knew that if I had simply said to that prospect a year or two earlier, "Hey, we should do some work together", not only could we have started to work together much earlier, but I could have gotten them over their roadblocks and achieving profitability much sooner.

Clients expediting your prospecting process

Prospects with need and not means will romance you. They will compliment you. They will ask you if you have time for just a quick coffee (which is code for "Can I suck out all of your information without paying for it?"). If they do it once, shame on them. If they do it twice, shame on you. You know better. That's why at Ghost CEO™ we have a saying that "everybody gets the time of day... once." You should be able to figure out in your initial meeting whether this is a prospect that has both need and means. If it's not obvious at the end of the first meeting, best to default them as not being a valid prospect and move on. They know where to find you when their circumstances change.

As you get more particular about who gets your time, validating prospects by quickly identifying whether they have both means and need becomes fun. You'll learn that the niche markets you are focused on are filled with existing clients and prospective clients that talk to each other all the time. If you deliver on your promises and fulfil your side of the client relationship then your clients can't help but talk about you with other members of the niche market. You become known for being a great provider and this information comes from someone buying from you, increasing the effectiveness of your credibility to prospective clients. As well your clients will share with these prospects how your offering is customised for the market they are in. This comes back to the way you answer the three questions. When done properly, these existing clients will introduce your messaging to others in the market.

When I decided to focus on business coaching for a female clientele, I knew that I had the opportunity to capture the attention of the market by specialising. Because all the other business coaching models at that time focused on men, something customised for women would stand out to a female audience. Women had been forced to learn content intended for men, and how to act 'like men' to be successful, which was ridiculous. In doing this, they abandoned the very skills that would enable them to grow much quicker than their male counterparts.

I realised the opportunity lay in tailoring content specifically for professional women in a way that didn't pull punches or sugar coat things, that was system-oriented, and that identified goals. Being a 6'6", 300 pound giant did not hurt as I was memorable and unique. Being a proven business professional who had built a reputation of being a proponent of business women, teaching them fundamental ways of developing business, extended my credibility. Speaking directly and bluntly to my female audience, I would share ways to avoid pitfalls when working with male counterparts in the workplace, and the secrets men had kept to themselves about getting ahead. Since the niche markets I focused on were professional women's groups, these clients and prospects spent a lot of time with each other. When one of my clients would start to break through and grow at a rapid pace, all the other women in her circle would ask what she was doing. The Ghost CEO™ would always feature in the description. In hindsight, when looking back at male clients that I had, they never wanted anyone to know that they had a business coach because they saw it as a weakness. Female counterparts loved sharing with their peers that they had a male business coach who was working with them on business development and dealing with men in business. Our clientele has always been our biggest source of new business. Women love to share best practices; men hide the advantages they have.

When you target a market that has a need for your customised offering, business development gets easy. Every Ghost CEO™ business coach and client go through a six-step process when developing business. Here are the six steps that we use, and I would encourage you to adapt them to your system:

1. **Credibility.** You have complete control over this. You get to decide if people know you or not, and you get to decide through your actions and words what that story is in order to establish credibility. The market doesn't control these first two steps; you do. If, for whatever reason, you're not getting traction, you can review what you are doing and adjust. No one else has to do this for you, nor can they. When you have established visibility and credibility, profitability automatically follows if you're talking to prospects with both means and need who understand that you can provide the solution to the problem they have.

2. **Sit down with prospects and give them a taste of what you do.** If you're in a product business let them touch or experience the product as much as possible. If you're in a service business give them a taste not only of the professional service that you offer but also the customer service that your company will deliver. Remember, the better you know the markets you're looking to service, the better a customised experience you can offer them.

3. **Qualify those prospects during your initial meeting.** Make sure that you have a list of questions that you used with prospects that will either validate or dismiss that prospect as

being viable. They have to have both means and need to get any further attention. Even if you're targeting the market properly, a majority of the people you talk to are going to have need but no means. This is just part of the process. If you find yourself talking to many people with means and no need, then you need to adjust the way you are targeting the market. The saying, "You have to kiss a lot of frogs to find a prince" is as true in business development as it is everywhere else. As your reputation as a Market Shark grows, people will start to self-select before they even come to talk to you. In most of our markets, distant clients and champions (gatekeepers) will tell prospective clients what they need to look like from a business point of view to sit with us. This cuts down on our time investment and most prospects are validated before our first visit together. Not a bad thing at all, but took years to develop.

4. **If the prospect is viable, invite them to do some work with you.** Don't hard sell them. Just ask the question, "Would you like to do some work together?" This is the question every business owner needs to make a part of their daily vocabulary. It's to be delivered only after a prospect has been validated. When used properly, it will become your favourite question and not be something that you're nervous to ask.

5. **Once you get that client, I want you to work hard to know everything about them.** The better you know them, the better you can serve them. When you solve their problems and blow them away with how to treat them, they will talk to others in the market when you aren't around. They become an unpaid sales force for you. They evangelise you and your company in your absence. They validate prospects by telling them why they need you and what resources they need to work with you. This is what will make you a legend and a true Market Shark.

6. Any validated prospect that doesn't close (and you know they have means and need) indicates an issue with credibility or your presentation. Do a post-mortem on your process and see if there is anything you can tighten up for future presentations. Do not chase the prospect if you screwed up because the only thing worse than doing a bad presentation is looking needy and chasing their car down the road asking for second chance. Market Sharks don't play that way. Take it as a lesson learned and move on.

Staying on Top – Your Monthly Checklist

Getting on top and becoming a Market Shark is only half the work. Staying on top is where the magic happens. Back in grade school we used to play King of the Hill. There'd be a big snow pile and someone would get on top and everyone else would try to rush the hill only to have the King of the Hill punt them off as they got close to the top. You had to grab the King by the leg and push them over and then ascend to position of King of the Hill and defend your territory. Good game for future capitalists.

In business, it's almost the same action but without the same physical aggression. Once you ascend to that top spot, you have to own it and make it so that other people who might consider challenging your spot will rethink things and decide whether it's really worth the effort of trying to knock you off. Most just go off to find their own hill. Those that topple from the top spot have taken that spot for granted. Without realising it, they find their hard-earned spot eroding under their feet. This is a sucker play. Don't be that sucker.

Not to be a super hypocrite, I've taken my markets for granted, on more occasions that I'd like to admit. Everything would be going swimmingly, only for me to suddenly feel the erosion of my position in the market happening quickly and unexpectedly. I would have to work my way back up to the top, and then work at being mindful not to let that happen again. Each and every time, it was because I took my eye off the ball. This happened a number of times, before I finally wised up. Like most of the things we're talking about in this book, this is completely within your control. Learn from my many, many mistakes. If things aren't working, it's because you're not doing something right. Take time to look at what you are doing (and not doing). Making the proper decisions, will get you and keep you on top. Don't get lazy or sit back thinking that things are never going to change once you hit the pinnacle. That's just when the work starts. Because you are going to get busy, you need to have a system in place to manage this.

I follow an eight-step process that I review every month, no matter how busy I am. Any of these points on their own are powerful, but when you bring them together they create a system for you to track what's going on in your markets. Start with one and then, in each subsequent month, add another one. By the time you are at Month 8 you'll have my full process in hand and you will see that it both gets you to the top and keeps you there.

1. **Knowing information about your markets is great, but be aware of the trends and anything that has influence over your markets.** I make notes on every account that I'm responsible for. Where did they come from? How long have we worked together? What have they bought from me? Why did they buy that from me? What did I learn about the market through working with them? Are they ideal or marginal clients? (To us, marginal clients are those that are theoretically good but that lack some fundamental piece that would put them at the top of the list).. I like to go back into my notes for both active and past clients and look for the trends I can distil about that particular market. One of the trends I found through this process concerned young female lawyers who have a focus on making partner. Those who are at a 5-year call or higher and considering having a family will

begin to explore becoming in-house counsel or starting their own firm after having the family. The firm is likely to lose them at this point. The trend I've discerned is that many female lawyers leave big firms at the 5-year call mark. Of course, this information is mirrored in industry reports. We know that if we don't have a client on partnership track by the time she decides to start having a family, we need to introduce the other options for her consideration. Too many women go on "Mommy Track" (where a firm stops a woman's advancement once she has kids) when they return and that isn't acceptable on any level for us. If a client is okay with this, we cease our work with her. This is just one of the trends we have adjusted our model for. Once these trends are identified, they continue to be tracked and are shared with other coaches as best practices. I have notes on every single coaching client I've ever worked with. Now it's become an encyclopaedia of how business models work, how they're developed, what strategies work for what personalities in which markets, what's the best recipe to implement strategies. This is valuable beyond belief for me. Especially moving forward with new clients. I know the 'recipe' for their profession.

2. **Sharing best practices between each other.** Remember, you are looking for trends. Your colleagues might see things differently from you and this difference in perception can be valuable to both of you. If you find that you have a lack of colleagues serving the same markets, consider joining industry groups, conferences, or even other monthly meetings of service providers like you in your markets. We've had clients join LinkedIn groups just to read what people are talking about. All of these situations are a great way to get a lot of aggregate information in a short amount of time to consider. As I shared earlier, my communications company serviced BIAs. There weren't many other vendors in this space to share

information with. Instead, I attended their yearly conference where they all got together in one place. I would talk with 60 BIA's over 2 days, all in the same location. I'd get to find out what they were working on, what they had on their wish list, and any challenges they were having. The added benefit was that many of our clients were in the room talking to our prospective clients about the work we were doing with them. A Market Shark loves shooting fish in a barrel and the conference was the 'barrel'. Today with Ghost CEO™, we use conferences and conversations with other service providers to identify trends that are happening in our markets. It has been key to our success in tailoring our offering to our markets.

3. **Be open to learning from your competition.** Your competitors can tell you as much if not more about market trends as your colleagues. To get this information, you need to dig a bit deeper than you would with colleagues. They aren't likely to be as forthcoming with information (as you can imagine). Websites, press releases, market conversations, market gossip and the like are all valuable resources for you to learn from them. During the recession of 2008 I spent a lot of time reviewing who was getting laid off or fired from competing coaching companies. This information offered insight into if they were losing clients. Companies don't downsize if things are going well. Once I realised these companies were trending downward, I'd start up conversations with their clients (if listed on their website), and call their top coaches and see if they wanted to cross the floor. It's always better to join growing team rather than staying with their existing company waiting to be euthanised. The information that competitive companies put into press releases can be used to your advantage.

4. **Watch news, and read magazines and blogs that relate to the markets that you serve.** I wanted to know what my clients are interested in and many them shared that they read O Magazine so I followed suit. Male friends who come over to my house always assume that the O Magazine is my wife's and when they find out it's mine I always get a good ribbing. I take the teasing happily; reading the magazine allows me to understand what's important to our clientele outside of business. By understanding what thought leaders and influencers in my markets are saying, I can better understand and serve our clients at any given time.

5. **Review your offering on a quarterly basis, but track your revenues monthly.** Has the market (or your clients) suggested things they'd like to buy from you? Is there a gap in service provision that would make your clients' lives easier? Always look at what you could add that will both make things better for your clients and build your bottom line. Ghost CEO™ was in business for almost 10 years before we finally took action on a comment we received repeatedly from clients that they did not understand how cash flow worked. As Ghost CEO™ has focused on business development and sales, we don't spend a lot of time on dissecting financials with clients. We do review their monthly statements to see that the profit model is on track but we don't go into how they are spending money, look at leases they are entering into, or any such thing. In 2010 we launched Fast Track CFO™, the sister company of Ghost CEO™. Fast Track CFO™ offers clients the cash flow side of business: How to leverage money, manage cash flow, put into place accounts payable and receivable, and the like. Where Ghost CEO™ teaches companies how to bring money in, Fast Track CFO™ teaches them how to keep it. It took 10 years of hearing these comments before I was sure that (1) clients truly needed this service in a way that we could deliver it, and (2) that it made

viable sense for us to be the ones to develop it as opposed to partnering with another organisation. For those 10 years we suggested that the client talk to their accountant about those issues. Time and time again, clients would come back saying that their accountants weren't interested in having those conversations. When we couldn't find a viable option to partner with, we developed one. That company is growing by leaps and bounds. As you can imagine, it has a great business development system.

6. **Reach out to alliances, colleagues, and even old clients that might need a bit of help.** Being empathetic to those who are struggling will remind you that business gives you a unique vantage point for helping others. Not only can this potentially build your business but it can affirm your position as a Market Shark others. Offering a helping hand to a past contact is good for your soul and good for the bottom line. Even if they don't become a client, they become an evangelist for you and your work. You get to be selfless and selfish all at the same time, which is something that I love doing.

7. **Serve those that support your business endeavours.** No one becomes successful on their own. It takes a group of people who rally around the professional and support them. Review these people who offered their assistance and reach out to do something nice for them at least once a month. This may be sending them a note, or forwarding an article to them that they may find interesting (while you're reviewing industry trade magazines and the like while working on Step 4 above), etc. This doesn't have to be a grand gesture, but just a little nod to them letting them know that you're thinking about them and that you're important to you. Many of these people will become 'Champions', which are educated referral sources that bring you clients. Champions know what you do, why it matters, and why people care. On top of that, they have

influence over a market (or markets) that you are a Market Shark in.

8. **Reach out to new contacts in the pond and welcome them.** The Market Shark is always part host and part bouncer in the market. Decide who will get into your own personal inner circle but be welcoming to everyone new to the market. You were once a new character on the scene and some person or people opened up time to talk with you and gave you an opportunity to earn your spot in the pond. Be gracious to others as others were once to you. If you weren't extended this courtesy when you joined your markets, remember that feeling and be the bigger person and be exclusively inclusive.

Those are the eight things that I do on a monthly basis to ensure that I'm staying on top. I'm not going to be hypocritical and say that some months I don't remember to do all eight things, but I will let you know that in those months where I had not done all eight things, I can detect a noticeable difference in how I'm perceived in the market. It may not be anything huge, but I can see in a person's face when they think I've forgotten about them. Be consistent, be mindful, and follow these eight steps (to the best of your ability) monthly. You won't be able to incorporate all eight steps the first month. If you try, you won't do them well, feel that you are failing and stop. Pace yourself. Start with one the first month, and add a new one each month as suggested.

Best Practices of the Market Shark

In high school I took one of two roads when it came to required literature course work: I either chose novels that had a Coles Notes version (that's Cliff Notes for Americans), or I dated a girl who was good at the course work. For you, dear reader, I offer the best practices of the Market Shark without having to take me for dinner and a movie. These best practices serve as a reminder of the key points that we have covered in this chapter. If you never read this book again, dog-ear this page and come back to it when you need to a little check-up on yourself. If you find that after you've ascended to the position of Market Shark the ground under your feet feels a bit unstable, grab this book, open it to this section, and go back through it. I want you to think of this as the cheat sheet for the book thus far.

Here's the list that I have printed out on the first page of my journal and I review it at least 3-4 times a week. It's a constant reminder to me that all the work I've put into becoming a Market Shark in my markets can be taken away almost immediately if I forget what and who got me there.

Clients, who use this list religiously, make a check mark beside each thing they do each week. Use this list in any way that serves you best, but use it!

Be yourself; people are watching. If you're a small fish or someone who is inconsequential, you don't have to watch your actions because no one gives a shit. When you ascend to being a Market Shark, everyone will be watching you and half of them will want you to do really well; the other half will be jealous and want you to fall on your face. Either way, you will be subject to critical gazes. Don't fake it. Don't be nice one day and nasty another. Be yourself, but understand which characteristics to highlight when in your different markets.

Consider the needs of others when you serve. Anyone who tells me their customers need them more than they need their customers is a dolt. The only reason you're in business is because people need what you offer and choose to buy it from you. With an ever growing market place there are more options for consumers than ever before. Don't buy into your own PR. It can be taken away from you as quickly as it came. Be mindful of those that you serve and be aware of their needs. Without them, you don't have a business. Never forget that.

Be active in your markets. Don't just go into your market, make a big splash, and then disappear. People trust those they can rely on, and relying on someone comes from consistency. Don't go to a meeting one month, ditch for three months, and then go back in expecting everyone to view you in the same way they did before your absence. Baby steps always trump grandiose action. When in doubt read the story of the turtle and the hare. Slow and steady (and consistent) wins the race. You'll find that the more often people see you and understand you, the more people start to buy from you.

Contribute to your market's knowledge base. Nobody likes someone who takes all the time, so look to share best practices and information with others in the market. For example, we might develop a tool for a particular client such as a worksheet, a to-do list, or a checklist. We'll have the client use this and, once we have worked out any kinks, we'll then make it available to other clients. Heck, we'll often release this stuff on our own website so other practitioners can use it, once we know that it works. We appreciate that we can't serve everyone who needs to be served so we'd rather our colleagues (competitors) use great tools than have those customers we can't serve suffer with tools that are subpar. Think of yourself as a part of the science community. If you discover something that works really well, share it with others. Keep some of your 'tricks' to yourself, but if it is general knowledge that would benefit all, put it out there. Scarcity mind-sets create scarce results.

Introduce vetted members of the market to each other. There's nothing worse than one of your great contacts introducing you to someone shitty. Not only does this waste your time but it makes you second guess that person you trust. Whenever anyone is introducing me, I'll connect with that person doing the introduction and say, "What do you want me to do with them? Is it a favour for you or a favour for them? Is it value for you or for me, or is it value for all of us?" When you pose the question in this manner people are quite honest. Often clients and colleagues will ask me to talk to one of their contacts as a favour that they can leverage off of down the road. As long as you know why, you can be prepared to do it. This works both ways. Any two people you introduce to each other are riding off of your reputation, and if one is a bonehead and the other is exceptional, the bonehead is going to think you're awesome (which you don't want) and the exceptional one will think that you're the bonehead (again, something you don't want). Be mindful when introducing two people to each other because you're co-signing on both of your reputations with your own reputation. Make sure it benefits both. If not, let the one not getting the benefit know what you need and tell them you are ready to reciprocate when they need it.

Leave things better than you find them (people, too). If you can't have a positive impact on the situation or the people involved, don't engage. There's no upside to being a bystander who can't get things done. Any time we meet with a prospective client, even if we vet them and realise that they're not a quality candidate for our practice (either don't have means or need), we still make sure we leave them with a couple of tools that they can implement to make their business better. A prospect that does not fit, should still be an evangelist for what we do. That's something we strive for in every meeting we have.

Look at market cross-over. How can you be the bridge between two markets? In most situations a business professional will have markets that have similarities with each other. It's key for you to look at how you might be able to bridge those groups together. It can start with connecting gatekeepers to each other or even by taking a member of one market as a guest to another market to let them have a look. We have taken many of our colleagues and strategic alliances into new markets that we are currently working in to let them experience it for them to see if it is a market they might want to come into. The best thing about this is that those favours are almost always returned by bringing you into market that you might not be familiar with but that are viable for your bottom line. If not entering their markets, when they enter yours, they become evangelists for you. Either way, "you are golden Pony Boy." Controlling the bridge is a powerful position to be in. Look for ways to flex this muscle.

What gets you busy, keeps you busy. Do not mess with the secret sauce. Once you see yourself ascending into the role of market shark, keep doing what you're doing. Don't try to get creative and artistic; keep doing the consistent work that's allowing you to ascend. Once you get to the top of the hill, and then continue to do the work on a consistent basis keep one eye on the work and one eye on the trends. The market trends will let you know what you need to do and where you need to focus your attention. I never hunted coaches out of existing coaching models until I saw the trend that coaching models were simply downsizing and euthanising key talent rather than engaging in business development. I shifted my course because the opportunity was in front of me and it made sense on every level. Many of the daily practices I follow today are the ones I used back when I started business coaching in 1999/2000. Once I realised something worked, I did not mess with it. I just kept on using it as long as it produced results.

Invite others into the market and avoid a scarcity mind-set. I know of people who find that honey hole (a fishing term that connotes a place with a lot of fish that few people know about). I'm not suggesting that you invite your competitors in, saying, "Hey, look. Here are a bunch of clients we can all fight over." However, when you find a good market, take a look at the people you're aligned with and invite them to come in and have a look. The more of you on the same team in the market, the more you can defend your position as a Market Shark. I have found that at any time I slide into a scarcity mind-set where I am looking to defend and protect something; I end up losing market share. When I act as that market's ambassador (Market Shark), inviting colleagues and like-minded people in to have a look, not only does my credibility increase, but my suggested influence over the market also increases. Both are great for my business as it will be for yours.

Engage with other Market Sharks and emerging Market Sharks. Birds of a feather flock together and if you want to fly with eagles, you know by now that you can't run with turkeys. If you see other Market Sharks in complementary services you should engage them. When you see up and coming Market Sharks (we call them "Bright Eyes"), engage them and talk about how you can build business together. Again, this is not a scarcity play but is rather an abundance mind-set knowing that more is more, not less. When you're choosing the right people to hang out with a multiplier effect happens. If you're hanging out with people and you're not getting a multiplier effect, you're probably hanging out with losers. Change your group. We are going to talk more about building Strategic Alliances in Chapter 7.

Don't forget all the support people that got you to where you are. When we get busy with work, just keeping in touch with clients and Champions can be challenging. Don't forget all the people (even the small ones) who have helped you get to where you are. This will take extra effort, but is time well spent. The same people that you pass on the ladder going up are the people you will pass on the ladder going down. When I worked for municipalities, the most important person at any city was not the mayor or the city manager; it was the mayor's secretary. Not only did they control access, but they would give me a heads up on any trends (i.e., important information) that I needed to know. Support people make the world go around so make sure to pay attention to them. They are often dismissed, ignored, or unappreciated. Make up for that by being attentive, interested, and appreciative.

As a Market Shark, please and thank you must be (and should remain) your two favourite words. Courtesy can be overlooked, but it's never forgotten by the person who should have received that courtesy and didn't. Remember your manners when dealing with anyone and everyone.

Be proud of your work but never think that you're too important. Anyone who gets too big for their britches often has their legs cut out from underneath them. My dad taught me never to believe the criticism and never to believe the accolades. You know you're doing a good job, and if you are doing a good job in the market's eyes, you will be rewarded with continued business. If you're losing business, no matter how high you think of your service, something you are doing sucks and needs to be changed.

Every business is a service business no matter what you sell. Most of what you do with any client will be managing expectations and the relationship. Never forget that. You put those two things on the back burner and you will quickly be marginalised by your audience and your market. If you aren't leaving them better than you find them, you are doing something wrong.

Don't over think things, but do put time into examining trends and performance. Math doesn't lie. If you're growing a particular client segment unintentionally, you need to spend time on figuring why they're coming in. If you are losing a particular segment and are not sure why, you have to do a post–mortem to figure out why they are leaving. Everything in business can be dissected but do not lie in bed asking what ifs; instead, work the numbers. Math doesn't lie. Ask the right questions.

Don't be jealous of others. Everyone is trying to build a business and some do it at different paces and in different ways. Some people hit really quickly and others take more time to become established. The only race you are running is a race with yourself. Anything else is both futile and amateur.

Never take your pond for granted. As soon as your market thinks that you think you are better than them, they will punt you out of the market. Any market that feels under-appreciated will wreak havoc on your business model. The only reason that you're in business and staying in business is because of them. Never, ever, ever take them for granted or you'll watch your bottom line vaporise. To feel the love; show the love.

Nobody does it alone. Acknowledge and honour all the people that currently and in the past have helped you build and guided you when you were figuring things out. None of us is born with the knowledge to be successful. We acquire it from watching people, being mentored by people, and learning best practices.

Don't ever forget where you started. It's easy to think that it's all shits and giggles when you're a Market Shark but you started as someone small and unsure in the market like the rest of us. That's where your humility lives. There was a time in my life when I lived in a shitty little apartment in the worst part of town. Now I live in a big house on a golf course in one of the most beautiful areas of the world. My home town is on people's 'bucket lists' of places to vacation before they take the 'dirt nap'. However, I keep a picture of that apartment building on my desk as a reminder not only of how far I've come, but what will happen if I take it for granted.

Solicit best practices and share best practices. Simply put, we are all here only for a blink in time. Make a contribution through your work and that contribution can live on long after you are gone. Being a Market Shark is about following best practices and being an example of best practices. Never lose track of that.

Those are your best practices to read, implement, and manage. As we've said before, you can't do it alone. Let's have a look now at finding some friends in the market to build with.

Chapter 7 – Swimming with other Big Fish

"The Death of the Entrepreneur is Solitude" – Ernesto Sirolli

Why Alliances Make Sense

Many entrepreneurs stop building their business not due to fatigue or failed plans, but because of loneliness. Building a business or being a high-level professional is a lonely experience and this only increases as you become successful. You will notice that less and less people have what it takes to get to the top of their game and become a Market Shark. In addition, successful business professionals will state they couldn't have done it on their own. They relied on a team of people, staff, and contractors and, equally important, on alliances they formed early on in their business model.

No business can offer everything that their markets need and stay at the top of their game. When two or more companies come together, operate at the same level, and service the same markets with complimentary services, they might decide to explore an alliance with one another. Such an undertaking can contribute to win-win-win situations; a win for you, a win for your alliance, and a win for the clients you commonly service.

Most businesses new to alliances get spooked when they hear "strategic alliance" because they think by entering one, they are committing to a monogamous business relationship (where they agree to go steady with someone, which may block opportunities from other companies). This simply is not the case. We define a strategic alliance as:

"two or more independent companies coming together to pursue agreed upon goals while remaining independent organisations. Companies in strategic alliances collaborate and may share resources, but remain distinct and separate from one another."

In layman terms, a strategic alliance happens when two companies come together to operate in a mutually beneficial relationship with one another, while staying independent of each other.

A strategic alliance is like having a roommate. Rather than incurring all the overhead yourself, paying all the utility bills and the rent; you have a few people move in with you to share the overhead and hopefully you will be interested in the same pursuits (i.e. Drinking Jägermeister, Ouija Boards, puppet shows, etc). While at university I had many different roommates in many different houses, but the goal we all shared was to graduate from university. In a sense, people who have lived together while at university have built a strategic alliance to get through something together, where they both share in some of the work/investment and individually benefit from the collective efforts.

Many strategic alliances go off the tracks before they even get started. People don't understand how they are supposed to work or how to implement them effectively. Instead, they wing it. We know from our discussions in earlier chapters that a bit of planning ahead of time will help avoid a lot of problems down the road.

This chapter will outline the way to find and explore potential relationships with strategic alliances, how to enter into those relationships, and how to manage those relationships, either in an ongoing capacity or to terminate them when they no longer work. One key thing I want you to remember: strategic alliances may be short term or they may be long term, but you only want to be involved with them while both you and the other party or parties involved have a selfish benefit that you can derive from the alliance.

Building strategic alliances is like any other practice that we discuss in this book; they take time and effort to develop. Some alliances look really great but just fizzle out; others may take a while to build but then become profitable and dependable over time. Before exploring what a strategic alliance delivers, let's first look at what you need to have done before engaging with them:

- You have to be very clear with the three niche markets that you are engaged with or are about to engage with.

- You have to have done your research to know where the watering holes are for each of those markets, and who the gatekeepers are.

- You have to have your answers to the three questions developed and finished for each niche markets.

- You have to have already established relationships with gatekeepers and/or other Market Sharks in those ponds.

- You have to be in Business Development mode.

The five statements above might seem like common sense, but most people enter into alliances looking for a lifeguard to save their business from drowning. Not only should you not be looking for a lifeguard, but you should not be suckered into becoming the lifeguard for someone else. If either you or the other business do not have the fundamentals in place, then do not engage in a strategic alliance until both of you are sorted out. Otherwise you will end up getting together to commiserate about 'how hard these things are' and it will end up as a self-made support group that people will talk about behind your back. Not good.

All your foundation work needs to be done in advance because you want the alliance to become active on day one. If you are still figuring out your tools when the alliance begins, the other side (if prepared) will get tired of waiting for you to get your shit together. A great strategic alliance will make you a better version of yourself. They will challenge you to play a bigger game so that you don't disappoint them and, hopefully, they will feel the same way and be the best version of themselves. You will end up getting the best out of each other, which is good for both of your business models and bottom lines.

One of my clients referred to strategic alliances as like having a workout partner at the gym. It is easy to go to the gym and fumble through your workout alone and maybe even do a bit of planning beforehand but still, if you decide not to show up, nobody will know. The strategic alliance relationship means that somebody will go to the gym with you, will be waiting for you, and know that you will be waiting for them. They won't let you play small, nor will you allow them to play small. When you show up together, you start to look like a powerhouse and people take notice. This is one of the key objectives you want to accomplish with your strategic alliances: accountability.

Assuming that you have all of your markets/communications/messaging sorted out as does your prospective alliance, let's go through six reasons why strategic alliances make sense for Market Sharks:

The alliance fills in a gap in service that you do not offer currently. When you have a good alliance or an alliance is in place, you can extend the service that you offer the market. As an example, a commercial realtor could form an alliance with a residential realtor. If they are going after business owners, one can fill their housing needs and the other can fill their commercial needs. Since the client will come in through one or the other, the client gets the benefit of both, and the providers can create an internal referral.

When you are starting to kick around the idea of who could be a strategic alliance, think about which other service providers or product providers could extend the value of what you offer. I know one such alliance between two consultants. One engages in market research and one writes business plans. By partnering together, they can go after bigger contracts that they might otherwise not be able to fulfil on their own. This becomes a symbiotic relationship and something that becomes very exciting for both parties.

The alliance fills in a gap in service for the prospective ally that isn't offered currently in their business. Again, many times business owners would like to offer other services but it's not viable for them to offer it themselves. Rather than hiring additional staff or even contractors, they can align with a company and form a partnership with it that will add the alliance's components to the overall mix. I know of one such alliance between a digital marketing firm and a social media management company. The social media company can sell itself as a bigger firm with a development arm, and the digital marketing firm can tell their clients that can also extend services in the social media platforms. Both companies individually look bigger to their markets without additional overhead of staff or contractors. Peanut butter and jelly; spaghetti and meatballs; mac and cheese: two separate components that go well together, as does a well thought out alliance.

Each company challenges the other to be the best version of itself. If you're doing business on your own you may not have anyone to challenge you, but when you're in a strategic alliance both sides should demand the very best from each other every time. Not unlike the gym partner example; both parties expect the very best work from each other every time they engage.

A strategic alliance may provide existing accounts that you can sell into. As both sides of the alliance should have an established clientele, there is an opportunity for some cross-promotion. With an existing clientele you've already developed visibility, credibility, and profitability and you can extend the credibility you have earned to your alliance, and vice versa. This shortens the sales cycle, especially if you're targeting the same niche markets (which you should be) and a client "for one becomes a client for both" (think Three Musketeers: "All for one; one for all). This works well, for example, between lawyers and accountants. When it comes to small business, most that have been incorporated should have a corporate lawyer and an accountant who does their year-end. When an alliance is formed between these two professions, the accountant can send out a letter to all their clients sharing some pertinent legal information developed by the lawyer (their alliance) and, vice versa, the lawyer can send out some tax tips developed by the accountant (their alliance) that would be interest to their corporate clients. Since each have the trust of their existing clientele, their clients will take seriously the fact that those two companies have aligned with each other to cross-promote. The assumption is that a vetting process has already happened (which it has) and that they can trust the new service provider as they do the existing one.

A strategic alliance may cover geographical territory that you want to move into. When I was first opening an office in Seattle I began developing alliances with bankers, financial planners, small business lawyers, accountants, personal coaches, and other business coaches by phone and the odd business trip there. Because what Ghost CEO™ offers is unique, I positioned the piece that we play clearly and concisely to those we were looking to partner with (the Three Questions) and found out from the other professions how their components would fit into the practice I was building. When I officially entered the Seattle market, I already had contracts in place that I could leverage for new clients. This added to quick development of credibility with this market. On top of that, those alliances told me about the best offices to find space in and which to avoid. As well, they gave me critical market intelligence that I wouldn't otherwise have been able to collect as I didn't live there. We've developed these types of relationships around the world now, so if we get a request for a business coach in Israel and Ghost CEO™ doesn't currently have one there or if a client requires a coach they can meet with face to face, then we can make an introduction to a company that we've already vetted, and vice versa.

A strategic alliance may have a service or product that will make you more attractive to prospective accounts. We've partnered with organisations that are certified Myers Briggs™ practitioners so that when we're working within a corporate environment and the HR team is hot-to-trot on Myers Briggs™, rather than having to go get certified in that area, we simply bring in our alliance to do that part for us. We bill the work under our company name and pay our alliance on the back end. We benefit from that knowledge base and expertise without having to put in the time or money to train our own people. Access to this specific expertise allows us to hunt in to companies that require a specialised knowledge base of assessments that we do not currently offer along with many of our service lines. In a lot of cases, these clients want to buy from one company. Having an alliance allows us to close this business and subcontract out the parts we don't do to someone we trust.

As we dive deeper into finding alliances and engaging them, remember that an alliance can also be a client or a champion. Sometimes this can seem a bit confusing until you realise that everyone you know in the business sphere could be an alliance. We have clients who are graphic designers, social media experts, architects, movers, professional organisers, and a hundred other professions. We align with those companies and if another client needs the service then we are quick to refer that business. This is easy for us to do, we get a unique insight into how that business conducts their operations, and we feel very comfortable in making that recommendation with credibility.

Our coaches have developed alliances with different accountants in our markets. Some specialise in small business, while others specialise in high net worth professionals. When a client has an accounting question outside our area of expertise, we are able to call our alliance and get our question answered. Not only does the client get an immediate answer, but the alliance gets exposure to our clientele. On the other hand, many of our accounting alliances will recognise when one of their client's profit models isn't doing as well as it did the year before and will ask us to spend a half hour with their client to help get things sorted out. Value is added from the accountant to their client and we gain exposure to a prospective client. Like I have noted before, once a client knows about us, they can't 'un-know' about us. Both benefit from serving that client and extending the service to each other. When you have a handful of great alliances, you will start to see the number of quality prospects increase exponentially because a client for one could be a client for all. (Remember Musketeers!)

What Makes a Good Alliance?

Thinking about working with someone else as a business development partner, after having spent a lot of time alone trying to develop your business, can get you all 'hot and bothered'. It's kind of like if you haven't dated for five years and somebody looks at you who has most of their teeth, all of their toes and on some micro level is attractive. You might jump on them right away. Whoa! Slow down and rein yourself in. This is a no-leg-humping zone. Take your time so that you find the right dance partner. Put in the effort, you want it to have the best chance of being successful.

Your strategic alliances must first make sense on paper and, once you have started to explore a potential alliance with this person, it must pass the 'gut check'. If any part of it starts to feel weird or gives you a bad feeling in your stomach (gut), stop.

There are too many good strategic alliances out there for you to settle for something is half-baked or half-assed. If your intuitive radar suggests that it is not a good fit, trust it. Do not invest a bunch of time into something that will not work. Much of what we pick up is non-verbal and it is better to keep looking than to invest in the wrong person and waste time and money on them.

I start with a scorecard, even before I start talking to someone. Similar to when I research niche markets and gatekeepers, I spend time behind the scenes exploring and researching a potential strategic alliance before fully engaging with them and having the conversation. I have a list of 15 components that I go through myself (this is not something I share with them) and I grade the potential alliance. When evaluating these 15 components, the more positive comments I have written down, the more likely I feel that the strategic alliance will work for both of us. It still has to pass the 'gut check', but this is the paper part of it. Here are the 15 things that I cover:

1. **The other person is in Business Development mode.** You are not a horse looking for a wagon. You're looking to run with a running mate. You want someone who is equally involved in building business who will be out there hunting every day just like you do. Even on the days you are not hunting together, they will still be out hunting. Remember that a client for one of you could be a client for both of you, so you want somebody who is directed, goal-oriented, a self-starter, and looking to build their bottom line. If they're building their bottom line, you'll be building yours through the alliance, and vice versa. Do not take on any charity cases or, as one of my mentors used to say, "Don't enter a three-legged race with a one-legged partner."

2. **They have an amazing reputation.** When you form an alliance, you will be leveraging your credibility for them and they will be leveraging their credibility for you. If their reputation is shit, then it's worth nothing for you. This will not develop new business for you and will have a cancerous effect on your reputation in your markets. Imagine you were an up-and-coming corporate Investment Banker who had aligned with Bernie Madoff. Talk about career suicide. When two companies with amazing reputations come together, it's like fire and gasoline. They can't be stopped. Do not align with anyone whose shoddy reputation will snuff out all the effort you have exerted into building your reputation.

3. **They are engaging and interested in partnerships that work.** You don't want an alliance with someone who's looking for an AA sponsor. You want someone who knows that they get the best out of themselves when somebody expects it from them, and vice versa. They do not 'suffer fools' and do not let anyone waste their time. They respect their time will respect your time. This is essential in an alliance.

4. **Their niche markets are the same as your niche markets.** If you hunt farmers and they hunt airplane pilots, no matter how good the alliance may seem, it will never work. You must be targeting the same markets for it to make sense because, remember, reputation is literally the "key" in this. All of their clients could be your clients, and all of your clients could be their clients. Your reputation will open doors for them, just as theirs will for you. When you walk into a networking event together, you should be looking like a power house to everyone in that room. You may have interests in additional markets that are not common, but your main focus must be the same.

5. **They are sustainable in their business model (not a drowning man).** Again, do not be a lifeguard to anyone; in fact, you do not even want to be swim instructor to your alliances. You want to work on a model with someone who knows how the model works. If you're spending time explaining or teaching, you've found yourself a mentorship relationship instead of a strategic alliance. They should be exceptional at what they do, you should be exceptional at what you do, and you share best practices with each other as you go out to hunt together. If any part of you senses that they are drowning, swim back to shore and let them drown. Most lifeguards who die on the job do so because the person they are trying to save drowns them. When I went through life guard training, this was drilled into our heads. After 20 years in business, I have seen many healthy businesses get capsized by bad alliances.

6. **They have the ability to refer business.** There are some professions and business models that cannot disclose who their clientele are. Make sure that anyone you talk to about a strategic alliance has the ability to refer. If they're not able or willing to refer then they won't make a good strategic alliance. Move on to somebody else.

7. **Your business models would be more powerful together than apart.** First on paper and then through personal conversations, it should become obvious that aligning these two companies will make each of them look more powerful than they do on their own. If you have to struggle to see how this could work, it's not a good alliance. For Ghost CEO™, partnering with qualified, personal coaches is a no brainer. Nine out of ten prospective clients that we see need a personal coach, not a business coach. This serves our reputation and it serves the prospective client through referral from us to be introduced to a personal coaching professional who can achieve results. Selfishly for us, once they have the personal

side sorted, they could come back to us and work on their business goals. That is why we never partner with personal coaches who also say they do business coaching. This is a fallacy. You can only be one or the other, and anyone who says they do both is a drowning professional. This is someone who is looking to grab any client that might come within their sphere of influence because they are not confident enough to stake one expertise. We refer to these types of professionals as "Pikers" and we treat them like the plague. If their only interaction with business is their coaching practice, they simply do not have the credentials to give out advice. It is like having a dating coach who cannot get a date; a running coach who can't run well, or a cooking instructor whose food tastes like dog shit.

8. **They have been in successful alliances in the past and know it takes work for alliances to produce measurable results for all parties involved.** Teaching someone how to be in a strategic alliance is a pain in the ass from a professional point of view. Again, you don't want to mentor your alliances; you want to build business with them. If you're spending time trying to teach them how to do business properly, this is time taken away from hunting up new accounts and clients. It's always great to work with someone who has been in, or currently is in, strategic alliances that work because they can share best practices with you and vice versa as you develop your relationship together.

9. **They are in locations that work for you (either in your city or in a city that you need coverage in).** Our initial step is to develop alliances in the communities in which we are currently active. After this is done, we focus our attention on communities where we are receiving leads about prospective clients, communities where we either do not yet have a physical presence, or where we do not currently have any

alliances. Our most recent example is Paris, France. Just a few months ago, we received six inquiries from Paris. We currently did not have coverage in that country, so I reached out to some business coaching professionals who had both English and French on their websites. We had initial conversations and after I vetted them, I found out they preferred to meet with clients in person and that they had received inquiries from Canada and the U.S. through their websites. We agreed that we would align together and when they had clients that needed coverage in North America they would refer to us; when we had prospective clients that needed coverage in France, we would refer to them. This alliance may not last forever if Ghost CEO™ expands to France, but in the short term it serves both of us because they can now say that they have coverage in North America and we can say that we have coverage in France. It really can be that simple.

10. **They are exceptional at making introductions between professionals.** While introverts are great, extroverts are slightly better at making introductions in my experience. You want somebody who is out there who moves and shakes, meets a lot of people, and who can discern real opportunities from the Pikers. Strategic alliances should not introduce Piker prospects to the other. They should only make introductions between qualified prospects and they should do so in a way that highlights your areas' of expertise and the ways in which they could serve that prospect. This is something that you work on together to make sure that you have the language properly developed to optimise the chance of new business coming in.

11. **They keep their word.** There isn't too much to say about this other than that the way somebody does one thing is how they do everything. If your alliance does not keep their word to

you then they probably won't keep it to the clients you introduce them to. If they don't keep their word to you, they look like shit. If they don't keep their word to people you've introduced them to, you look like shit. So be cautious.

12. **They can clearly outline the value that they bring to their clients so it's easy for you to refer.** Not unlike the three questions (again, What do you do? Why does it matter? and Who cares?), they have to be able to give you the same, concise, on-message content that you can share with people you meet. If you struggle to define what it is they do in business then it's not a good alliance and they haven't done their job. Make sure that they do the heavy lifting on that part, just like you have done on your part. Right?

13. **They clearly understand the value you bring to the table and know how to selfishly benefit from selflessly promoting you.** You've shared with them the answers to your three questions and the way that you introduce yourself to prospects and they've taken it upon themselves to learn that verbiage so that they can represent you effectively. You'll know you've dialled this in when you hear them talking about you and a smile creeps across your face. They have now become an evangelist for you and, hopefully, you for them.

14. **They have control over their time (they're not buried in work).** The last thing you want to do is have an alliance with someone who doesn't have control of their company. If they are currently swamped with paperwork or running around at the last minute putting out fires then that stress will transfer itself onto your relationship. Beware. If they don't have control, you will have to handle them to get things done and it's just not worth it.

15. **They're looking for a long-term play.** If things are working, they're going to keep them working with you for years. You don't want somebody who is fickle and jumps in and out of alliances as often as they change their underwear. You want somebody who is going to cautiously date you, then propose to you, then marry you and have a great relationship that is mutually beneficial.

Those are the 15 points I consider when evaluating a strategic alliance. While it probably takes a lot of the romance out of it, if you can't measure it then you can't manage it. Everything a Market Shark does must be done methodically and with intention. We do not hope for the best or guess about things; rather, we invest time to make sure that whatever we engage with will create a financial benefit to our bottom line. Alliances that work are worth their weight in gold but they take time to set up. It is common for me to explore ten prospective alliances and, after doing my initial review, decide to meet with only four of them and, after meeting with those four, find only one (or sometimes none) that make sense to align with. This is okay. I would rather have one great strategic alliance than ten shitty ones, and I'd rather meet with 50 prospective alliances and not take them on, than to partner with two that make me want to slit my wrists.

Before talking to any prospective alliance personally, do your homework. It is most uncomfortable when you suggest talking about a strategic alliance with someone only to discover they're looking for a lifeguard to rescue their business. On a weekly basis, people suggest to me "We should form an alliance and you can bring all your clients to my business. It would be good for them." When I hear this, the sentiment that pops into my mind is, "Please...rescue me...I don't know how to do this alone..." They know nothing about my business, just as they know nothing about their business. They just know that I have many clients and I could leverage to fulfil their business development function. I don't think so! If you are not at least as strong as me, or have the potential to be as strong as me, then I don't have the time for you and I sure as hell don't have the time to align with you. If I see someone drowning and they don't want to fix the situation, my first suggestion is for them to start gulping water. Life is too short to play around with people who aren't serious.

Dating Prospective Alliances

Take a big breath. You've done all of your prep work. You've marked the score card.   Now it's time to call that special someone. Your heart will pitter patter when your sweaty palms pick up the phone. Winners want to do business with winners; Market Sharks with Market Sharks. When entering into a conversation about an alliance, you have to be strong and project strength. Make sure that you are very clear about what you do (you know your three niche markets and have clear answers to the three questions) and know as much about their business model as humanly possible.

I invite a prospective alliance for coffee to discuss doing some business together. Keep an eye on how they respond because some people are too cool for school. Some act disinterested which leads me to burn them and move on right away. The disinterest is often because they think they are better than I am or, more often, they are insecure about what they do and they do not want to embarrass themselves. So they do not engage. When you call, some will start dry humping your leg on the phone. Treat them like you would a horny puppy and kick them off and move on. If they are dry humping right off the bat, they are needy and too hungry. Others will act like they're doing you a favour by meeting with them; with those, just move on. These are the people who say that they've really busy but can meet you in a month or two, or they may say that they can probably cut out 15 minutes to hear what you have to say. If they are acting 'douchey' at this point, then that is likely how they will treat the clientele you would introduce them to. It is better to save your time and your reputation, so thank them and move on.

The fourth response is the one that you're looking for, and it is one where they show genuine interest in meeting with you to talk about possibilities. If you get a feeling of warm interest without the dry hump, this is somebody that you want to talk to. Remember! "The death of an entrepreneur is solitude." Many successful people have yet to find a key alliance that is not a leg humper or a drowning swimmer. They might be cautiously optimistic that you could be a true running partner for them to move with in the market.

When you've found this fourth group, it's best to choose a neutral location for the initial discussion. Don't meet at your office or their office. A coffee shop works very well and keeps this first meeting casual. This isn't getting serious yet. This is just you being curious to see whether; (a) this is someone you would like to build business with, and (b) they have a business you could endorse and put your reputation behind, and that they would be willing to do the same for you. The single and primary goal for the first meeting is to see if the two of you are heading in the same direction.

Not to take all the romance out of it, but you might have guessed that I have a list of questions (10 of them) that I want answered in that initial meeting. I do not bring this list along with me; rather, I spend time role playing these questions with a colleague, friend, or family member until I am comfortable with the flow of the questions. I don't want to be obsessed with asking the questions, though, because I need to focus equally on how the prospective alliance answers my questions. I monitor not just what they say but how they say it. How they act with me is how they will act with people I introduce them to. I need to make sure that I'm comfortable with how they engage with others.

Here are my questions. Feel free to make your own versions, but this is the basic content that you want to get from that first meeting:

- **What markets are you interested in expanding and/or entering?** This question is important because it lets you know how aligned they are with niche markets. If they are currently in your niche markets but looking to move out of them, that's telling. If they are in niche markets similar to yours but want to dial in and your markets would make obvious sense, that's exciting. You're looking to find out (1) if they target markets, and (2) how close those markets are to the ones you're focused on.

- **What are you currently doing for business development?** Yes, this is a trick question. If they say nothing, I want you to smile and start deciding what you'll make for supper. If they have strategies that they implement on a regular basis that includes engaging with the ponds, this is where you might get excited. A great strategic alliance for you is someone who is active in business development. Listen carefully, not only to the strategies that they say they use but to how they use them. Many people will bullshit, telling you about all the things that they do and you'll find out down the road that they don't do any of those things.

- **Are there niche markets that you are established in?** Again, this is another trick question. You want to see if they already have currency in their markets and if they have cache and credibility. This is what you'll be looking to leverage off of. If they have a reputation in those markets and it's a reputation that can be leveraged by you, this is attractive. If they just seem to skim in and out ponds and haven't entrenched themselves as a Market Shark, this is telling.

- Do you have experience aligning with another company? This is where we check to see if they've had a relationship before. Do they know how a strategic alliance works, or is this their first time? Sometimes working with virginal businesses that have never had an alliance relationship can work but it is a lot more work than you might want to sign on for. You will end up teaching them as you align with them. However, if they've established pretty deep roots in markets that you're interested in, in might be worth the investment. Proceed with caution.

- Are you partnering with anyone else in my market space, or have you in the past? This is exactly like asking your boyfriend or girlfriend who their exes are. If they've already aligned with your competitor, an alliance is unlikely to work. If, however, they've partnered with companies in other markets then you'll want to hear about how that went it, whether it's ongoing and if they've stopped, you want to hear why. If an alliance ended, you want to hear that the reason was because somebody changed direction or it started to feel one-sided so the person you're talking to decided to call it off. If they called it off because it wasn't working for them this is a good thing. You want a selfish strategic alliance who will serve you so that you can serve them. Greed isn't good but selfishness is.

- What's the big picture for your company? We want to know if they're looking to sell their company and get out, to expand, to achieve explosive growth, to coast for a while, etc. You want to gauge their mind-set if you are going to be working with them. Again, you don't want to be the horse and them the wagon you're dragging behind you. You want a running mate who's doing exciting stuff that will marry well with the exciting stuff you do.

- What does a successful alliance look like to you? Hear what they have to say about what their expectations are of an alliance and then decide if that fits for you. Keep in mind our report card as you go through this process. If they say that a successful alliance is one where they are working with a business that's established in their markets, with someone who keeps their word, who can clearly outline what they do, who can refer business and get business referred to them, then these are all great things that we want to hear. If they say, "Oh, I get a bit lonely so it would be nice to have someone to talk to" then smile, thank them, and leave.

- **How do you see us best aligning?** Check if they have learned anything about your business model prior to the meeting. There are a lot of lazy people out there. Have they spent time on your website and/or talking to people in the market about what you do? Have they put in any preparation time or are they winging it?

- **In what areas could we be in conflict?** Are any services that either of you offer that overlap each other? This isn't necessarily a bad thing but you want to disclose it ahead of time. We had an alliance with an HR company which also offered business development coaching for corporations. Conflict only exists when it's not disclosed so we talked about what this company offered and agreed that anytime we did business if we referred the client, they wouldn't bring up their business coaching offering, and if they referred the client we would just do corporate training and no one-on-one training. These were the ground rules we put in ahead of time and we've had no issues with this alliance which has been in place in Los Angeles since 2006.

- **Are there any strategic alliances that either of us is currently partnering with that might be in conflict with the other's business model?** This builds on the last question. Let's say that I'm partnering with that HR firm in Los Angeles and I'm considering partnering with an HR firm in Seattle; however, I hear that that Seattle firm is expanding to Los Angeles. That can put me into conflict. So it's best for us to have a conversation about any alliances that are current, that are in conflict or could be in conflict. Forewarned is forearmed. Don't be afraid of conflict; rather, be afraid of undisclosed conflict.

Remember that the way that they answer these questions is as important as what they say. If you leave the meeting feeling good, proceed to the next step. If any part of you doesn't feel it, move on. Your gut reaction or intuition is key when it comes to alliances.

If it is a 'go', suggest dating a little bit. At the completion of your first meeting, suggest you connect again in two weeks or so to discuss details around how to get started. It's like the three-day waiting permit to buy a gun. It's better for you to think about buying a gun and then come back to it in a week or two than it is to buy a gun impulsively. If it's worth doing, it's worth waiting for. If it's right today, it's going to be right in two weeks. Two weeks later, you will come back together to see (1) if you are both still interested, and (2) what steps you will take to begin establishing the alliance.

If at any point during that two-week period they bail or turtle, consider it a good thing. You do not want to invest time and resources into an alliance that is not going to produce fruit. If they say "No," take it as graciously as if they had said "Yes." During these two weeks, if anything sends up a red flag for you, honour that and state that the alliance probably is not a fit for you at this time. You won't be a fit for everyone that you're considering, nor will they be for you. If there isn't a fit, thank them for meeting with you and move on. It doesn't mean that you can't still know each other in the market and maybe even leverage each other, but you're not going to enter a formal arrangement.

Finally, when you're dating these prospective alliances you need to be discerning. Choosing the right person will make you money while the wrong person will cost you your hard-earned reputation. Be mindful as you explore this process.

Getting to Second Base: Rules of Engagement

A couple of weeks have passed and you are both still showing a willingness to connect, it is time to go a bit deeper. Good strategic alliances are based on clear rules on how the relationship will work. We alpha males refer to this as the "rules of engagement." A strategic alliance isn't about making friends or commiserating about business. It's about making money with each other, not for each other.

Here are some questions to discuss in your second meeting. Remember that there are no wrong answers and it's better to be honest with each other now than it is to waste time and resources figuring out that the fit wasn't there. These are some questions to lead the conversation and I recommend sending an agenda and these questions to the alliance so that they have time to think about them and come up with thoughtful answers. As well, doing this illustrates that you're serious, organised, and not looking to piss around.

- **Will you be exclusive vendors to one another?** This question addresses the situation of if you are a lawyer and they are an accountant, will they be aligning with other lawyers in different practice areas? Again, there's no right or wrong answer but nobody wants to have their hands tied, nor do they want their alliances developing relationships with competitors. This is a question should come up right at the beginning.

• Will you share your client list with each other and, if so, how? With my alliances, because we have confidentiality considerations, this is a sensitive topic. Instead of disclosing who my clients are, I might invite an alliance to join me at a client event and give them a chance to meet clients one-on-one. This is also true for those in the financial services and legal fields. They are governed by confidentiality responsibilities so the alliance needs to talk about how to respect those requirements and still highlight each other's service or product in a way that will be noticed by the clientele.

• Will you offer preferred rates to each other's clients? Using the example of the alliance we have with an accountant, we offer that accountant a one-time 45 minute session of business coaching for each of their business clients. Their clients don't necessarily know that we're comping these sessions; instead, the accountant tells their clientele that they are booking a meeting for the client with us to talk about their profit model and how to ensure that it's trending in the right direction. This is something we don't offer anyone outside an alliance but it's a value-add that we bring to the table. In return, that accountant makes time available when a financial question arises during a session with one of our clients and we need to access their knowledge base. We've worked out an arrangement where we can call and talk to them or one of their colleagues in the firm to have our question answered. Not only does this extend our reach of service to our clients, but it gives our clients some exposure to our alliance.

• Will you pay each other a percentage on deals brought in for the other? Sometimes a referral system can be put into place between alliances; sometimes a finder fee is used. Depending upon your industry this may or may not work, but it's a great conversation to have. This will often equal out if the arrangement starts to tip in someone's favour. If somebody happens to be getting more clients but the person referring is getting some financial recognition, the alliance can survive. If there is no type of remuneration in place then the person referring may start to get bitter, see things as one-sided, and leave the alliance. If it can be avoided, don't be stingy with each other.

- Will you bring each other in on projects and, if so, will you each be subcontractors to the other or will you both work directly with the client? Again, this will depend on your industry but using the example of the digital marketing company and the social media management company, they just became vendors for each other underneath the company project. So the client only has one touch point and only has to pay one bill. The person managing that client relationship manages all of it so that there's no cross-information or opinions that contradict.

- Will you have a system for managing client relations and client interactions? This relates to the previous point, but if you are working on a client together, how will you share that information? For alliances we have with small business lawyers where we might be working on the same client together, both of us are managed through confidentiality agreements. We ask the client for permission to talk with the other about the account. I can't think of any client that said no, but if they did then you'd have to figure out another way to get the communication through. This could be as simple as one of us talking to the client and asking them to forward that information to the other part of the alliance. No matter how exciting the alliance is, your clients and your professional responsibilities always come first.

- What are some of the reasons you would refer outside of the alliance? Because we work predominantly with female business owners, there are occasions when they choose to have either a male or female professional as a lawyer and/or accountant. In any particular market we might have an alliance with a male accountant but if the client prefers a female accountant we let our alliance know that the client has made that request and then we refer the client out to another company. We do this so that the alliance knows that we are respecting the alliance; however, the client's wishes come first. This also gives the alliance valuable market intelligence around the fact that some businesses might be bypassing them because they don't have a female accountant on staff. In your ponds you have responsibility to share best practices and contribute to the knowledge base. If your strategic alliances are hearing through the grapevine that you're referring outside of them and you haven't disclosed this to them, things can get a bit mucky. It's best to have an open conversation. Not to divulge who the client is, but that a client is looking for X which is not offered by the alliance so you referred that client to Company X. You can suggest the alliance may want to consider building some bandwidth so that you're able to send those referrals to them in the future.

When building alliance with this person, it is best practice to commit to meeting on a regular basis. My suggestion is that you meet monthly. You'll both be measuring the relationship to make sure that it's making sense for both of you. Some alliances start of strong then fizzle out, mainly because it becomes one-sided. At the beginning you need to agree with each other to disband the alliance if either party isn't happy or it becomes too one-sided. If possible, figure out whether some type of remuneration can be agreed for referrals, especially if one party is referring more than the other.

As well, you should do a six-month review of the relationship. You'll have some hot months and some cold months, so you'll want to look at the overall trend of the relationship over two quarters. This isn't like declaring a major in university. It's okay to shake things up, shift things up, or quit.

When I'm forming a new alliance, I suggest that we answer five questions at every monthly meeting.

1. Are we both benefitting from this alliance?

2. Are we still focused on the same markets?

3. Has either of us added or taken away any products or services that the other needs to know about?

4. For the clients that we've shared or the introductions that we've made, how did those experiences go?

5. What can we do moving forward to keep the value high in our relationship?

You will find as you get to know each other better that you can become blunter about what is working and what is not. If you both have the sincere intention to build great business together then you're not going to want to be in a relationship that doesn't work. Invite the other party to let you know whether anything happening is bothering them and ask their permission for you to do the same. Set the ground rules to manage the relationship at the beginning. When things go off track, they can do so quickly and normally in an environment void of rules. Deal with any and all issues immediately. Remember that disclosure is key for a relationship to be healthy.

When entering into these relationships, as well as all the others, we have this rule:

Get into them slowly and get out of the quickly.

Take the time to really know the person you're aligning with and how they do business. If any part starts to feel wrong or feels like it could have a negative financial impact on your business, terminate the relationship. Do not stay too long and have your reputation toasted.

Assume that the first and every subsequent alliance you go into will be healthy and profitable. Let's dig a little deeper into management of these relationships.

Management: Dating, Mating, and Divorcing

All strategic alliances go through two and sometimes three stages. The first stage is dating (honeymoon), the second stage is mating (marriage), and in some unfortunate situations (and more often than not) the third stage involves the termination of the relationship (divorce).

In the dating phase, the sun is shiny, butterflies flit around your head, and unicorns gallop merrily through your markets. You're happy to have found each other, you're talking about future plans and sometimes you're even planning on cohabiting in the future (co-location). Everything is wonderful and life is good. The two of you skip in unison around the market picking up clients together and braiding each other's hair. This is an exciting time in the relationship. You aren't alone anymore. There is someone sharing the work with you. You're getting great prospects coming in and your clients are getting more service than you could deliver on your own. People see the relationship you have with your alliance and they wish they were part of it. If only they could be that happy. This stage lasts for about the first six months and then, like anything, the new becomes familiar. As familiarity sets in, we move on to marriage.

In marriage, things are good. Why not fully commit? Let's move in together and share a sock drawer. Let's go to networking events together as 'besties' and sit in the car before it starts to talk about our strategy. We're going to work the room either together or solo, driving prospects to each other and then after the event, drive home together or talk on the phone later about who to follow up with, what worked, what didn't, and what we'll do next time. It truly feels like you're part of a team. The marriage phase can last for many, many years. As long as both companies are growing, both are in business development mode, and both are evolving with the markets they share, then they can ride together.

I've experienced some alliances that have lasted in excess of eight years where every month there is a financial benefit to being in that relationship. Just like in a real marriage, this takes work on a weekly basis. We communicate well, we share best practices, we contribute to one another, and we look at how to serve ourselves and each other. It becomes a partnership of two independent companies doing great work for the same market.

It's key to make sure that neither partner is taking the other for granted. If this happens, the relationship starts to hit the rocks. Review the five questions on a monthly basis to avoid this. Are you both benefiting? Are you both focused on the same markets? Has anything changed in your offering? How are things going with the introductions you're making? And what do you need to do to continue to add value to the relationship? This might sound a little foo foo, but it works! Don't mess with the secret sauce recipe.

If one party in the alliance starts to take the other for granted, the one who feels taken advantage of will start stepping out on the other. They will start to explore other alliances because they will want to get back into a relationship that's good. In that case, you will feel like you're being cheated on. You will be sitting at home with their box of Kleenex, wondering what went wrong? When did the music die? Where did the love go? And then the bitterness will set in. You'll start to get pissed about all the time you've have put into the relationship and the other party will do the same. You will start to resent all the introductions you've made and how you helped build their business. At the same time, they'll start to minimise all of the contributions that they made towards you. Even though they were great, part of you will want to minimise them to show how damaged you are by their actions.

Once the alliance goes off the tracks and doesn't look like it will get back on, it's time for the divorce. If there's a real reason that the alliance isn't working, and upon review neither of you can figure out how to get it back on track or don't want to, then it's time to break up officially. Sometimes one part of the alliance will feel like everything is fine and the other will feel like they are being taken advantage of or that they're not getting a fair deal. This happens when the five monthly questions haven't been addressed or information hasn't been disclosed about how clients are moving in and out. The easy thing to do is just to let the relationship die on the vine. Just stop meeting, stop talking, and pretend it never happened. That's not a great idea. You need to step out officially from the relationship. There's a reason to break up, there has to be a reason to stay broken up, and the two of you need to decide how you will move forward independently when people ask if you're aligned. Rather than raining on each other's parade, you want to figure out want your common story will be about why you're now aligning with different people. This is not unlike how a couple tell their friends and family that the relationship is over and that they're now seeing other people. It's not really anybody else's business, but Market Sharks need to control their reputation and the conversations that happen when they're not in the room. If you do not set the intention then the market will come up with their own story and most times this will not show you in the light that you want.

It doesn't have to come to this. Managing your strategic alliances actively is key. Any relationship worth having is worth putting time into. It's like having a puppy. You need to teach the puppy how to go pee outside, how to obey what you want them to do, and give them enough attention to build loyalty. On the other hand you need to watch what they're doing to see what their needs are. There is no master and servant relationship in an alliance. It is two powerful people coming together to master the model of being aligned with one another. There's no boss. If there's a boss, there's an inequality of power in which a true strategic alliance cannot exist.

In the beginning, and throughout the relationship, you must both agree to do things in the best interest of the alliance and address any challenges immediately. You will listen with open ears and give each other the benefit of the doubt that you are acting in the best interest of the alliance. Any of us can get pissed off about things that we've interpreted incorrectly because we're looking through selfish eyes. If you know the person is a genuinely good person and not out to screw you over, then give the benefit of the doubt on any action that you see as 'questionable'. Seek to get additional understanding when things are making you uncomfortable. Most can be cleared up immediately with extra information. Do your best to add value to the relationship and to make sure that it's easy for them to do the same. Be clear with them about what you're working on and what type of support you need from them. This support may change over time, both for you and for them.

If things start to feel like they're going off kilter, address it with them immediately. Don't wait for the monthly meeting because four weeks can wreak havoc on a relationship. If something feels off, suggest that you meet for a coffee and have a conversation about it. The longer you leave something to fester, the worse it gets (most times only in your mind). Your default should be that it is a 'misunderstanding' rather than 'malicious intent'.

I know I use the singular when talking about an alliance. Do not misunderstand; I want you to be in many alliances. In any given market, a Ghost CEO™ might be aligned with an accountant, a lawyer, a financial planner, a commercial realtor, a personal trainer, personal coaches, etc. Each relationship will yield measurable benefit if managed effectively. You have to have the expectation that they will bear fruit for you and vice versa. As you might have guessed, as your alliances develop, then you can start to introduce your various alliances to one another. As long as they aren't in alliances that are in conflict with that particular profession, you can start to get a true multiplier effect moving forward.

As you add alliances after your first one, try to be sensitive that any new alliance doesn't jeopardise existing alliances you have in place. Almost all issues that lead to an alliance divorce are caused by things that started small in the beginning (and swept easily under the carpet) but then festered and became big things. I have found that sharing with my alliance (right at the beginning) that I get into alliances slowly and out of them quickly is helpful. Having a 'tension' in the relationship wherein they know that you're not going to put up with shit and you know they won't either is very helpful in both sides being considerate of the other. You will both be able to focus on the relationship if you want to keep it, knowing that if you do not focus and put in the required time and effort, it is likely to go away and all the time and resources invested to that point will be lost.

Finding the right alliances for your business model will further your position as a Market Shark and make things easier for you. With just a handful of alliances, every client that you have can be serviced more fully than you could on your own. Every client that your alliances have could be a client for your business. Community plays a large role in building a profitable and sustainable business. My favourite part about alliances is that you get to choose who is in your community. It's like picking the players for your sports team. You get to be discerning about who will be part of your family, and who gets left out in the cold.

Chapter 8 – Managing Fish that Bite

When Something Bumps Into You

Sadly we can't live in a vacuum. Any pond worth swimming will already have competitors in it. If you enter first, competitors will follow. Besides being a major pain in your ass, this reaffirms the market you are entering does have value and that there are opportunities in it. That said, it is important to be aware of everyone else in the water and how to handle them. Many companies have gone out of business by focusing attention on combating their competitors rather than on gaining market share and keeping clients happy. Your focus should not be on driving out other fish, but rather on positioning against them and engaging the market. Focusing on your clientele, while remaining aware of competitors in the market, will enable your business to thrive and provide the sustainability feature that many companies forget.

When we talk about these other fish, we are talking about fishes: there is a huge variety. Some are going to nip at you. Some will just get in your way. A few might actually attack you, either head on, from underneath, or even from behind. You must categorise them quickly, so you know how to deal with them. A Market Shark is not afraid of any fish. He or she knows how to quickly identify the competition in the water and handle them (which we will cover later on in the chapter). As you spend more time in your ponds, engaging with your clientele and understanding who else is in the water, you will appreciate and enjoy engaging with your competition. It can actually be fun, when it is done with intention and respect.

Before we begin to identify the different species and how to handle them, we need to look at how to dial in your competitor radar.

- Determine what constitutes a competitor versus someone who is just taking up space (a hobbyist). Don't pay attention to other companies who are swimming in the water but not accomplishing anything.

- **Know where you sit in the food chain.** Are you at the top? Are you making your way to the top? Are you sinking slowly to the bottom? (Yes, this does happen.) Or are you just floating? When you enter the pond, you need to know what the pecking order is so that you can start to move up. Failing to know this will mean that you end up watching competitors ascend above you while you wonder what is going on.

- **What is it that you need to know about your competitors?** Who they are targeting? Key staff? Key clients? Service delivery? Their pricing? Their service levels? Their locations? If they're expanding or contracting? Remember that competitors can be a valuable source of market information, so make a list of everything you'd like to know that tells you what they're doing and how they're interacting with the market.

- **Make a list of all the concerns you have about your competitors.** Are you worried that they will take clients? Are you worried that they might have a negative effect on your reputation either by badmouthing you behind your back or by sullying the reputation of your industry as a whole? Are you concerned that they will undercut your pricing? Is there any way that they could put you in a shadow? Fear is an acronym that stands for False Expectations Assumed Real. Many times people will upset themselves by having a whole story in their head about what their competitors are doing or not doing without taking five minutes to explore what it is that could happen and how they could mitigate that risk. Market Sharks do not allow this to happen. They are intentional with everything they do and they think through their processes so that they do not have to do things twice.

- Knowing your concerns from the previous point, what can you do or what have you done to position yourself strongly? When we started offering business coaching for women, we were the trailblazers. I knew that competitors would show up over time. Sadly, it took other companies up to five years to realise the market was there and as they started to come in, some of our coaches expressed concern that the market might become saturated. Of course, we employed positioning statements so that we would remain the Market Shark in that particular pond. Simply put, we were first in the market, we wrote the book on coaching business women, we had seen thousands of clients, and we had customised all of our curricula for women instead of offering curricula designed for men to women, which is a big difference.

- How often do you want to keep track of your competition? Monthly? Bimonthly? (Don't do it weekly, you stalker. Don't you have better things to do?) Don't tell yourself that you'll just keep an eye out and look to see if the competition does something; instead be intentional by scheduling time every month (or every other week if you're like me) to have a look at what they're doing. You can look at their website, look at any press releases issued, or talk with the market to find out information about what your competitors are doing.

- Who do you have in your current network that can keep an eye out for you and share information they receive? We're thankful that, with the thousands of clients we have around the globe, we receive information all the time about new competitors moving into our different geographical markets. Our clients effectively become bird dogs for us and let us know when other people are offering them something and the terms of that offer.

The Killer Whale

When we think of Killer Whales we think of something big and majestic. They swim through the ocean with dominance. We see them at aquariums playing and frolicking with each other, but do not be deceived. They are killers. From a business point of view, the Killer Whale is very noticeable when they enter a room. They are unbelievably engaging but also quickly crush people who get in their way. Their personalities are larger than life and they are filled with confidence. There's a lot of jumping around and playing in a business sense because they want a lot of attention to be on them. I always think of politicians when I think of Killer Whales. Walking into a room smiling, shaking hands, kissing babies, patting people on the back, congratulating people – they seem to be able to snake charm the overall market. They act very nice but within is the core of a cold-blooded killer. Everyone is excited about the Killer Whale until they see it eating and slamming a trainer into the water. "Mommy! Why is that orca eating the man?"

How they hunt

They move into a pack and hit their prey from underneath or body slam it. They look really cute but their teeth will tear you apart. They use words to inflict damage to those who are in their way.

Where they are in the food chain

They are right near the top. They have that killer instinct that many people lack and when they are hungry, they are willing to travel for the game. When in a target-rich environment, they can get very lazy because they know they just need to swim out, eat, and go back to resting. Since they don't have much competition besides other whales in their territory, they can seem docile but can quickly turn on a dime if you get in the way of their food supply (aka clients).

Danger they pose to you

The biggest danger that a Killer Whale can pose to you is that they will run right over you if you get in their way. They don't care what you are or are not doing; they will just hit you from the side and eat your lunch. These are not people who will respect any existing relationship you have with a client or any time you have invested into a prospect. If you have something they want, they're going to try to take it. These types of business people can go in quickly with a powerful burst, but they run out of energy just as fast and they need to rest for a while. Your opportunity is in their resting period and staying out of their way. It is best to let them tire themselves out and to work around them.[2]

What to feed them

Big fat client types who are full of bureaucracy and red tape. They are attracted by these fat contracts which often have a long and expensive process of procurement. They love this process so it's best to leave these types of projects/clients to them. The Market Shark knows that these types of contracts are usually a waste of time and better left to the Killer Whales who like to do a big burst of energy and then feed over it for the next while. A busy Killer Whale is a safe Killer Whale to a Market Shark, kind of like well-fed guard dog.

Other companies that they feel are impeding on their territory are another good food source to offer.   When you offer up information about other companies that are servicing their markets, Killer Whales will quickly divert their attention from what they're doing to go and attack anyone who seems to be eating their lunch. So grab yourself a bag of peanuts and a beer because this is really fun to watch.

---

[2] I know many of you who are reading this are thinking that a Killer Whale isn't a fish. Just go with me on this. It's for the purpose of the analogy.

How to manage them

One of my favourite quotations is,

"The big take from the small. The quick take from the big."

When dealing with Killer Whales in your pond, remember to move faster than they do. You want to act like a hungry sea lion. Dip in, get fed, dip back out. Don't give the Killer Whales enough time to sink their teeth into you or slam into the side of your business model. They are lazy so they're going to go after slower moving competition or prey. When you are in a heavily populated Killer Whale pond, watch for the submarkets that the Killer Whales swim by and focus your attention on those markets instead.

When I first started Think Tank Communications, there were a lot of consultants in the British Columbia market who I would consider as Killer Whales. They hunted into Vancouver and Victoria but they dismissed all the secondary communities like Kamloops, Prince George, Kelowna, Prince Rupert and so on. Rather than trying to swim into the big bureaucratic mess of closing contracts with the City of Vancouver, I went after the smaller cities and, on many occasions, the mayors and city managers told me that I was the first consultant that had ever come to see them from outside of their town. I went into those smaller communities to avoid Killer Whales and, once I had entered them, the local consultants probably felt that I was the Killer Whale. This wasn't a bad thing.

Steps to engagement

- Identify them and their patterns.

- Look at what they consider their territory to be.

- Look at what they are and are not eating. Even within that market that they're focused on there will be many opportunities they do not target.

• Go after what they are not eating.

• Position yourself to be the second quicker option for their main clientele.

Remember, the big take from the small but the quick take from the big. The way that I was able to start engaging the larger cities like Los Angeles, New York and Miami was by building my reputation in the smaller markets and then being prepared to step into the larger markets when the Killer Whales were being lazy with their clients.

The Piranhas

These are the little sons of bitches that flash in and out of the picture in your pond. They're easy to dismiss because they're small on their own but when they and their friends start to sink their teeth into you, you're going to notice. Impotent on their own, they are always surrounded by cronies. Once they get the numbers on their side, they become very dangerous. They simply kill you by eating through your market credibility.

How they hunt

They have to hunt in packs because they are small. They lurk behind the scenes, waiting to orchestrate an attack on a competitor by repeatedly saying the same shitty things into the ears of clients in the market. If you split them up, they try to get away from you as fast as possible. They are cowards with razor sharp teeth. They attack you by creating a consensus of other

Piranhas who then go out and try to piss on your reputation in the market.

Where they are in the food chain

On their own they are at the bottom. When in a group, they are right up near the top. The big don't normally take notice of them until they see the damage they are inflicting. Everyone has seen those nature documentaries where the water buffalo walks into the water and two minutes later all that's left is a skeleton. That's not because of one Piranha but is because he and all his buddies decided to go after that water buffalo together. As you can imagine, if you have ten different people bad mouthing you in the market in the same way, the market will start to embrace that information as true. This is very, very dangerous. Because they are easy to dismiss as individuals, nobody identifies them as predatory.

Danger they pose to you

- They bad mouth you to the market.

- They make up rumours or stories about you and your business that are less than perfect.

- They highlight any mistakes or hiccups you've had.

- Many present themselves as "frenemies." They know just enough about you to be dangerous (which is why we never show professional colleagues behind the curtain. They can use it against you).

I'm reminded of a story of a woman who managed a women's group in Texas. From the outside she looked fine and always professional but from gossip in the business community it was my understanding that she had struggled with some mental health issues. After getting to know her, she shared with me that she did, in fact, struggle with some mental health issues but was managing them in a very effective way. Some of the other community managers of different groups, started to spread the message that she struggled with mental illness, which resulted in her organisation shutting down not too long after. This is a prime example of a scarcity mind−set; the other women's groups felt someone had to lose in order for them to win. Very, very sad for both the lady running the organisation that closed and the members she served.

What to feed them

Nothing. Starve the Piranhas out. They are parasites and they deal in the negative speak of others. It is important for you to root them out and take them apart one by one.

How to manage them

• Atomic winter. Do what you can to isolate them both from the market and from each other.

• Share information with them that is so ludicrous that when it comes out they will look like dumb asses. We call this "testing the lead balloon." You share with them a story that is so crazy that when it circles back around to you, not only can you immediately dismiss it, but you can go back to them (because they are the only person you told that story to) and call them on their inability to keep their mouth shut. This is very effective on both sides.

• When they have a misstep, track it and bring it to their attention that you have seen it and have documented it. Now you have something on them to use for leverage should they decide to take a bite of you.

Sample Script:

"I noticed that your company was serving two direct competitors and was curious if your clients realised that you are playing them off one another. While it certainly isn't my business to encourage you to do business properly, it would devastating to your reputation and bottom line if your market questioned their ability to trust you. Be careful. Someone is always watching." – Remember you aren't threatening them; you are putting them on notice that you have information that would not bode well with their market.

• No matter what, always be on the full offensive with them. Never go into defensive mode. If they want to take a run at you, you take the run right back at them. Don't back down to Piranhas or they will eat you alive.

Steps to engagement

• Find the ringleader of the particular Piranha group and single them out.

• Let them know that you know what they do and how they do it and that if they choose to make you a target that it will be the worst decision of their life.

• Track all their cronies and put them on notice.

• Let them know that you go all in when people challenge your reputation.

• Any misstep you see by them you immediately address in an assertive manner. Do not give them any lenience. Piranhas like to prey on the weak and on people who do not stand up to those who say bad things about them. Do not allow yourself to be a target.

The Barracudas

These are voracious and opportunistic hunters. This is the type of person that hits on your date when you go to the bathroom. They can move quickly and attack from behind, and the attack can be lethal.

When I was a kid our family doctor was a man named Dr Chu. I remember him telling us the story about a friend of his who went water skiing in Fiji and a Barracuda jumped out the water and bit his Achilles heel, tearing it out, and then the fish took off. This is exactly like Barracudas in business. They take a really nasty bite out of you and then swim away while you think to yourself, "What the hell just happened?"

How they hunt

They mostly hunt alone, but have also been known to pack up if they are taking on someone really big. They wound you and then swim back around to eat what is left. In practical terms, they will come up and embarrass you in front of one of your clients and then call that client the next day suggesting that that client consider changing providers.

Further, Barracudas are known to move fast. When they start moving in on your territory and going after your clients, you need to get to those clients faster than they can.

Where they are on the food chain

Well, they're a predator. They take great enjoyment in killing other fish in the pond and some do it for business, but some do it for sport. They deal in influence and like throwing people under the bus. They think this is what gives them power. They aren't right on the top but they are very near the top. Barracuda types have been known to take down Killer Whales, so if they bite in the right place often enough they can topple giants.

Danger they pose to you

They can sully your reputation. They can embarrass you in front of your clients. They can call your clients and try to steal their business from you. They can try to take away your key staff and contractors to make it impossible for you to compete. They've been known to attack when you're on vacation, away from your desk, or at any opportunity where your back is turned and they can wiggle into any client relationship you have that isn't strong or where loyalty and intimacy has not been built. Barracudas prey on the weak points. They do find that Achilles heel and they will bite it.

What to feed them

• Marginalise them. Do not feed them.

• Send them hints about easy prey to go after but the better option is always to starve them out.

• Information is power so try to get as much information from them and about them as you can, but don't give them anything unless it is meant to misdirect.

How to manage them

• Look them in the eyes. Don't show them your back or weaknesses or allow them ever to speak behind your back.

• If you're speaking with a client and they come up trying to engage, look them in the eye and say to them, "Excuse us. We're having a conversation. I'll come and talk with you later." Then dismiss them. There is no immediate recovery for them so they will slink away. Then go over and address them privately so they know you aren't messing around with others that try to poach clients.

Sample Script.

"Bob you obviously had something extremely important to say that caused you to think interrupting me and my client was appropriate. It wasn't. What was so important that you had to interrupt?"

• Do not give them an opportunity to engage with your clients because they will not extend the same graciousness to you.

With Barracudas, I would encourage you to feel free to hunt into some of their markets. Taking their clients is fun. When they see that they've drawn your attention and you're now capturing some of their market share, they will end up leaving you alone for fear that you will continue to erode their client base.

Steps to engagement

• Identify them.

• Let them know through actions and words that you don't take shit from anyone, nor will you allow yourself to be disrespected.

• Watch them carefully and see what you can find out about them as leverage. Knowing who their key clients are is very important. I like to go so far as to getting those clients' direct phone numbers and information about their business, then letting the Barracuda know that if they get in my way I will invest hours daily in eroding their client base. Remember that they don't like to fight head on. By putting up a solid front they will likely turn and go after weaker prey (i.e., other businesses that won't stand up for themselves).

• Any time you see them take a run at anyone, call them on it. Don't just defend your territory, but put them back down. Barracudas can act very much like bullies.

Sample Script:

"I noticed that you had an issue with Tom. I found it curious how you decided to go full steam into it with him. Were you doing that for theatrical value or was there intention behind it? I'm always curious when someone puts their reputation at risk acting like that, if it is premeditated or just an emotional break?"

The Drunk Shark

The Drunk Shark attacks just to attack. Think about the guy at the bar who has had too many beers, watched a Mike Tyson fight, and has now decided that he is the king of the world. He wants to pick a fight at anyone, swing at everyone, talk back to everyone, and hopes that someone will fight back. Drunk sharks love to fight more than they like to do business and for them, competition is not building the bottom line but is trying to make somebody lose so that they can win. They've been known to interrupt business models by taking your attention off of your business to defend yourself.

How they hunt

They just swim around biting at people. Some might say Drunk Sharks are bristly or they have bad attitudes but in truth, they really are the true school yard bully. They will confront you face-to-face and in front of crowds to embarrass you and get you to engage with them. They get their power from making you nervous, uncomfortable, or fearful of running in to them.

Where they are in the food chain

Slightly above average because aggressive trumps passive in their minds so they are ahead of anyone who is uncomfortable with confrontation. A true Market Shark is neither aggressive nor passive but is assertive, and assertion beats all. When the Drunk Shark comes in, the smaller fish swim away, the larger fish stay clear, but the Market Shark doesn't take any shit from Drunk Sharks. In fact, Market Sharks handle them for the rest of the pond and, when required, in front of the pond.

Danger they pose to you

The biggest danger they can pose to you is that they can embarrass you if you don't stand up to them. They are quick to dress down or critique other people's business models and this makes everybody uncomfortable.

What to feed them

I like to put them onto the scent of other Drunk Sharks. I let them duke it out together. If someone is cruising for a fight, I look for someone else who's cruising for a fight and tell them that they are looking for each other. It's best to allow them to spar in the corner so they stay out of the way of the people who are getting real business done.

How to manage them

Simply put, immediately and privately, if possible. If you see them acting up, get them away from everyone and have a conversation with them. If that's impossible, then in front of the group, you should identify what needs to change and ask the Drunk Shark either to change or invite him or her to leave. Bullies lose their power when people stand up to them.

Steps to engagement

When a Drunk Shark acts up:

• Escort them to a place where you can talk privately.

• Address the situation in a clear, concise and measured tone.

Sample Script:

> "I want to offer you a bit of uninvited advice. The way you are acting right now is both offensive and crippling to your reputation. You need to sort yourself out. I'm not the only one having this conversation; the difference is I'm having it with you while they are having it with each other."

Years ago I was attending a conference in Florida with a number of dynamic speakers from across North America. In the green room where the speakers waited to go on stage, there was one particular person from the Northeast, who decided to walk around and critique each person's speaking topic, commented on the way that some of the speakers were dressed, and offered a variety of other "insights" that he had. It wasn't that he was singling out any particular person; he decided to go through each person's speaking topic and tell them why he thought it didn't work, why he thought it needed more work, why he thought the title didn't play, and on and on. Sitting there and trying to mind my own business, I heard him spewing this shit at people and the other speakers, being professionals, just dismissed him without engaging him. As he moved on to his fourth victim, a woman whose specialty was business gesturing and eye contact, I said to him from across the room, "that might be enough." He turned to look at me and said, "That's enough of what?" I stood up and I looked him in the eyes and said, "Enough of your un-invited commentary on how others are running their speaking business. Not only is it uninvited, it is bullshit. The definition of candour is to know when to shut your mouth so somebody doesn't have to shut it for you. I've seen you speak on many occasions. You would be better served spending more time on making your content relevant than making comments about how other people deliver theirs." He looked at me, a bit shocked, and he grabbed his bag and jacket and walked out. I know that I had made the rest of the room feel uncomfortable but it needed to be addressed.

The question arises: Was it my place to address that behaviour, or should each of the three previous targets and the current one have stood up to him? I think that is for each of us to decide. For me, watching someone bully someone else to feel good is not something that I am prepared to witness. Even though it was uncomfortable, I'm hopeful that, as he continues to be on the speakers' circuit, each time he opens his mouth to another speaker, he thinks about whether he will be called out again. As Market Sharks, we are all supposed to leave business better than we find it and to support the building of the community as a whole. If some Drunk Shark is tearing down the people in the pond, you have a responsibility to do something about it. It doesn't have to follow the same course I did in this example, but you should find something that addresses the situation and positions you as a true leader. Leaders don't allow others to be bullied in their presence.

The Guppy

Guppies are either the new fish in the market or failed professionals who are trying for a second chance. They posture like they are inside the inner circle but everyone knows that they aren't. From time to time, they swim in your way and you need to gently nudge them out of the way in order to do real business. This is bad for your pond but it's good for you because you look exceptional when compared to them. Universities are filled with Guppies. Talk to an MBA class today and you will see what I mean. There are always one or two Market Shark potentials and lots and lots of Guppies. These Guppies will go hide in the holes of big business and do grinder work.

How they hunt

They don't hunt. Weren't you listening? Didn't you hear me? They're Guppies. They can't bite into markets but they can try to gum the arm of the market. They are like little puppies running around shitting on the floor, biting at your feet, and tumbling over each other. Cute, but harmless.

Where they are on the food chain

Slightly above the Sucker Fish because they don't eat poop, but sadly very near the bottom. While they love the idea of being a Market Shark, the fear and danger of being around Barracudas, Piranhas, and Killer Whales married with inexperience and lack of talent sentences them to Guppyville.

Danger they pose to you

They are really hard not to help. It's easy to let them eat up your time at events, time that would be better spent hunting up clients or valuable contacts for your business. They inundate you with compliments and really stupid questions. When you're moving around, you can end up tripping over them because they're all over the place. They will try to leverage off of your credibility by either dropping your name or asking you to sit on their advisory board which they believe would lend some credibility to their business model. Unfortunately, having a great advisor does not mean that you will immediately have talent in business. There has to be some innate ability, somewhere.

What to feed them

This kind of fish needs more schooling

• Offer book suggestions on how to increase their skill set.

• Suggest places to go to increase their skill set such as training, seminars, workshops, keynotes.

• Suggest mentorships with people in the market that you want the Guppies to keep busy, like your competitors.

OR

• You can put them to work on getting you information on the market and show them how you use it. This is a form of new age indentured servitude. They go and do all the required prep work for you and then you interpret it with them in the room to teach them the skill of how to do just that. Then you're not wasting your time because you have to interpret the data anyway, but you're showing them the real application of knowledge for their grunt work of going out and collecting the content.

How to manage them

Limit the time you give to them. Tell them that they need to figure out what value they can bring to you in order for your time together to make sense. If they do work hard at trying to increase their value to you, and if they do some of the work that you need done, give them some additional direction about what to learn, where to learn it, and how to get stronger. Remember that we were all Guppies once, even if we thought that we were Market Sharks from birth.

When I first started Think Tank Communications I remember being in way over my head and feeling unsure what to do. I had a hundred ideas about what I could do but I didn't know what to do first or in what order to do it. I was lucky enough to have Market Sharks that I showed value to by doing a lot of their shit work who then allowed me to have a glimpse inside of what it was like to be a Market Shark. As I increased my value to them, they increased the time they allowed me to hang out with them. It is shocking and amazing how much you can learn by osmosis when you're in the room with great people.

Steps to engagement

• Limit your engagement time with them.

• Try to meet with a bunch of Guppies all at once. This is efficient for you and beneficial for them.

• If they want to chat, suggest you do so by email. Remember to show them some love but on your timetable. Do not allow the Guppies to eat into your own business development time. They will send you messages saying, "I need advice right away", or "Can I have five minutes right now?" Don't divert your day to serve your Guppies. The Guppies have to learn that if they want to be Market Sharks they need to plan properly. By looking for last minute advice on things that they don't understand, this doesn't serve either you or them. You have to model best behaviour for your markets.

The Sucker Fish

Sucker fish are the bottom feeders of your pond. When you think about your kid's aquarium, you think of all the goldfish, clownfish and everything else swimming around and then you have that little grey fish that swims along the bottom sucking and cleaning the sides of the aquarium glass. I think of the ambulance-chasing lawyers, the relationship coach who can't find a date, the depressed counsellor, or the financial planner who dry humps everyone's leg and begs for referrals to anyone (alive or dead, they aren't choosy). Maybe it's the accountant who has the revenue service freezing his or her account. Overall, the Sucker Fish is a hypocritical train wreck who only works with the worst of the worst clients because they are the only ones that will hire him or her. In those markets you, as a Market Shark, are throwing half-eaten sandwiches into the garbage and the Sucker Fish are trying to catch that sandwich mid-air before it hits the garbage can, but they're not above sticking their hand in and invoking the 5-second rule. The Sucker Fish is the person who disappears when the lunch bill comes. I think you're starting to get the idea and I'm sure most of you know Sucker Fish in your ponds.

How they hunt

Sucker fish hunt by friction and conviction. Friction in that they think if they hump your leg enough it will catch fire and you'll give them clients; conviction in that they think that they can wear you down by asking for business and business referrals over and over again.

Where they are in the food chain

Just below Guppies and just above poop.

Danger they pose to you

Aside from setting your trousers on fire from the friction of dry humping, not much. They will use you and try to close your contacts. They drop your name to people who know you and try to use you as leverage. It is icky (yes, I just said icky).

While posing no real danger, they do give you a gift and that gift is practising saying the word "No." We have a guy in our neighbourhood who sells meat and he comes door-to-door about twice a year with his big refrigerated van trying to sell seafood and filets, etc. I've made a conscious decision not to buy meat from the back of a truck that drives up to my house. When he knocks on my door he names all of my neighbours and says they have suggested he come talk to me. Part of his shtick is that when he comes to the door, he holds out his hand, introduces himself, and gives his name which would, in most cases, encourage the other person to shake his hand and give their name. I haven't done this and thus he hasn't been able to use me as leverage with my neighbours, but I tease my neighbours about sending the meat man after me.

What to feed them

• Your in-laws.("Hi, Andy and Viv!")

• People you don't like.

• Competitors who look like they need a good leg humping.

Years ago when we first bought life insurance, we bought from a man named Miles. Miles did a pretty good job at giving us the plan that we had researched on our own. We walked into his office after booking an appointment, told him about the package that we wanted, told him what the terms were that we wanted to agree to, and wrote him a cheque. Miles did very little for the business and he won the lottery that day because he simply was the name that we first saw on their website. After doing this transaction, whereby we did 90 percent of the work and he basically just filled out the paperwork, he looked me in the eyes and said, "Chris, can you think of three people who would appreciate having me plan their life insurance for them?" I looked back at him and said, "Miles, I can't think of three; I can think of three hundred." His eyes became wide, like a child on Christmas morning and he said, "Oh, my gosh, you're kidding! Three hundred?" And I said, "Yes. Easily three hundred people. But Miles, my job is not to sell for you. Your job is to sell for you, and you didn't close this deal, you just wrote the paper. So how about you take your commission from the business I just gave you and get yourself some sales training on how not to ask for referrals in a cheesy way." Miles looked at me, nodded, and let it go.

Three months later I got a letter from Miles asking for referrals. Although I'm sure that he's a lovely guy, he is a Sucker Fish and when the term of that insurance comes up I won't be able to bring myself to renew with him because I think that every time you give business to a Sucker Fish, a unicorn dies and an angel loses its wings.

How to manage them

Tell them that you aren't interested, will never be interested, and likely in the afterlife you will still have a bad taste in your ghost mouth when it comes to what they're selling. You'll lean over and say to Casper, "Do you have breath mint?"

Steps to engagement

• No eye contact.

• Tell them that you're horribly busy doing very important things that you aren't at liberty to discuss due to national security and tell them that [insert competitor's name] was looking for them.

The Clown Fish

Clown Fish are the 'people version' of knock-off Gucci purses on Canal Street in New York City. Their websites start to look like yours. Their business cards try to look like yours. Even their presentations start to look like yours. They are your own personal version of the movie, Single White Female. While they say that imitation is the better part of flattery, the truth is that Clown Fish can't figure out their own game so they try to duplicate yours and in most cases do it really poorly.

How they hunt

They hunt like you. They are your numbskull version of a doppelgänger. They are at the same events you attend, watching how you act and trying to duplicate your actions. It's a little bit flattering and a lot uncomfortable. They have hero worship and infatuation all wrapped up in a bundle of insecurity and crazy.

Where they are in the food chain

On the food chain of business, they are just a tick above Guppy. They possess a really bad need to be successful and take action to learn what they think you know so they can act the way that you act. They could move higher up in the food chain but desperation smells bad and Clown Fish come across as being very desperate. They have a huge need to be relevant and because this supersedes everything else that they do, they never truly get the work they require. It's the perfect example of focusing on the goal rather than on the work that will get them to the goal.

Years ago I brought a coach into the Ghost CEO™ model who had come from the pharmaceutical industry. She was a relatively well-established sales professional, although she had hopped around from company to company, either because her feet went to sleep or she was looking for new challenges. I had initially worked with her as a client and her work was pretty good. When given really clear instruction, she was able to get results. After a couple of years working together it just happened to coincide that I started licensing the Ghost CEO™ model and she was a very willing candidate to come in and start practising what we preach. The challenge was that she, like many, was much more interested in being famous than in being successful. People have a belief system around celebrity, thinking that once you become well known and famous, life will become very easy. In reality, when you start to get true acknowledgement from the markets that you serve, you end up under a magnifying glass. Anything that you do that isn't perfect is what ends up in the spotlight. Therefore it's important that you be an exceptional technician before you step onto that bigger stage.

This particular coach was so enthralled with trying to become a big player that she forgot that the technical side of the business is what launches you and keeps you on that platform. Since I was touring in the U.S. under a visa, she started finding ways to tour the U.S. without a visa. I would book an office in a particular building and she would get an office just down the hall. Any event that I would talk at, the next month she'd be trying to talk at it. It began to create a bit of weird dynamic in the company because rather than collaborating to penetrate the market, she was in a constant state of competing with me and other coaches in trying to be the top dog. We were forced to part ways when her ego couldn't be kept in check.

This type of thing can happen both inside your company and with competitors, so be mindful. It's doesn't just happen with fish outside of your model.

Danger they Pose to you

If the Clown Fish starts to look a bit like you and then they start to screw up in the market, it will begin to sully your industry as a whole. The Clown Fish will hang around at the events you attend, trying to look like part of the in-crowd. You end up looking like someone who smells something bad and needs to get some fresh air whenever they are around you. You'll sit down at a table and they'll quickly try to get a seat at the same table. They want to be seen with you not only so they can try to ride your credibility, but also so they can pick up some of your tips and techniques so they can emulate them. This is one of my biggest criticisms of personal coaches who try to say they are business coaches. They tell their clients that they can coach on anything but many of them have yet to understand how business works. Therefore they end up giving half-assed advice that the clients follow and then don't achieve results. Then that client will go out into the market saying that business coaching doesn't work, when they were only getting business coaching from a personal coach who didn't know what he or she was doing and who was unethically selling expertise that they didn't actually have. It makes us all look bad when personal coaches emulate business coaches without the ability to deliver.

What to feed them

When I see Clown Fish circling around me or the company I always like to give them suggestions about how they can get more business using different strategies than we use. I let them know that it's important to distinguish themselves from competitors so that the market knows where they sit.

If that doesn't work, then I move into a misinformation phase where I tell them that I'm going to particular events that I'm not going to and then ditching events that are not strategically valuable to me if I know that they will be attending them. Truthfully, I give them a bit of a run around because I do not like to have a tagalong when I am doing business.

Clown Fish always make me think of the movie, Austin Powers, with the Mini Me character. Dressing the same, looking the same, talking the same, acting the same, but not the same.

How to manage them

You want to manage Clown Fish with courtesy but at an arm's length. Like the Guppies, they are trying to move into **Market Sharkdom**, but they lack some of the core abilities to make this happen. Don't give them too much information about anything that you are doing because they will quickly try to emulate and be first to market on some of those strategies. Often this can happen because you're busy building and managing a clientele and if the Clown Fish isn't busy with a clientele (which most aren't) then they will have the extra time to develop the model. Granted, it won't be as good as yours but they will be first to market which could sully the market's consideration of the offering.

I always prefer that Clown Fish find out from the market what it is that I'm doing, rather than following what I'm doing. They have to work for the information and I know that by working to do the research they're likely staying away of messing with the markets that I'm entering.

When you find that other people in the market are comparing you and the Clown Fish to each other, tell people that how honoured you are that a person like them would like to be like you as they obviously use your model of business as inspiration for their own. Make sure that you position yourself as the

Market Shark within that pond, and not as one of the Market Sharks with the Clown Fish being assumed to be one as well.

Steps to engagement

• Be kind but cautious. Assume that everything you tell them about what you're doing, they will try to do as well.

• Ask lots of questions of them, but don't answer too many of theirs. I like to keep them busy sharing what they're doing so that there's not enough time for me to talk about what I'm doing. You can only dodge their questions for so long.

• Point them in the direction of markets you are not interested in. This isn't meant to be mean spirited. Instead, look at what they, in theory, would be good at in regards to market identification, and suggest those markets to them. If they're not excited about them, tell them that you're going to be going after those markets in the next couple of months and if they don't want to go after them, you will. Many times this will light a fire under them and they'll be out of your way.

• When they say that you two are alike, tell them that that type of comparison will be confusing to the market and that you don't want them to be seen as a cheaper version of you. Encourage them to get clear about what they do that's different from what you do, and how the value they bring to the table is also different. This will make you both successful.

• Help them find their own place to sit in the market. Following on the last point, it never hurts to help the Clown Fish find a home. One of our coaches refers to the Clown Fish as the little sister who follows her big brother around the house wanting to do everything that he does. This can be cute and endearing for the first couple of days but the big brother will slowly get tired of being followed around and will strike out and do something stupid that ends up getting him into trouble. It would be better for him to get his little sister focused on something that she would enjoy thereby giving him space to do what he enjoys.

The Great White

This is the Mac Daddy of any pond. The Great White is the business professional that is loved by the market and held in reverence. Think Amazon, Apple, Walmart and Ferrari. While they will have their equal share of fans and critics, they are the company or companies that everyone else wants to be and compares themselves against. They seem to be infallible and they are, but everyone runs their course and every dog has its day. These companies become so big and dialled into the ponds they serve that they can destroy smaller competitors or new entrants to the market in a matter of months if not weeks. The Great White truly is the ideal Market Shark.

How they hunt

Great Whites are symbolic of what companies want to achieve when managing a niche market. As well, they can become symbiotic with smaller fish who might also be Market Sharks and who will fill in the holes that they have in their business model (remember when we talked about strategic alliances?). Often it is easier for the Great White to partner with smaller Market Sharks than to develop those business models and manage them on their own. When they enter into new markets, they go all in. They are fully loaded with lots of cash, lots of strategy, and much bandwidth to make things happen.

This is what we all aspire to be. As you spend more time in your markets learning to understand how they work and how to apply the tools that we've discussed in this book, your proficiency with those tools and strategies will become so great that, as you enter new ponds, it will take weeks rather than months for you to establish yourself as the Market Shark. What a great position to be in.

Where they are on the food chain

The Great White is at the absolute top of the food chain. There is no one above them. That said, their market can still take them down a notch for a misstep. From the outside looking in, they seem to be holding that top spot for the foreseeable future. It's theirs to lose, not to gain. Those who challenge them for that Market Shark position are unsuccessful almost all the time, and the failure rate of their competitors becomes widely known lore throughout the market.

Danger they pose to you

The biggest danger a Great White poses to you is you getting too close or in their way and they eat your lunch. They can run you out of time and money simply by flexing some if not all of their resources. They are so intentional with their actions and have planned so thoughtfully for every possible outcome that by the time you're implementing a strategy they are already four levels ahead of you, blocking you off. It is like a cat playing with a mouse.

Years ago I was having drinks with a couple of colleagues and Howard Schultz of Starbucks joined us. It came up in conversation that Starbucks was the true Great White of coffee companies and, in particular, that it was the belle of the ball for the Pacific Northwest. It was shared that the largest competitor to Starbucks then was none other than McDonalds, another Great White. McDonalds had become a big coffee competitor to Starbucks because they were serving really good coffee and they already had an enormous supply chain of stores that they could sell coffee from and a loyal following of clients who were already buying at their stores. Isn't it a curious problem to have when two Great Whites are nudging each other to see if they can grab market share from each other? Of course, on the other side, we know that Starbucks now offers quick serve fast food in the form of sandwiches, pastries, and other goodies. I wonder how much that is eating into the McDonalds' breakfast market.

What to feed them

Feed Great Whites opportunities. Sourcing opportunities for them makes you valuable to them. Niche out something that you are an expert on or that you own intellectual property (IP) on, and have a conversation with the Great Whites in your pond. Microsoft, Google, and many other tech companies have made other companies tens and hundreds of millions of dollars by leveraging the smaller companies' IP into the larger company's platform. This benefits everyone involved, including the consumer.

How to manage them

Manage them respectfully. Look for gaps in what they offer and see how you might be able to fill those gaps in a mutually beneficial way. It's your job to figure out how you can make money together. It's up to you to put the pieces together. If it makes sense to them, there's probably a deal to be had. If you're trying to get them to come up with a solution that serves both of you, they'll likely leave you in the dark. The key characteristic of all the Great Whites I know is that they don't suffer fools at all. You get one chance to make an impression and if it isn't great, then you likely won't get a second chance.

Steps to engagement

- Know your place and how it can work with them. You are not equals. This is not a bad thing. In every business model, in every business pond, and even in every business relationship there's a pecking order that gets established. Build a relationship with them respectfully and find out more about how they do business, where they're moving their businesses towards, and how this might be complementary to you and your goals.

- Remember to be wary of the Great White's teeth. One wrong step could be your last. You need to make sure that the relationship serves you and serves them. Lose sight of their needs and you'll lose sight of the opportunity.

Many times business owners will say, "Hey, hold on. I'm an equal to that company." Well, the truth is, you're not. If you were a true equal you'd be exploring them as an alliance, not as the big fish in your pond. Remember that we all start somewhere and there's nothing wrong with standing in the footsteps of the giants ahead of you.

Just the Beginning

You will meet many fish in the different markets that you enter, and it will feel like one of those massive public aquariums. The ones where you can barely keep track of all the different colours, sizes, and characteristics of the fish you see swimming in front of you. In this chapter we've covered only a few of these types of fish as these are the ones you should be most aware of. Further, it's important for you to know which types of fish will be important for you to engage with (i.e., Killer Whales and Great Whites) and which ones to stay clear of (i.e., Drunk Sharks, Clown Fish, Guppies, and Sucker Fish).

The Market Shark engages everyone and because you are standing in the position of leadership within your pond, everybody gets the time of day from you once. No one should feel like you are dismissing them or don't have time for them, so it's important that that emotional intelligence side of your business is high. Those who are getting in your way, you need to gracefully shift out of your way and into the path of others; those you want to swim and keep up with have to see the value of putting time into you and creating space for you to be part of their business. Some fish will get very little resources from you, while others will get most of your full attention. For those who are truly undesirable to you, send them off to eat other people's resources.

Kindness only goes so far. It's not personal; it's business. You need to manage all the fish in your pond right from the beginning, so that you can use them (or avoid them) to grow into your true role as the Market Shark of that pond.

Chapter 9 – Managing Pond Problems

Market Movement – Eye on the Prize

Never take for granted the importance of watching what your ponds are doing once you are active in them? The only thing consistent about the ponds is that they are going to change over time. Sometimes these changes occur gradually over the year; other times within the week. When changes come, you will have to make one of two decisions. You can choose to adapt to those changes and, in doing so, you will win. Or you can decide to pretend that nothing is changing. You will find yourself out of business, just like many other companies have when they decided to ignore market indicators.

Most changes don't happen overnight so you will have some advance notice and time to devise a plan. The farther out you can see the change coming from, the more time you'll have to plan for it.

In this chapter we will consider examples of the most common situations that you're likely to encounter in your ponds. For each situation, we will address what it is, why it happens, what impact it could have on your business, and what steps you can take to manage the change effectively.

With every situation you come across, consider that what you see is a real adjustment and not just a blip on the screen (of which there are many). Your gut feeling will know whether it is a real change or just a quick shift but always sleep on any decision before making a serious adjustment regarding the ponds you service or how you service any particular pond. You don't want to be too rash or sensitive about things that are happening in your pond because you may end up leaping out of a perfectly good pond.

You need to find the perfect balance between being really vigilant and sensitive to what is happening in your pond and not screaming the "sky is falling" like Henny Penny. Even if the sky is falling (which it isn't), Market Sharks never look like they're having an emotional episode and losing control. Your pond will look to see what you are doing and if you start to panic, they'll start to panic. The Market Shark is cool, calm, and collected. Everything done is intentional.

Market Saturation (Too many Market Sharks in a pond)

If you have chosen your ponds properly, they will be filled with many opportunities. This makes them attractive to you and also to other Market Sharks looking for opportunities. As you establish your markets, you will find that other Market Sharks will start to follow you and look around, and if they think an opportunity exists, they will set up camp. More will follow, once they smell the blood in the water. Being the original Market Shark in a pond is a key benefit but other aggressive sharks can start to erode your market share. This is a serious situation and one that requires immediate action you first notice it.

Obviously, you do not automatically jump out of a pond when another Market Shark swims in, but you need to be mindful about how big the pond is, how many prospective clients there are, and how many competitors the pond could hold without tripping over each other. This is all part of the assessment work you did earlier some of the information that you will continue to consider as you collect data on your markets moving forward.

Why it happens

Markets get saturated when more and more competitors see an opportunity within the same pond. When you entered the pond, you educated your customers on what you do, why it matters, and who cares. Unfortunately, a lot of this information will automatically be transferred to other people and other companies that look like yours. An educated market shortens the sales cycle of any business. In being the first one in, it's important for you to educate your market about what you offer and how to buy from you and, as importantly, why you are the person that they should continue to buy from and how you saw the opportunity to work with them while the rest of your competitors were asleep at the wheel. All of those Market Sharks that follow you in will have a considerably shorter sales cycle because of the efforts you've already put into in educating the market. However, you might have followed others into the market that were not Market Shark material so you were able to capture the spot. This can be a great situation. When other Market Sharks swim in, they will see many service providers already in place and will move back out.

The greater the opportunity coupled with smaller the competition increases the attractiveness of a market. Imagine that you are a plumber and you have three options of where to open up your business:

A: A big city with a ton of plumbers,

B: A smaller city with many plumbers, or

C: A smaller town with no plumbers.

Where do you think you're likely to have your highest ratio of success? It is C, being a plumber in a small town with no plumbers. Your second best opportunity is the big city with a lot of plumbers because the last and least attractive option of a small city with many plumbers means that the market is already saturated. With that option, you are destined to spend half of your time trying to get clients, and the other half trying to seem different from everyone else who is already in the market.

When entering a pond that already has Market Sharks in it, or if you're the lead shark with others following you in, remind yourself that every dog has its day. Others will look to come in and build on your foundation, in the same way that you'll be entering into ponds and building on the foundation of others. This is what makes the world of business go around.

The impact it can have on your business

Market saturation confuses the market. Period. Having too many opportunities is almost as bad as not having enough opportunities. More sharks appearing can create an immediate loss of your market share. As well, even though the new businesses coming in might experience a shortened sales cycle because they are now talking to a market you have educated, it can result in an overall lengthening of the sales cycle because now customers have more options. If you buy a computer from an electronics store it will take you much longer if there are 15 options than if there is only one option.

My grandmother used to say that if you're ever trying to feed an old person, don't ask them what they want for dinner: just offer, "Chicken, beef, or fish." That's the only choice you give them because if you give them all the options then they can't decide on anything, and every option you give to them they won't want because they'll want to hear what else you might have.

The same holds true for a saturated market. Consumers will hold out because they are worried they might miss something better. However, if there are only one or two considerations, they will choose the one that most closely fits and makes them feel like they're not missing anything.

Saturated markets can force you to offer terms you would not otherwise offer. Back when Amazon was the king of electronic books, they were able to set pricing of $9.99 for all books on their Kindle format. Because they were the only real game in town (there were many smaller competitors that couldn't get it done), they were able to put publishers over a barrel with pricing and the option was either to sell the book at the price they specified to the consumer or they just wouldn't list the book as an electronic option. Publishers took the beating and bowed down to Amazon because they had no other choice. However, others began offering competition to Amazon: Apple got involved with their iBooks program, Barnes and Noble offered their format, Kobo books entered the market and other bookstore formats followed suit. This saturation increased competition for electronically published titles. Amazon was forced to increase the price of their ebooks because publishers with options informed them that if Amazon did not sell their books at their list price, they simply wouldn't make them available on Kindle. Evidently, the market dynamic had shifted enormously. If Amazon was not in the book business at all, they might have considered leaving the pond because at some level they had lost the control that they once enjoyed.

Finally, as the market continues to saturate, your marketing resources (that were intended to educate the market on your particular offering) now must be used to teach the market how you are different from your newly-arrived competitors. Until you are truly entrenched in the loyalty of your clientele, you will always be fighting with the fresh face on the scene. Your game plan, coming in early, is that you were the first in and the longest standing. If you followed other Market Sharks into a pond, you will position yourself as having the fresh ideas and the most exciting offering because everything you do is going to be perceived as innovative.

Steps to managing the situation effectively

When you find your market saturated, there are seven steps that you can implement to manage how you do business internally and to manage the communication externally.

Relax. You are already the top dog so it's yours to lose, not to win. Now is not the time to act out of character.

Circle the wagons. Get all of your clients, champions, alliances, and contacts on the same page. Remind them about all the good work you have done together and how you are going to be together in the market long after this new blood decides to leave.

Watch carefully what the competition offers. If they come in with low ball pricing, do not adjust your pricing; instead focus on how you will show the value difference in what you offer compared to what they offer. When facing this type of change in the market, I like to use the following statement, "You will find cheaper, but you will not find better." When you automatically adjust your pricing, you send a message to your market that you were overcharging and have been called to the mat by the competition.

If they are truly different, engage with them and discuss working on the same side. If they are direct competitors, however, engage them with full efforts to drive them back out. Let them know about how entrenched your relationships are and how long it takes to create a profitable market within that pond.

Showcase your time and expertise in the market. Highlight how long you have been in the market, your level of customisation to the clients you serve, and the way that you had the foresight to be in the market long before others decided to pay attention. Nobody likes a bandwagon jumper, so make the new Market

Shark's entry into the market look like they're jumping on the bandwagon to take advantage of the markets that you so carefully service.

If competitors try to undercut your pricing, let your clients know that those competitors are guinea pigging their pricing with the markets, and those prices aren't sustainable. Anyone choosing to do business with them will have to come up with another option once your competitor runs out of money for not charging enough. I like to tell markets, "If you want them to learn how to service the market by using you as a guinea pig, it's your decision. You know what you're getting from us."

You want competitors to look into the pond, see that you have things sewn up, and then look for other ponds that are more easily available. Nothing drives this home better than the lore of the companies who have dipped into your territory only to have their operations extinguished because they weren't able to get traction. You want all competitors a little bit worse for the wear when they couldn't develop a market within your pond.

Years ago when we were first entering into the First Nations market in British Columbia, we heard stories about all the companies that had come in before us, had been unsuccessful, and had been driven out. By listening to the stories about what their failed practices were, we developed a list of best practices to engage that market in a responsible and respectful way. We ended up growing that market successfully. Once people had heard about our success within First Nations, we started to see competitors enter our different ponds. Anytime I heard about a competitor coming in, I would call the Chief of that particular community and ask them how the meeting went. Then I would remind the Chief about all the other companies that come in before us that weren't interested in building relationships but instead were looking to pump and dump the communities for cash. I'd tell the Chief that I was happy to be vigilant and watching to make sure that, if they were to work with that company, the community wouldn't be screwed over by that new contractor. This was often enough for the Chief to be reminded of previous bad times when working with competing firms that weren't focused on the service to the community. In almost all cases, any competition was driven back from the door. The beautiful thing was that the gatekeeper of that pond wasn't us but ended up being one of main clients.

Market Melt (It's all going bye–bye)

One of the major market corrections you may experience in your pond is market melt. This is when you notice that your clients are moving, going out of business, or shrinking. The pond that used to be so lucrative seems to become smaller by the month and there are fewer and fewer prospects for you to develop and clients to service. Existing competitors (if there are any) will change their direction and take their attention outside of the pond. All signs will indicate that the pond is shrinking or dying. This is not a happy thing, especially if you enjoy the pond and the clients that you serve. There's always a little bit of mourning that happens because of all the time put into developing the market. Part of you won't believe that it is changing and will grasp on in the hope that this is just a little ripple and that it is going to come back.

Why it happens

There are many reasons why markets start to melt away. It can be a larger market correction, such as in a stock market crash. Technologies and markets can start to demand different things. Wallpaper was a hot design feature in the 1980's but it was hard to find a wallpaper hanger twenty years later. Lots of companies made a tonne of money and then found themselves out of business when the market dried up. Today wallpaper seems to be heating up again and the cycle continues (as it often does with style). Videographers were really hot in the 1990's but now people can shoot video on their iPhones. Technology is the killer of business models. Look at the film business: Kodak used to have a huge business selling people film and cameras but now film has been replace by digital cards that do the same thing as film but at a price point that is much more attractive to the market. All of these are examples of markets melting away.

The impact it can have on your business

The largest impact is that staying in a pond to long will force you to go out of business if your other two ponds can't keep you buoyant. If you don't change what you offer, or change the market you are offering it to, your bottom line will melt just like the market.

Steps to managing the situation effectively

Take note of any dip in your sales. While some businesses may experience seasonality in their profit models, there should be a growth tract for every business of at least ten percent per year. If you stay consistent from year to year then it is likely that you are losing ten percent of your clients every year. Businesses rarely stay neutrally buoyant. They are either growing or shrinking. If your numbers are the same year after year, trust me when I tell you that your business is shrinking. Your sales will be a great indicator about what's happening with the market and your performance within the market. Math doesn't lie.

Sit down with all of your accounts and find out what's happening with them. Not only is this part of building further intimacy with your clientele, but it finds out exactly what's going on. If they are having a dip now in their sales, down the road that could trickle down to you. You want to be aware of any problems they are having because it will have an impact on you moving forward. As well, sometimes you might be able to support your clients in making a correction so that their profit model stays in line which, in turn, will keep your profit model in line.

Make sure that you have current, relevant research and intelligence about your backup ponds. If any part of you thinks that a pond might be going sideways in the future, you need to look at those other ponds that you have been interested in doing research on and start to warm them up on the back burner. Building your work around these models is like doing a fire drill. You hope not to use them but, if you have to, you know what to do. As well, you likely still have one dog within those three niche markets. I want you to practise identifying your markets as tigers, ponies, and dogs because I want you to always make sure that you have another emerging market ready to step into if something go so sideways that you need to jump off the boat quickly.

Start warming up additional markets just in case. Find out who the gatekeepers are, where the watering holes are within that pond, and start working on your three questions to make sure that you're dialled into each of these new potential markets. It wouldn't hurt for you to go to that first meeting to explore them a bit more or send one of your ambassadors to do it on your behalf.

If you continue to see accounts in a particular market getting smaller or dropping off, start increasing your attention on your backup markets to bring them up to speed. We call this the "mine shaft canary" strategy. Back in the old days, miners used to hang cages with canaries in the mine shafts and the canaries would sing away. However, if the canary stopped singing this signalled to the miners that the oxygen might be running out and it was time to go topside. While you might not entirely stop singing to the markets that you're in, you do need to find a new way to get topside so that you don't run out of air in your business.

Continue to act normally and do business development in the markets that you are in. Sometimes a handful of isolated clients can suggest to you that there's a market correction happening, but they might not be representative of the market as a whole. If you are still picking up new accounts within that market you might be okay, but dial up your sensitivity a bit and keep a watchful eye. During the recession, restaurants saw a major dive in the number of clients that they had while quick-serves and pubs started to see an increase. Anyone in food service would have been better off taking a little bit of their attention off restaurants and put a bit more into quick-serves and pubs. They wouldn't be leaving the pond; they would just be diverting their attention slightly towards a smaller niche group within the pond.

If the market in question starts to look like a real dog, bring your backup up to speed. As soon as that backup produces as much as the "dog" pond, kill the dog (you can still serve existing clients, just do not continue to invest resources). In theory, you want to step off the elevator that's going down and onto the elevator going up. Do not wait for that backup market to reach the peak the dog market was at in its prime. You're trying to get off the losing team and onto the winning team.

Accept it. This will happen. It happens to all of us. You need to be ready to make this shift when your backup market takes off. You're here for a good time but maybe not a long time, so appreciate it while you can and be prepared to hop into the next market if required. This is why it's important for us to continually develop new potential markets should we need to leverage them.

Market Disappearance (Where did it all go?)

Occasionally, a market will disappear within in a matter of days. The travel industry took a major hit in the days after the September 11, 2001, attacks in New York City. Not only did the US have a major correction in markets, but the ripple was felt around the globe. Companies, airlines, and industries lost 90 percent plus of their business overnight. While this is a drastic example, we only need to look back to the market crash of 2008 to be reminded of how many companies started going out of business seemingly overnight. When a major market correction happens the first thing that most businesses and professionals do is turtle. They tuck and cover and hope that the bad man stops. They sit back hopelessly watching the explosion happen, in a state of shock. They don't know what to do, they weren't expecting it, and they have no contingency plan. Instead, they just hope, if it is the death of their company, that it will be quick and painless. What a sad way to look at a huge opportunity. Companies that can make the best out of a horrible situation are those that, in time, will see the benefit of stepping up and rising to that occasion. Not only is there a huge upside to being proactive but the life of your company depends on it.

Why it happens

Major issues happen first on a macro level and then quickly filter down to a micro level. Imagine a mill closing down in a small town without any advance notice. Overnight the major employer in the area has shut and now the labour force and community most dependent on that mill is left in a state of shock. Rather at looking at what else they could do or where they need to move to get gainful employment, the employees sit back and wait, hoping that somehow the mill will reopen, or that there might be a new buyer to take over operation of the mill. The only plan they have is closing their eyes, placing their heads in the sand, and hoping (praying) for the best.

A second example comes from the financial markets. When a stock market crashes, as it has on many occasions in history, everybody goes into a frenzy. We saw this with the dot bomb fiasco in the late 1990's, and again in 2007–2008 with the subprime mortgage industry. Overnight markets can lose 10 to 20 percent of their value which equates to people's retirement funds and money that they may have been saving for 20 to 30 years. Real Estate panics, employers panic, employees panic, and the general public panics. The effect of all these people not spending money filters down, thereby impacting the business and providers they buy from, their families, where they go on holidays, the schools they send their kids to. You can see that a major market fiasco can have an effect on everybody.

A third example is when governments turn, change, or shift in a fundamental way. I know that in British Columbia there's always a back and forth between the two major parties, the New Democratic Party of BC and the Liberal Party of BC. When the New Democratic Party has power, there is a concern about the negative impact to small business and corporations, but there is an upside to social programming and education. When the Liberal Party gains power, there is a concern about social programming cuts and the impact on those who are less fortunate, but excitement in business because the pro–business party has been elected and tax cuts and tax breaks are in the near future. Either way there is always a dynamic shift in particular markets, with some being more sensitive than others.

The impact it can have on your business

It can be a giant–killer. Depending on how big the correction, this can kill your business model in any particular pond. Truthfully, your entire business model can change overnight. The only insurance you have against this is to develop a Plan B before it happens and then deploy that Plan B to ensure your survival. This is why I'm a big proponent (and a broken record) of the value of having three niche markets. While they can be complementary, I like them to be a little bit separate from one another so that they are not collectively impacted by a major shift. You would not want your three markets to be corporate lawyers, tax lawyers, and wills and estates lawyers. They would be too closely connected. If you're focusing on professional services, you might want to target lawyers running their own business, major accounting firms, and architects doing government contracts. While these are all white collar professional services that are being targeted, they each have a different market that will have an influence over how they do business.

Steps for managing the situation effectively

Here are the steps you should take, if you discover yourself in a market that is falling out from underneath you:

Accept that what has happened, happened. Acceptance is the first step. You might be in a state of stock and those around you may be in the same state. Go have lunch, take a walk, sit in a quiet room for a couple of hours, and let it sink in that this just happened. You cannot make decisions in an effective and profitable way when you are emotionally charged. It's easy enough to for me to say don't be emotional, but I know that when I faced this type of situation at first I couldn't believe that it had really happened. I had to take a few hours just to process the fact that an unbelievably profitable market just went away.

Look at all of your options. What other things you could have your company do immediately to help it survive the storm? This isn't about turtling, but about jumping on opportunities that might not have seemed so exciting yesterday but now will be the key to your survival.

Look at each of those options and rank them from most viable to least viable, considering potential short-term cash flow. As well, you should make a note of how long it will take them to become cash flow positive and how long it will take you to access a clientele that will convert immediately. You need to take a timeout right when a market suddenly disappears so that you can do this step with as clear and objective a mind-set as possible.

Put any and all resources into shifting the course immediately. If you see that the iceberg is right in front of you, you need to take a hard left now. This will be one of the most aggressive and assertive market corrections you will ever make.

Halt putting any resources into the market that no longer exists. Nothing you do can bring back that market (remember, you've accepted this) and you need to stem the flow of any financial bleeding that is happening in that now disappeared market.

Go into full business development mode. You need to get new clients coming in immediately and systems built that will support that model on the back end. In my situation, I spent from 8:00 in the morning until 5:00 in the afternoon calling on and closing new business, and from 5:00 p.m. until bedtime each night building the systems that would support new model. When your markets are available (i.e. 8AM-5PM), engage them; when they aren't, spend that time building the systems and doing the housekeeping of your business.

Remember that this, too, shall pass. The companies that rise to the challenge will survive and thrive. Those who put their heads in the sand will die along with the market. I remember prior to the financial crash of 2007-2008, we were starting to get a glimpse that there might be a small hiccup in the markets due to some imploding mortgage models. Little did we know that markets would turn overnight and we lost 90 percent of our corporate training business. Once these companies knew that they were haemorrhaging cash at a much greater speed than first realised, they shut down all discretionary spending which included business development and sales training. In a very short timeframe, 80 percent of our revenues went away.

While our colleagues, who also offered training decided just to live off of savings and wait for the market to come back, we quickly diverted out attention from the corporate world directly to small businesses that were looking to survive this market correction. We also knew that companies would be laying off some of their key professionals. We quickly reached out to any of those professionals who had previously shown an interest in self–employment. We knew that they would be getting packaged out of their companies as the process of downsizing commenced to secure some cash flow for these corporations. We ended up building a robust clientele of professionals starting their own firms after being let go from their corporate jobs. On top of that, other coaching companies who held contracts started losing some of their key business coaches because they couldn't afford to keep them on. These proven professionals were people we warmly welcomed into our licensed model and who now started servicing this increasing clientele who were exiting corporate America and Canada.

In hindsight, I admit that adrenaline pushed many of those decisions the first year, but our company came out unbelievably stronger on the back end. Not only that, but the markets where we had huge competition (especially in financial services, legal, and accounting) were left barren in regard to competitors so that in 2011and 2012 when corporate training picked up again, we not only got back all of our contracts but also acquired new contracts that former (and now out of business) competitors held. What a beautiful opportunity that came from such a horrific and unexpected shift in the market. This is the benefit of being prepared, being able to be objective, thinking quickly on your feet, and implementing a plan that focuses on the bottom line.

Market Adjustment (The market wants something different)

The tastes of your market will evolve as their business models do. Some will want to shop online, some will want niche offerings that don't make sense for you to carry or provide, or your market may want you to become something that you currently are not. When any of these things happen, you need to decide whether the adjustment is something that you want to offer. It is your business, but they are your market. Not changing what you offer to your existing markets when they want an adjustment can lead that market to move in a direction that you can't follow. This is okay as long as it is a conscious decision on your part. Your market will give you valuable information about how to keep them as a market or tell you when it's time for you to move on and make an adjustment.

You are not in the business of chasing your markets. Businesses go bankrupt chasing the moving goalpost. It's sometimes just easier to change markets to one that wants exactly what you are offering now. Customisation can be a bitch and custom companies rarely make money. You need to have a set service or product line that it is interesting and viable to the greatest audience and that feels customised to them so that they see you as their Market Shark.

I've been caught in this situation many times where three or four of my clients would say that they'd really like me to offer something new. When it made sense, both professionally and viably, I'd start to build it only to find out that once it was built they had changed their minds. Now we don't do spec work on anything. If a client wants something custom outside of what we currently offer, we are happy to oblige them as long as they are prepared to pay for it. We don't pay for development hoping they like it. We take instructions on what they'd like developed and if it is within our capacity then we will build it for them for at a price.

Why it happens

There is no particular reason why tastes change over time. It can happen for a variety of reasons, which can be very hard to track. When you ask a client why a particular interest has changed, you discover they often have a hard time putting it into words. It's just that they want something different. You need to determine if this is a passing fancy or a trend indicating they are moving in a different direction that you need to acknowledge. Sometimes it happens because the market needs to change. Something going on with the dynamics of your clientele has caused an evolution which has changed what they're looking to buy. Sometimes they go from outsourcing something to insourcing it, and then back to outsourcing.

Going back to the dot bomb crash and then the financial crisis of 2008, many of our small business clients were outsourcing all of their bookkeeping and accounting. When the shit hit the fan and everyone was battening down the hatches their first inclination was to try to insource everything that they had paying out. They wanted to take on their own bookkeeping, or deal with discount accountants rather than proven professionals, and one even went so far as to suggest she start printing her own marketing collateral rather than using a printing company she had used for many years. Our key message at that point was that they shouldn't take on work that didn't make them money but, instead, to increase their business development activities because there was a gold rush happening. All the competitors that they had fought hard against would now be turtling and this would be a chance for them to pick up all the remaining accounts. Fortunately for us and our clients, they agreed to follow the strategy and came out of the recession stronger than they went into it.

Another shift that we're all aware of is people wanting shop online. In the late 1990's people thought that online shopping was crazy. Even into the early 2000's people still preferred to do their research online but would then go into the stores to touch, feel, and experience the product or service that they were engaging in. In 2013 our family did almost of its Christmas shopping online. While hanging out in malls can get you into the Christmas spirit, standing in long lines to fight over unavailable toys won't. Instead, we were able to go to our favourite websites and order products which were then wrapped, packaged, tagged, boxed and sent to our front door. We were free to enjoy lunches and drinks with friends and family while our "worker elves" did the work on our behalf. Even five years ago, thinking about doing such a thing would have been crazy to me. Today doing things the traditional way seems crazy.

When we look at this from an impact point of view, we are buying from large companies instead of from small shops. That's not to say that we don't spread the wealth around but at Christmastime those with the best and most efficient offering for us (in this case, proven e-commerce providers) received 95 percent of our Christmas budget. That's obviously going to have an impact on small vendors who would otherwise have gotten the money if the online option wasn't available. Lucky for us, many of the small shops we like, have an e-commerce opportunity so we didn't have to choose.

The impact it can have on your business

Changing your model for the right reason not only can preserve your market but further engage them with you. Changing for the wrong reasons (and I speak from personal experience) can make you miserable and cause you to lose much of the profit model you established in the past. If you change and the market still doesn't buy, you now have an offering that no one is interested in buying. That's death waiting to happen.

When you hear about companies that have overdeveloped their line, developed too many SKU's, or made too big of a menu of service offerings, it's important to acknowledge now that everything that they've created or offered that's not being sold has lost them money. This isn't a smart thing to do if you want to stay in business.

Steps to managing the system effectively

Listen carefully to what the market wants. You're not in business if you don't have a market. However, markets can tell you that that want something but they're actually just interested in sharing ideas that they think might be cool. You're not in the business of building cool things; you're in the business of building things that people will buy, whether it is a product or a service. Listen carefully to carefully to what the market wants but make sure that you weigh the pros and cons of adding that to your existing offering.

Consider how your operations would have to change to offer what your market is requesting. If you are the community bakery and the community tells you that they would like you to offer pizzas that might not be that big of a jump. However, if you're a plumber and your clients tell you they'd also like you to be an electrician, that's a very different choice to make. For some things that the market wants you can make the adjustment overnight, but other things might require months or years of development.

Make sure to run the revenue model on any build out you're considering and figure out what would add to your bottom line. In the past, we've seen clients establish a whole new line of business only for it to take five to six years just to recapture the capital expenditure of making that offering available. When you look at something taking six years just to break even, the smarter choice would have been entering a new market that is already looking for what they offer.

Once you've determined whether it is a viable option for you to offer, go back to your clients and poll them. Find out what they would buy from you if you offered the new model they suggested, how much of it they would buy, and how frequently they would buy it. If it's a one-off and the price isn't high, then maybe this idea isn't that interesting. If the clients promise (by promise, I mean they are prepared to sign a purchase order) to buy a certain amount of business from you then it might be worth looking at. If, after talking to your clients and the numbers make sense, it's worthwhile to test the model with what we call a "minimum viable product" to see what your market does. To illustrate this point, we had an accountant client who ran a small book of business. Her clients kept telling her that they would love her to offer bookkeeping services. Since her space was somewhat limited, she started to think about moving into a bigger space, incurring all the expenses involved in doing that, leasing new furniture, leasehold improvements, and getting out the current lease that she was in. The numbers started to become overwhelming when considering the return on $25 per hour bookkeeping fees. We suggested that instead she talk to her five key clients and offering them ten hours of bookkeeping a week for $25 per hour. She then went to a bookkeeper and offered to subcontract the work for $20 per hour. She would make a $5 span on every hour that the bookkeeper did work for her clients. She had eight clients take her up on this offer. If you do the math, 80 hours a week is a bit much for one bookkeeper to do so she had to find a second bookkeeper who was also outsourced out of their home office. Within two weeks, our client realised that she had billed 160 hours, generated an additional $4,000 in revenue from her existing clientele per bookkeeper, and made a gross profit herself of $400 per bookkeeper. All of this happened without changing her office space, adding any overhead, or incurring any other expenses. That's $1,600 per month by offering a new service that was complementary to the service she was already offering her clientele. We ended up building her clientele for bookkeeping to 30 clients who bought an average of 20 bookkeeping hours per month at an hourly rate of $25. She hired contract bookkeepers at $15 per hour. She was generating gross revenues of $15,000 per month (or $180,000 per year) which generated a gross profit of $6,000 per month, and added $72,000 to her bottom line. She had the bookkeepers working out their own home offices. Their only required travel was coming to her place to pick up and drop off client books. Talk about a helluva way to add to her bottom line by making a small adjustment when the market wanted something that she wasn't currently offering.

If what your clients want isn't a viable option for you to offer, consider what other markets you could enter that would be interested in your current offering. As well, you might look back and develop a strategic alliance with a company that can offer the components you're not prepared to offer. Strategic alliances can allow you extend what you're offering without having to incur the overhead.

Start warming up any new market on your radar that wants your current offering, then wait to see whether your market corrects at all when you decide not to make their suggestion available. If so, then keep on working with existing clients but invest all of your resources into developing the new market that isn't looking for something different from what you're offering now. When the new market out performs the one that you're in, change your focus.

Don't get stressed out about this. In the end, it's your business model. You decide what you're going to do with it. While it is important to be mindful of what the market wants, you don't have to be anything you don't want to be. There is a lot of market out there and Market Sharks can always find other ponds to make money in.

Sometimes shifts in the market are a gift. You can evolve using good information coming in from your markets so always be open to what they have to say.

While working on this chapter, I started thinking about suggestions that our markets had made to us and how they had impacted the way that we do business. There are three things that came to my mind immediately: ePACKS, group coaching, and Coaches' Corners all came from market recommendations. ePACKS are documents we sell that are industry-specific around a do-it-yourself business builder model. From photographers to chiropractors, people can buy ePACKS and self-study how to do business. We got this recommendation through speaking at a conference of new business owners. While they weren't in the position to buy one-on-one coaching, they didn't want to have to wait to learn to have cash flow, so we created a $100 model where they could buy the documents they would normally get from one of our coaches and do a self-study.

For our group coaching program, we found that we were working with many franchisors who wanted to learn not only how to sell their franchise but also to inspire their franchisees to build more business. One of those clients said to us, "You really should come up with a group coaching program." We thought about this for a while and then, when we got him to commit to enrolling all 55 of his franchisees in a program at a particular price point with particular deliverables, we built it out. Now, all of our coaches around the globe offer some type of a group coaching program.

Finally, Coaches' Corner is where, once a month, our coaches sit down in a coffee shop with a group of business owners composed of our clients and non-clients and we talk about a particular business topic that somebody has suggested. It's a great way for us to give back to our community, plus it allows us to connect our clients with each other in hope that they may explore partnerships and alliances together.

I know above I said there were only three, but the fourth example is this book. Often I heard clients say that they didn't want to be a big fish in a small pond, and I told them that that is exactly what they wanted to be. Their ears would perk up when I'd say that and at least a dozen clients said, "You should write a book" and so here it is.

Market Migraine (These people are pissing me off)

Sometimes you fall out of love with your markets. What once attracted you to them now makes you crazy and frustrated. As you evolve as a business professional, so too will the tastes that you have in the markets that you want to serve. It's easy enough to warm up a new market and jump into it, but I think you need to show due respect to the markets that you're leaving and that you've built your success on. Reputation is key in business and if one day you just walk away from your market that reputation will carry into your next market. You don't want to acquire the reputation of being someone who bails on the people who learn to count on you.

When you manage your transition with a bit of grace and a lot of thought, those in the market that you're leaving will be left with a good feeling about you and what you contributed during your time there. A key cornerstone to being a great Market Shark is to leave your things better than you find them, and leave people better than you find them.

Why it happens

We often fall out of love with our markets if we spend too long in the same market and things start to feel stale. It can seem like we keep on doing the same things repeatedly and every day starts to feel redundant. I'm always reminded of that Bill Murray movie, Groundhog Day, where he wakes up every day at the same time and watches his day play out in the same way. I think that every professional needs to feel challenged when doing business. If you're no longer feeling challenged by your market then it's time to have a "come to Jesus" moment with yourself. If you look at your work and it starts to feel mechanised and no longer exciting, it's time for you to find something that will float your boat.

You need to be aware of when you're having these types of feelings, and make note of them. For me, vacations tell me a lot about my markets. If I can't wait to get on vacation, there is something wrong with my market mix. If I can't wait for my vacation to finish so I can jump back in, I've got the right mix. I like to try to take vacations a couple times a year just to test how I'm feeling about my business. For me, it seems to be a trend that I shift my markets every 24 months or so. It isn't uncommon, however, for me to go back to markets I've previously serviced, which is why it's important to keep up relations with the people in that pond.

The impact it can have on your business

Life is too short to do work you don't enjoy. Market Sharks have the skills and the techniques to develop any market they want, so once you have honed the skills offered to you in this book, the world will be your oyster. When you are unhappy, your work and clients will suffer. You owe it to them and to yourself to serve them only if you are excited and, if not, to find a replacement market for you and a replacement provider for them. This takes courage. Many stay too long in a market that they don't enjoy and become bitter and eventually are punted by the market. It's best to leave on your own terms.

Steps to managing the situation effectively

When you wake up each day, gauge your excitement level around going to work. If you're happy and excited, are looking forward to the people you'll be meeting with and talking to, and are pleased to be doing the work required to keep your business going, then you're probably on the right path. If you dread the day and would prefer to pull the sheets up over your head, it is time to make an adjustment.

At the end of each day, consider whether you feel a sense of accomplishment from your work. Burnout happens when people feel like they're doing the same thing repeatedly without having any measurable outcome. I've always felt that if you're doing meaningful work for people who appreciate it then you'll both be paid well and will enjoy the time you spend working. No amount of money can make it make sense if you're miserable and are dealing with shitheads.

If you find yourself watching the clock like you did in high school, you are in the wrong markets; if, however, you find that your day is slipping away from you and you cannot believe what time it is, you are probably in the right markets. I find that on Sunday night I'm excited for Monday morning to come, and on Friday afternoons I'm rushing to try to get everything done I want to accomplish and often feeling like I'm stuck in the penalty box for the two days of the weekend, waiting to get back on the ice to play. This tells me that I'm in the right market. At other times, on a Sunday night I've found myself wishing that I had one more day for the weekend. That's when I postpone any meetings I have booked on the Monday morning and take a sober look at the markets I'm serving to determine which ones aren't floating my boat.

Let's be honest: You know. You know if you're enjoying the work, and you know if you're not. The question I ask myself (and I want you to ask yourself now) is, "If I had a year left in my life to work, would this be the work I'd want to be doing with these particular people?" If the answer is "No" on any level, you need to make a correction. Don't let the market correct for you. You correct the market.

About three years after I started Think Tank Communications I fell out of love with economic development. It wasn't because the work wasn't fun or exciting; rather, I was dealing with politicians and bureaucrats who made the most exciting process feel like lying on a bed of nails. They tended to talk to death about common sense solutions that could be implemented for almost no money. If any of you have been in a situation with a room of bureaucrats who love to meet to talk about "what if" then you know what I'm talking about. So I decided to team up and get more people in the company to do that work while I explored going out to be a professional speaker. This was in 2003.

As I did more speaking gigs, I found that got more coaching clients. As I coached more corporations, I got more corporate training gigs. I ended up in a cycle of more clients, more speaking, more training, and 90 percent of my time went to that side of the business with 10 percent overseeing Think Tank Communications, with the people I'd hired to work on Think Tank really taking on that work. For seven years I ran the speaking, training, and coaching model with much passion and fervour. In 2010 I found, after three years of being on speaking tour to support my first book, What Men Don't Tell Women About Business (Wiley, 2007), that I was tired of planes, trains, automobiles, and hotels. I know what you're thinking, "I feel really sorry for the guy who flies first class and stays in five-star hotels." However, anyone who has been a road warrior for 100 plus nights a year will realise that the best bed in the world is the one that has your own duvet on it. In 2010, as I was going out the door to the next speaking gig that I wasn't looking forward to, I made the conscious decision to shift course. From the end of 2010 to the beginning of 2013 I barely toured. If a group wanted me to speak I was prepared to video conference in to their location from one of the local universities near where I live, or to send one of the Ghost CEO's on my behalf to deliver the content. I made the conscious decision that I didn't want to be on speaking circuit any more. Servicing that market became a barrier to doing other work like writing more books and further developing Ghost CEO™ in other countries.

Now, just over three years after making that decision, I find that I'm jonesing to speak in front of groups again. As I admitted earlier, it's not uncommon for me to go back to past markets and re-engage them. It's not like I'm swimming back into those ponds after three years as an absentee Market Shark. I've been in contact with those people the whole time, introducing them to other great speakers because, remember, a Market Shark has a responsibility to find replacement service providers for the markets that they leave behind. I find that I'm being welcomed back with open arms to those groups, plus those groups are now introducing me to other groups.

In business you get to choose your own adventure. Markets that you're in love with today might give you a migraine tomorrow but in years to come, it might be like running into an old friend. Keep your mind open and remember that time is short. The work has to make sense and you have to love it to be effective with it.

Chapter 10 – Building a Bigger Aquarium

Why Bigger is Better

Being a big fish in a small pond is what we are all looking to achieve. To mitigate risk around shifting markets (as discussed in the last chapter) we need to give ourselves different options. More options mean more power over your company's profitability and sustainability. The larger the number of ponds you can enter without much effort, the more powerful your business model becomes. For each business model, there is a perfect size where you have enough markets to offer fair coverage but not so many that you diminish your impact on any given one. We start with three markets because they are a manageable number to practise and master the skills of developing and managing markets.

Overcoming apathy to new business development once you have established your three great markets can be a challenge. You always have the Tiger, the Horse, and the Dog. Through diligent work you could actually have three Tiger markets. When you have these markets that are performing and profitable, it is hard to think about doing more work after all the heavy lifting you have done to build them. Since complacency is easy (and something I struggle with myself), we need to remember that things happen in the markets and we would rather be the ones influencing what we do in the markets than have the market determine what we do with them. So those great ponds, where you enjoy swimming freely as a Market Shark without encountering too much resistance, are not something to take for granted, especially when they may not always be there or you might tire of them.

This is why we decide to build a bigger aquarium. More ponds equal more options, which equal more profits, which in turn equals greater sustainability. Even though you might be tired from all the heavy lifting to develop three Tiger markets, getting bigger is good for you and for the markets. As you gained in professional strength, your clients, colleagues, and the ponds themselves benefit from your development. When you can leverage more influence, make more connections, and engage people on a higher level, everybody benefits – you, your team, your clients, your alliances, and pretty much anyone else you decide to swim with.

This does not happen magically. Set an intention and put in the time to extend your reach. Exercise a careful balance between managing the work you are responsible for today and extending your reach into new markets, cities, and even countries tomorrow. This action, like everything else, requires small, consistent steps to master the technique of accomplishing this. Extending your reach should only be done after you have done all the previous work. Do not attempt to establish additional markets until you have three Tiger markets that fire on all cylinders. The work required to develop your three Tiger markets is what will result in your having a bullet-proof reputation. This reputation makes it easier for you to extend your reach because you can leverage it to develop great connections who can provide endorsements.

Connected people are attractive people in business. You already know that true Market Sharks have an amazing network of people they can leverage. A true symbiotic relationship that is mutually beneficial is a beautiful thing in business. It isn't about quantity; it's about quality. You can have a bunch of boat anchors weighing down your network (read: Guppies and Bottom Feeders) and that is not good for anyone. You want Market Sharks to fill your network coffers. Birds of a feather flock together or, in our case, fish of a type swim together. As you learn to master the development and management of additional markets, you will see your bottom line grow in direct proportion to your ability to manage it.

What the Larger Circle Looks Like

Having a big, powerful circle of influence can look like those rings on the inside of a tree. Your core group, the inner ring is filled with your high valued clients, champions, and alliances. Everything else builds out from there. The next ring out is your three niche markets and the general clientele that your company services on a regular basis. This could also be where the champions—in—training are, as well as strategic alliances that are good but not great. The next ring outside of that is comprised of the gatekeepers of your three niche markets, and all the prospects in your active markets. The next ring out has the markets you are warming up to replace any of the active markets that need changing well as alliances and champions in different markets and in different geographical locations. The outer ring is the business world as a whole.

Most professionals focus too much time on the first two or three rings. This is not bad, but it is limiting. You want to extend the reach of your work physically (shy of working the phones like a madman or going on speaking tour, both of which I've done). It can be challenging if you are busy servicing your existing markets. To extend your reach efficiently, develop and deploy a platform for yourself. This platform should be designed so it can deliver your content/information and is efficient and scalable for you to build and to manage. One unit of your work could now create a ripple effect in your ponds and outlying ponds if delivered through your platform. Let's look at a current example of someone who has built an unbelievable platform with a whole lot of substance. This is not something I suggest you do but it does showcase the power of platform in creating visibility and notoriety for an individual.

Think about Nicole Elizabeth "Snooki" Polizzi from the reality show, The Jersey Shore. Snooki is not popular because she is a 'revolutionary thinker,' but because she has established and grown a platform. First, the show was aired on MTV, which is a huge platform, and then she did a huge number of media interviews for hundreds of news outlets and magazines. Then came a New York Times bestselling book (I just vomited in my mouth a little bit), which doesn't suggest that she's a good writer but that she has a huge following of people who want to know what she is doing.

Now, I know what you are thinking. You want to run out and schedule a session with your tattoo artist to update your tramp stamp, or enter yourself into an online twerking competition. This is not what I'm suggesting. Just examine the process. I am not necessarily suggesting you follow Snooki's doctrine. Snooki is clear about what she wants to put out there and there is an obvious, but somewhat surprising, appetite for it. She knows there is an appetite and she exploits it in a way that serves her.

Now, what if you did the same, but in a positive and professional way? If your stuff is good, exploit it. Exploitation is not a four-letter word. Do not think of it as shipping illegal migrant workers to pick fruit for a dollar a day. Consider its alternative definition: "The action of making use of and benefiting from resources." If you have created the resource (intellectual property and business model) then you should benefit from it. This is how you extend the power and the profitability of your work. If you have your own version of the secret sauce, why not extend it outside of your trade markets to bring brand awareness for you and your work while benefitting others who might not have the opportunity to work with you directly?

Preparing Your Platform

Ted Talks have done a fantastic job of highlighting thought leaders in various areas of life. They showcase speakers that range from bestselling authors to global political leaders to high school students talking about a change in education. I contend that every professional can be a thought leader once they realise what they do that is successful and different from others. Most of us struggle with this because we take for granted those things that are easy for us to do.

That said, it is a relatively straightforward process to figure out what your platform could be. You can always make little tweaks as you go, but you want to know the main premise that you are building on top of. If you dramatically change it down the road, you will need to start again, from the beginning, and re-educate the markets about what you are known for.

When I think back to when I was establishing my platform, insecurity played a big role in why I neglected many of the strengths I brought to the table. Back in 2003, I was a 29-year-old hillbilly from Kamloops who took seven years attending full-time to complete a four year degree. I had a lot of creative things that I wanted to say about myself, but I was concerned that someone would look behind the curtain and realise that I was full of shit. I remember the frustration of repeatedly sitting down and trying to figure out what I wanted to be known for and getting stuck on this every time. Since my work of business building and developing profit models came easy to me, I did not find it particularly exciting or sexy. When others would get excited about my abilities in developing profit models and strategies very quickly, part of me thought that they were just paying lip service. I did not give as much weight in the gift that I was given as did others. Yet, people continued to come to me and pay me.

When getting coached through that process, and my coach said to me, "I want you to start a journal and on the front cover write, 'The things I know but do not say." I thought this was a bit foo foo at first, but out of sheer desperation, I decided to do the exercise because I could not figure out my platform. The first thing I wrote down in that journal was, "I'm fucking tired of women giving up their power in business!" Now, it's likely that I could have had a particularly challenging client right before doing this homework, but I found it immensely frustrating to watch women give up their power to men in business. I continued to write in the journal but always ended up coming back to that first page each time I opened it. The statement stuck with me, and I identified that the platform that I could build and would be happy to get behind would be one of levelling the playing field of business. Not making men wrong, and not making women wrong, but ensuring that everyone had the same information so that they could compete on a semi-level playing field. I do not suggest that certain groups of people do not have an obvious advantage over others in business, but I don't believe having an advantage by keeping the other side in the dark in regard to important information is a game that anyone should want to win. So that was the platform that I started to create, being a 300 lb., 6' 6" alpha male who was sharing with women what men talk about what they're not in the room, and welcoming any wrath from men or their groups who wanted to challenge me about sharing the "secrets."

From a marketer's perspective, that's a pretty good platform, but I can't believe how well it actually turned out. That platform led to a speaking tour, to the re-engineering of Ghost CEO™, which led to a book entitled, What Men Don't Tell Women About Business: Opening Up the Heavily Guarded Alpha Male Playbook (Wiley, 2007), which led to the book being translated into 17 languages, and now to a business coaching model that works with thousands of entrepreneurs around the globe. My platform extended further by me being someone who doesn't sugar coat things (hence, some of the language in this book). My mandate to you, as it is with every client, partner, and colleague, is to speak to you like I would to a good friend, to not hold my tongue or sugar coat anything because I believe that people crave honesty and authenticity. Therefore, the voice you hear when you read this book is the same voice you would hear if you have a cup of coffee with me. And that is someone who desperately wants the playing field of business to be level and who, every day, tries to move that mandate ahead.

Not only does it feel great to have that mandate, and that platform from which I build everything, in place, but that mandate also became a tool for me to calibrate all my actions. Any decision I make, new business I invest in, or activity I undertake is measured against the platform. Is what I'm doing supporting or confusing the platform? I can't begin to tell you how easy this makes a lot of my decision processes. When you look at my portfolio of businesses, you will note that they are all focused on supporting professional women and levelling the playing field in business through education.

Here are my steps for developing a platform:

1. Make a list of all the things you do that are exceptional compared to others who do what you do. This can be challenging, so get yourself a little notebook and as you do things that you know other people struggle with, write it down. A platform isn't built in a day. It might take you weeks or even months to fully distill what you're trying to build.

2. If you get stuck, look at the feedback that you get from others. What do they think you're great at? Objective opinions work well when you're struggling. I don't recommend you ask your mom and dad, or your spouse, as they may share with you things that you want to hear. Instead, ask clients, colleagues, partners, staff, or anyone else you do business with, what they think you are particularly good at compared to others. Being a good writer is not a

component of a good platform. Writing in a particular way that creates an emotional response in the market is. Don't go after generic stuff; rather, go after things that are unique to you. Review my platform: there aren't a lot of 300 lb. ex-bouncers who are sharing with women what men talk about when they leave the room.

3. Once you have an idea of what makes you exceptional, start to pencil in the platform around it. Using myself as an example, one thing that was exceptional about me was that I didn't come from an Ivy League school, I wasn't a particularly good student, and I had failed way more than I had succeeded. On top of that, I had a strong female role model for a mother, I wasn't a big fan of people keeping secrets from each other in business, and I was a proponent of women moving ahead in business. When you mix all of these components together, you get something really unique and in high demand. Due to my time sitting in the boardrooms of Fortune 500 companies and then having had, at that time, experience of working with hundreds of professional women, I was in a unique position to share the best practices from my experience working with these groups.

4. Here's the hard part: Make a list of anything that you're bashful about or get embarrassed about when people compliment you on them. These are the things that we take for granted or that we don't think are that big of a deal. Some of the core parts of your platform will be found here. One client used to describe me as taking on business bullies on behalf of women, and I would always blush a little bit because I thought it wasn't true. After the fifth or sixth time hearing her say this, I asked her not to say it anymore and explained I didn't really feel that it was representative of who I was. She said to me, "Aren't you somebody who picks a fight when you think things aren't fair?" I replied, "Well, yes,

but it's not really so much picking a fight as standing up to somebody." She said, "So, you stand up for people who don't know how to or can't stand up for themselves." I said, "Well, to an extent. My job is to teach them how to stand up for themselves." She replied, "Yes. So you stand up for people who can't stand up for themselves, and then teach them how to do that. And, on top of that, you don't let bullies take advantage of people just because they don't know something." I nodded, but I still remember my cheeks flushing when she said this. Anyone who knows me knows that I remain quick to pick a fight with anyone who is taking advantage of someone who doesn't necessarily know any better or who doesn't have a voice to stand up for themselves.

5. For you, it starts with what you want to be known for. Determine the story people will tell about you when you are not in the room. Once you know the story you want them to have, make sure you back that up with talent (i.e., walking the walk). Too many times we hear stories about people doing great things only to see them in that environment and witness them shitting the bed. Talk about total credibility killer. Years ago, I met Richard Branson at an event in New York City and all the stories about him talked about how gracious he was to entrepreneurs. Sitting at his table, I was surprised the stories didn't do him justice. His generosity of sharing best practices and connecting people is unmatched by anyone I've met before or since. I'm happy to share that story about him because it's well deserved.

6. Look at those whom you hold in high regard and look at the platform that they have developed. About the same that I was developing my platform as Ghost CEO™, Richard Branson had the show on TV called Rebel Billionaire. What I liked more about Richard Branson's show than Donald Trump's show, The Apprentice (which was airing at the same time),

was the treatment of people. Donald became popular for yelling at people that they were fired, while Richard Branson would highlight to the people he had leaving the show the different contributions they had made and give them a hug on the way out. He reminded me that you do not have to be nasty in business to be a leader, which is something that I struggled with early on in my career but I was able to model when I had somebody that I admired doing so.

7. Explore what you can emulate from the people that you respect and use them as your role models. Because Richard Branson was out evangelising what he did for Virgin, I knew that I had to do the same thing for Ghost CEO™, so I quickly got myself onto a speaking tour and started talking to audiences around North American on the topic of What Men Don't Tell Women About Business.

8. Look at the platforms of the people that we all admire and/or know. Johnny Cash was The Man in Black. He came from poor folks and he understood the challenges of inmates. Anyone who watches video footage from his concert at Folsom Prison can see the connection between him and the audience. Donald Trump is the no-bullshit, brash, real estate developer from New York City. If he started to act like Richard Branson, giving people hugs on the way out, we would all think that he had lost his mind. So anytime that he picks a fight with someone, understand that is a deliberate decision for him. He does not do things off the cuff; he is extremely intentional with building and defending his brand. Let's get our bible thump on in the next example: the last three Popes the Catholic Church has had. Each had a unique platform. John Paul II was the shepherd who was very kind to people and had a happy face. Benedict XVI was more academic in trying to draw the Catholic rank and file into order; and now, as I write this book, Pope Francis (in my

opinion, the Super Pope), is someone who is trying to bring humility back to the church and lead it into present times. In everything he does, from not wearing the fancy robes, getting rid of the Pope Throne, and sneaking out at night to give mass at small churches – he supports the platform of a Pope who is looking to change and make the church more accessible to the people. All three of these Popes held the same position and had the same responsibilities, but they developed very different platforms for themselves.

9. The way you tailor your platform as an expert in a particular area will allow you to expand your influence outside of your existing ponds and markets. Your reputation will become a calling card to new markets and will allow those within your centre of influence (the rings of your tree) to speak about you in a cohesive way. The stories that a person hears from one of your contacts should be similar to ones they hear from your other contacts.

10. Be mindful of the big game so that you don't paint yourself into a corner by being "too niche." Did I just say that? Too niche? Yes, I did. You want your reputation, platform, and niche markets all to be big enough for you to expand in, small enough for you to be the Market Shark in, and big enough for you never to run out of business.

Helping Your Content Hop Ponds with Minimal Tweaking

When expanding your platform, look to ponds that are most likely to connect with your existing services. It is not uncommon for gatekeepers you already know, to know others who are running markets complementary to them. Dig into the networks of your existing gatekeepers wherever you can (Hello again, LinkedIn). You are not trying to recreate yourself by getting your content into new ponds. You are simply seeking markets you can gain quick traction in without much rebuilding and where you can use your existing networks and contacts to build credibility with the new markets quickly. It's better to move down, not up in markets, so if you've been servicing big markets in the past then look at the market that's one size smaller. It's much harder to jump from Minot, North Dakota to Chicago than it is to jump from New York City to Chicago. A big part of all of this is perception and everybody wants someone with big market experience.

Markets love when their Market Sharks have been in the big game and then have started swimming in a smaller pond. Markets feel like they're getting access to someone or something unexpected and it is exciting. An example of this is when I came out of the gate with Think Tank Communications. I used my time at BC Hydro, planning Province-wide events and strategies, to leverage contacts with smaller cities (who were impressed by this pedigree). I let these smaller cities know that I had been trained well at BC Hydro and that they were getting "a ringer" when working with me (which they were, of course). As a speaker, when groups around the continent found out that I've been on the Today Show, in the New York Times, and on some of their favourite radio stations, they extended to me a lot of courtesy that I might otherwise not received if I was in the 4-H newsletter, on podcast radio, or on a campus network.

Whenever I aim to get my content into complementary ponds, I follow these steps to make sure that the new ponds make sense and are worth my effort:

1. I make a list of all the prospective ponds that I can think of and determine how close they are to ponds that I'm already in. I like to be truly efficient with my time now, so I look for low-hanging fruit. If there is a complete redesign required, or I have to translate it into another language, or there is some

other big obstacle involved, then I just go back to looking. I know that there are hundreds of markets at my fingertips that I'll never have the time to go after, so anytime it starts to feel hard, I go back to the drawing board and find something easy.

2. **I determine which of my existing contacts are also in the pond that I'm looking at or know someone who is in that pond.** Think of the six degrees of separation. We aren't that far away from anyone that we need to talk to. Put in the effort by looking at the contacts of your existing contacts. If you have built yourself a powerful network, this will be easy. If you have a hard time with this then you will need to go back and rework your network building activities to make sure you're hanging with the right crowd.

3. **Do your preliminary research.** Make sure the market is big enough for you to keep busy, small enough for you to take on the position of Market Shark, and large enough for you to grow in and have ample clients and opportunities. If you're stuck on how to do this, go back to Chapter 3 where we talk about doing due diligence on your ponds.

4. **Start the process of finding out more about that market directly.** Talk to people who are in that market. Talk to other service providers who deliver services or products to that market. Find out everything you can from the horse's mouth about that market.

5. **Meet with the gatekeepers of those ponds or markets and begin to develop credibility with them.** This is always much easier if you are being endorsed by an existing relationship who is a gatekeeper and who has credibility with the person you are talking to. Don't forego making these connections.

You've invested the time and resources to develop credibility with your gatekeepers, so put them to work for you.

6. Offer to share best practices with those new ponds, give a talk, or be a resource to them or their members should they need support. Since one of my areas of expertise is licensing, every new pond I talk to might see me as an evangelist for Ghost CEO™, but I always let the individuals responsible for those ponds know that I also am one of a handful of people who have expertise in licensing business models in North America. Should any of their members be thinking about licensing, I let the gatekeepers know that I'd be happy to have a quick conversation with those people. This is now an additional tool that gatekeeper can put in their tool belt and offer to their members, and it endears me to them in that I'm looking to be an asset, not a liability.

7. **Don't show yourself as coming into the market.** You want to be seen as already having markets that you serve but looking to support these new markets in what they're doing. Everyone is going to assume that you're there for selfish reasons (which you are) but you don't want to be seen as marching in and taking market share without being invited. Let them know that you're already busy with the ponds you're in but are happy to help out if you can if any questions or needs arise.

8. **For each of the three main markets you are servicing currently, you want a goal of having three ancillary markets that your messaging is spilling over into.** Here's an example. One of our main markets in Seattle is financial services. We've worked with all the big accounting firms and most of the large banks. As this a market that we've owned since 2006, it's a Tiger. The clients are great, it's very profitable, and we get great results with those we work with. Some of the ancillary ponds that we have now developed are those that

are alternative to financial services in our focus. Our content spills over to credit unions, smaller brokerage, hedge funds, venture pools, and angel groups. Because the way we build and assess business models is proprietary to us, not only do we share this with our accounting and investment clients, but with the market as a whole. They see us working with the big companies so they're always grateful to spend a bit of time with us, as we are with them. These ancillary markets almost equal the amount of revenue we derive from the traditional markets that we focused on.

In Miami, a lot of our client business is around hotels and restaurants but our ancillary markets have now been established around tour operators who offer unique experiences, such as bed and breakfasts, and catering companies who will feed your family when you rent a house in South Beach rather than stay in a hotel. Since business modelling is business modelling in this industry, we allow the content to drip over the sides of our existing market into emerging ancillary markets. I always like to think of it as a fountain where the water comes up through the centre to the top basin and then washes over the sides down into the next basin, and so on. This is how your information and expertise should hop between ponds.

Flash Your Fins – Getting Media Attention and Being Relevant

I know that the fear of public speaking surpasses almost everything but a close second must be speaking to the media. I'm often surprised at how many people are intimidated by the thought of engaging the media in a conversation. Whenever I talk to a client and suggest that they reach out to a particular reporter to pitch a story, they look like deer caught in headlights. They've forgotten, or don't know, that the media is in the story telling business. The media are always on the lookout for good stories to tell. Many pros I know, including those who work at the New

York Times and other major media outlets are always scanning other stories and things they hear about, looking for new story ideas. Many of them spend a big chunk of their time on social media looking for angles to cover. If you can make yourself interesting, and your area of expertise is engaging enough to a broad audience, you, too, can wield the power of the media. Take care though, you don't want to engage the media before you have a solid platform in place or you will waste the opportunity.

By using some of these simple and straightforward techniques, I've had my work covered by the New York Times, Entrepreneur Magazine, The Guardian, the Today Show, Fox, CNBC, and dozens of other network shows. It feels like I've done a lot of radio over the last five years (my guess would be I've done 250 plus radio stations), and every one of them showed interest in my topics right off the bat. Granted, I did get rejected by some but they ended up keeping my information and calling weeks or sometimes months later. One radio station in Vancouver wasn't that interested in the topic of my book but, a month later, they called me to do a Valentine's Day show covering the topic, "Why You Shouldn't Have Sex with Your Co-workers at Work". Talk about a racy title and one that I could use to extend my platform in suggesting to women why workplace romances never serve the woman involved (it's not fair, but it's true).

Most of the press I have received came from a first phone call, but also knowing how to pitch properly and manage the relationship has allowed me to build relationships with these professionals, to be called back by them, and to be given the opportunity to pitch to them repeatedly. I have been fortunate to have met a handful of public relations experts and been able to model (modestly) their expertise by watching them and seeing them in action. **Beth Grossman,** a PR professional in New York City, is awesome and someone I greatly admire (bethgrossmanmakesthingshappen.com). Her ability to source the right media for her clients and build phenomenal relationships with high-level media, is unmatched. On the West Coast, **AHA Creative Strategies Inc.** (www.ahacreative.com) is, in a word, exceptional. When I started touring heavily in 2007, AHA (Ruth and Paul) gave me a lot of guidance that I will now share with you, with their permission. Their words of wisdom always played in my head when I was dealing with the media and have served me very well. Here are some of the key points that they share with clients (with their permission):

- **Build long-term relationships.** It's important always to be respectful, available, and on time with all media connections. Make sure that you're building a mutually beneficial relationship and you will earn media coverage from those professionals for years to come.

- **Don't discount online offerings.** Social media, bloggers, and citizen journalists all should be an important part of your media relations strategy. Treat them with the same respect that you give traditional journalists as many of them have larger readerships than the traditional media in their geographical locations.

- **Connect with journalists if you can help them out.** Even if there is nothing in it for you, it's important to reach out to reporters and offer them resources to help with a story. If the only time you contact them is when you want something, you won't be their favourite person and you likely won't be at their top of their list of sources. Being a relevant reporter is harder than ever, so look to be helpful even if it isn't within your wheelhouse.

- **If you have the opportunity, ask journalists questions about what they think about your industry.** They have a wealth of knowledge derived from talking to many people and asking questions of others. If you can, try to get a chance to buy a journalist a cup of coffee and ask them what they think. It's amazing what you might learn. Not only are they educated, but they have sourced a lot of different resource points and look at things objectively. There's a lot of value in this for you.

- **Realise that they have a job to do.** Reporters will ask some tough questions. Make sure that you have the answers. Don't blame the journalist if you are not prepared or if you or your organisation has done something that is being questioned. The upside of media is that you get put into the spotlight. The downside of media is that what you do and all the decisions you have made will be put under that same spotlight. Be prepared.

- **Review the journalist's previous work.** If you're going to engage with a reporter, it's likely that they will learn as much as they can about you and it is common courtesy for you to do the same. Read through some of their previous articles, look at the types of questions that they ask, and try to understand their style. The better you can fit into how they do their reporting, the more likely they are to use you in the present and the future.

- **Don't be self-promotional.** Provide the journalist with interesting, valuable, and solid information around the topic you've been asked to comment on. Talk about the industry and trends as a whole, consumer demand, and global shifts that you might be noticing. If all you want to do is talk about how great you are, then it's better to buy advertising.

- **Never lie to a journalist. Ever.** No matter what, if you can't say something, just explain that you're not able to comment at this time. If you don't know a piece of information they've asked about, tell them so but that you'll find out and get back to them. If you lie, it will be found out and you will lose all credibility not only with that media person, but with everyone they know.

- **There's no such thing as "off the record."** If you don't want it on the evening news, in the newspaper, or on Twitter, don't say it. There are very few reasons to speak to a reporter off the record and, if you have a reason, get a professional communications person on your team. You need expert advice. We don't have to look far to find a growing list of politicians that have shot themselves in the foot saying things that were "off the record."

- **Take the interview seriously.** The reporter doing the interview will be taking it seriously so you should do the same. Go through all the potential questions you think they might ask and have answers ready for those questions. Refine your answers so they play like sound bites. They are short, informative, and responsive. Rehearse what you want to communicate. Those we watch in the media that seem well-groomed didn't happen naturally. They've invested much time into being prepared to show as media-ready and polished.

- **Don't ask to review the piece before it is printed or aired.** Keep in mind that the reporter doesn't work for you; they work for the publication or media source that is interviewing you. Asking if you can review a piece before it's printed, put online, or broadcast not only paints you as an amateur, but will irritate the journalist. A journalist may fact check parts with you but they will never let you review the piece and ask for your input. Media is supposed to be unbiased, meaning that they report on what they hear or what they see. Collaborating with you on the piece makes it an advertorial rather than a news piece.

• **If there is an error about you in the piece, decide how important that error is.** Don't go to the journalist or their editor and ask them for a correction unless it is crucial to your business model. If you do this, chances are that you won't be put on their source list or be interviewed again. Consider what you can live with and what could have an enormous detriment on your business. Unless the impact on your business will be huge, just let it go. A bad story is better than no story, in most cases. When in doubt seek the advice of a professional.

Those are the key points I keep in mind when dealing with the media. I like to remind myself that business professionals and the media can have a mutually beneficial and symbiotic relationship, but the that the onus is on the professional to figure out whether it will work for both of them (remember your lessons from the strategic alliance chapter).

Don't pitch stories if the reporter doesn't cover that area. It's rude to do so. Take the time to figure out who covers your area of expertise and reach out to them.

Remember to be grateful. Taking time to research and interview you is work for them. If you take them for granted either you won't make the cut or you won't be invited to speak with them again. I like to send a thank you note after every piece and I often get feedback from those reporters that it is rare for them to get any type of appreciation from somebody they cover. That's ludicrous to me. I like to keep in contact with many of the reporters that I've engaged with who were kind to me, and many of these reporters are from major outlets that add a lot of value to me and my clients. I will, on occasion, introduce my clients to these media sources once I know that the clients are well prepared and have something interesting going on that I believe the reporter will want to know about.

As you start to expand your platform into new ponds, the increased media attention is an immediate credibility developer.

Consider what you would think about an author who made an appearance on Oprah. How do you feel about a local business professional who was profiled in Fortune Magazine? Getting covered by mainstream media, as well as online, sets an expectation that you are different from the rest and that's what a Market Shark wants to be known for – being exceptional, and being noteworthy. I've found that business groups love to bring in people who have high profiles and they love dropping the media outlet's name that covered their speaker when they are promoting their programming. They love to use my name and say, "As covered in the New York Times, the Wall Street Journal," and so on.

All it takes is a phone call or an email to pique the interest of a reporter, once you are ready. If you can offer value to the reporter then they will engage you. Sometimes this can set off a chain reaction. I remember that when my book was coming out, I flew to New York to take a marketing meeting and I told the team that I wanted to be covered in the New York Times and on the Today Show. My group, who were from Boston, thought it was a little premature for me to want to hit these outlets.

I called a friend who had a contact at the New York Times in the business section and requested that contact information and explained I was going to call and offer to drop off a copy of my book to the business editor. My friend, who knows that I know how to pitch, gave me the name and contact information and, in the boardroom in front of the firm, I called the business editor and told him a little bit about my book. He suggested that I might want to talk to the business editor, but I told him that the slant was that this was, in fact, the first book every written by a man disclosing what men in business talk about when women leave the room. He asked me to send over a copy and I offered to drop it off as I was heading to Manhattan. Next, I made a couple of calls and acquired the contact details for one of the producers of the Today Show. I called and let her know that I was going to be in New York City and that I might be a great story for the show. She hemmed and hawed a bit because who the hell was I, this hillbilly from Canada, so I mentioned that I would love to just have a coffee with her, and if she had 15 minutes I'd try to see her after I dropped off some copies of the book to the business editor of the New York Times. Once she heard that she quickly made time for me and the following weekend we taped my segment. Sometimes the media don't know what you have but if they see other media sniffing around, their interest level goes up. I'm often asked by other professionals how I got covered in the New York Times and on the Today Show, and truthfully it was done by making two phone calls, each of which took less than five minutes, which gave me exposure to millions of readers and viewers. I've had harder times getting into local, secondary market newspapers than I did getting into the New York Times and on the Wall Street Journal. To the bold go the spoils, but you must be prepared.

Create a Piece of IP You can Release into the Wild

Market Sharks own the top spot by spreading their ideas and work to others. When you are producing great content and leaving your ponds better than you find them people, other ponds, and the media as a whole are going to want to hear about it. Consider how you would like to efficiently share your information with the market. With today's technology the options are limitless for professionals and businesses of all sizes. It is up to you to determine which vehicle or vehicles will best represent your content and be most attractive to the people that you are looking to engage.

Here are some of the most popular ways to release your IP out into the world but by no means does this constitute an entire list. It's really just the top vehicles that a majority of professionals use on a regular basis. You do not have to choose just one; you can use multiples from this list. You should probably choose a vehicle to experiment with and then expand your exposure by adding additional tools later on. All of them are meant to extend your influence both inside your current markets and in the ancillary markets we want you to engage with.

- **Website.** I understand that websites can generate a lot of business and a lot of money goes into SEO, developing leads, and attracting people to your website by getting a high ranking. I can't speak all that intelligently about any of that because I don't actually understand how it works. For me, a website is a secondary marketing tool that people get driven to after they hear about you somewhere else. While I have heard of people that buy advertising online to drive people to their websites, I have found that the best way to get eyes on your website is to deliver content that is relevant and engaging to the markets you are looking to serve. We like to post a lot of free content on our website for people to download. All of it is relevant to business development and offers prospects a taste of what we do. I can tell you that the number of new clients that we receive is outside the proportion of the number of hits that we get on website. Web experts constantly tell me that they can help me capture more eyeballs. The only challenge is... the techniques we use to capture eyeballs work better than we can handle. All things being considered, our website extends our credibility by allowing prospective clients to go in and read a bit more about us before they start to work with us. It is an extension of our sales cycle.

- **eNewsletter.** eNewsletters are another great way to share your information with the market. Allowing people to sign up for your newsletter online when visiting your website, blog, or other social media is a great strategy for capturing eyeballs and getting permission to send people information. You can increase the value by ensuring that, every time you engage with the market, you give them something. I'm not talking about hawking your wares or spamming the shit out of them, but instead giving them something of practical value. We've all signed up for newsletters only to get hit too regularly by their spam and then have to unsubscribe or just set them to go into trash in your email settings. That's because all they're doing is self-promotion and offering no real value to the consumer or prospect to leave them better than they found them. When designing an eNewsletter, sure to give something of value and leave the reader better off than they were before they read it.

- **Keynote.** Delivering a keynote is a great way to extend your presence into larger markets. The larger the audience, the larger the ripple can be in the pond because individuals who come to hear you speak represent additional ponds outside of the pond that you're speaking to. For us, we love speaking to professional women's groups because they're composed of professionals from a variety of industries. When you talk to one group of 100 women, you might have 40 or 50 industries represented. These women then take the information back to their industries and start to share it with them. Your keynote needs to be engaging, entertaining, and deliver value, and it should avoid what I call "speaker's hangover." That is when the speaker gets up and does a big rah-rah and people get all excited only for them to wake up the next morning thinking, "What the hell happened last night?" and then going back to the way that they've always done things.

- **Workshop and Seminar.** Workshops and seminars deliver a similar outcome to a keynote but in a more intimate setting. Seminars are where I cut my teeth as a speaker. What's great about seminars is that you can deliver your content and then get immediate feedback about what is hitting and what isn't from the group you're talking to. As well, the participants have the opportunity to ask questions which you can answer right there, and then after the seminar you can go back and rework your content to make sure that next time the questions get answered before they get asked. I like workshop and seminar groups that are anywhere from 12–20 people in size and, where possible, I like to have the group 50/50, with half of the group people who know me (clients and colleagues), and the other half strangers who are as part of a group. It's less threatening to the strangers to be part of a group, often more affordable for them, and it allows them to engage with people who are already doing business with the speaker. Again, these professionals then go back to their ponds and share what they've learned from those workshops and seminars.

NOTE: I believe that great keynotes and workshops need to have two components – content and context. Content means providing education for the audience that you're talking to, and context which shows them how to use the information you've just taught them about. Application is key when delivering a keynote so make sure that your content is useable and relevant.

- Magazine Article. It's very easy to get a chance to write a magazine article if you have expertise in an area that that publication likes to cover. Look at your area of expertise and decide how you could apply it in different industries that might not otherwise bring in articles by professionals like you. On a number of occasions I have written for a jeweller magazine that specialises in jewellery retailers. While most of the articles are about sourcing the best product lines, I suggested to the editor that they may want to offer some business management techniques for their retailers. I've written articles on client engagement, negotiation, and motivating staff to sell. All of these articles were reworked from previous articles that I wrote for traditional business journals and were extremely well received in this industry and produced measurable results for us in the form of clientele and revenue.

- **eBook.** An ebook is a smaller electronic book that outlines a core idea or group of ideas to your audience. A lot of people serve up ebooks for free as a way to get names for their newsletter or to give prospective clients a little taste of what they do. For us, we developed something called "ePACKs." They are small, 65-page, self-coaching guides to support people in a variety of industries that we've written them for. We have ePACKs for therapists, photographers, realtors, mortgage brokers, and the like, and we often make one of these available to an association for raffling off at an event or offer preferred rates to members of their association. Not only does it expand our reach within those industries for a minimal investment, but it gets us in front of people we might otherwise not have been exposed to.

- **Newspaper Column.** Going back to being a small fish in a big pond, you may not want to pitch an article to the New York Times but maybe to your local newspaper or trade magazine. These publications are coming under tighter budgets and can have difficulty paying writers to do articles. You may want to write three or four articles using your best skills (and probably have someone edit them for you) and then call the editor of a local publication offering them the articles for review. Many times editors are happy to take a well-written article in exchange for a by-line that states your name, your company's name, and your website address. Get enough of these going and you can build credibility to go after bigger publications or syndication, but that's a whole different topic.

- **Radio Show.** As we discussed in the last section, there are lots of opportunities to get media attention. There are also opportunities to host your own radio show. This can be much more affordable than you think and all you're required to do is generate enough advertising for the studio to pay for the production of the show. It's worth enquiring at your local stations about what it could look like to have your own weekly show. Having a radio show offers you an interesting opportunity to connect with people and have them on your show. Not only can you create a great show but you can build relationships with these professionals that can be extended into alliances or other mutually beneficial arrangements. This is absolutely worth exploring and each show creates an inventory of IP for you to leverage down the road.

- **Podcast.** It's seems that more and more people are doing podcasts, from small start—ups right up to big stars in movies and television. You can conceive of a podcast right now and by dinner time have the content online and available for download. The technology is affordable and accessible, the equipment required can be found at almost any local electronics store, and there are millions of pages out there explaining how to host good podcasts. It's worth exploring if you are comfortable with technology. Some of our clients do podcasts and have a huge following from them. There will hear from people from all around the world who are downloading their content online.

- **Blogs.** There are more and more bloggers showing up all the time. I recently heard someone say that there are upwards of 100 million active blogs being syndicated at any given time. Platforms like WordPress make it easy and, in many cases, they are free. This is worth exploring if you have something that you'd like to say. I used a WordPress blog back in 2006–2007 to build my platform of groups and got upwards of 30,000 readers on some of my most popular posts. This comes from people reading your blog and then reposting the link to it through social media venues, their own blog, and the like.

- **Social Media (Facebook, Twitter, and LinkedIn).** All of us seem to be really connected on social media, and social media can be an extension of your platform. Some people have built their platform entirely on social media but I find that they have a hard time monetizing it. Social media is an extension of your physical world work, not a replacement of it. Just because you have 5,000 Facebook friends, 1,000 LinkedIn contacts, and tens of thousands of Twitter followers does not mean that you will make money. You have to have a platform that extends online but that can be monetized offline. At the time of writing this, we had about 850 Facebook friends for our Ghost CEO™ page and, when I looked through those people, every one of those individuals either was a client or had referred clients. I have colleagues who have maxed out their Facebook friends at 5,000 and have upwards of 20,000 or 30,000 people following their page but are doing a mere fraction of the business, if any at all. They invest a ton of time and money building that online readership and following but it doesn't seem to convert to dollars, so beware of that.

- **Sharing Thoughts on Other People's Work.** This is an aggregate of all the above. This could be commenting on other people's blogs, sharing best practices when attending a seminar, writing a follow-up piece to something you read in a newspaper or a magazine, calling in when someone hosts a radio show, being a guest on a podcast, and so on. If you're not inclined to do it yourself, think about who you could guest with on their platform.

- **Writing a Book.** For me, writing a book was a game changer in business. I got the book deal because I had a platform, and my platform grew because of the book. It's funny to me how many people are writing books at any given time, yet few of them seem to complete them. Life gets in the way, work gets in the way, busy-ness gets in the way. Even though they may talk passionately about it, years go by and they never get words to paper. Writing a book is both the easiest and the hardest things you'll ever do. It is easiest when you get into the groove; it's really quite straightforward to get your thoughts down on paper. It is hardest to make it a priority when you're doubtful that you'll ever sell a copy of your book. Some stats suggest that most books sell fewer than 100 copies. And that's including the couple that your mom buys, so how sad is that? Having a book and being a published author is a game changer, and the options are greater now than they have ever been before. It's worth looking at. Please be cautious, though. Don't tell people you're writing a book unless you actually are writing a book, because everybody is writing a book just like everybody is losing weight. Rather than talking about it, just do it.

Your IP can extend the reach of your reputation and influence others by getting it into their hands and letting them experience you. It extends your reach to markets that may never be able to engage with you personally, hear you speak, or talk to anybody who knows you. When you create intellectual property, you can use it as a messenger into your existing markets, as well as into those markets that are two or three rings out from those markets. Let me get a bit biblical on you for a minute. Market Sharks evangelise and they create content which others can spread on their behalf. Think of it like the gospel (gospel means "good news"), so create the good stuff that adds value to others and that will allow them to know your name. If a book seems like too big of task to take on, consider doing an article first. If you don't like to write, consider interviewing an industry leader. If writing isn't your thing at all, think about recording a podcast or doing some other type of media. It's important to create messaging that conveys value to others, speaks to your expertise, and positions you as a leader. Once you've created that message then you can find the vehicle that will get that content into the hands of people you want to do business with.

I started off doing workshops and keynotes, then the book came out, then I started doing mass media, and now I continue to do select keynotes because of their power to reach a large audience in a short amount of time. Every time I speak to a new group, two to three new ancillary markets tend to show up. Technology has allowed me to deliver presentations around the globe through videoconference. Now, when I travel, it's for pleasure, not for business, unlike before when it was the other way around. Don't let the stories in your head about how hard it is to do this, prevent you from creating IP that can extend the reach of your expertise and reputation.

Regardless of which direction you choose to go in to extend the reach of your platform, you must reach. Staying small will not allow you to fill your full potential as a Market Shark. You want to bend, but not break, but challenging yourself to be better known, by larger markets, for interesting things. Aside from writing a book, the rest can be tested easily and you can see if you enjoy doing them, or if there are other techniques that suit you better. A measurement you can use to manage your growth is asking one simple question at the end of each month: how many more people know about me this month compared to the month before? If that number isn't growing substantially, you need to do more to expand your reach.

Epilogue

It's been six years since my last book and while that time was not wasted, I did think of many topics and titles that I wanted to work on that I felt would deliver the most impact to a serious business builder and something that I would have fun working on. Writing a book like this is difficult because as I get into it, I start thinking of tangents, stories, business cases, tips, tricks, and fun facts. But I held myself to periodic tongue-in-cheek comments to you as I know that part of picture needs to be painted by your hand. Business, like art, has suggestions, rather than rules, and it is up to the artist (business professionals) to decide what tools they want to use depending on the picture they are painting. What I can tell you is that the more you practice the pieces of this book, the more you'll see that the picture begins to emerge. You'll see how something you did a month ago is now positioning you to do something today and that a new client that called today, came from someone who was a stranger at a networking event a year ago.

When you target the markets that make the most sense for you, communicate with them effectively, and stand in a position of respect (the Market Shark), you are rewarded with more business than any competitors that might be in your trade area. There is nothing magical in here. It is simply the techniques that a select group of professionals have been using to great success over the decades. You are now invited into that group and you will ascend to the level of Market Shark by the focused, sequential, and committed application of this information.

May your ponds be full of clients, sparse with competitors, and may they afford you all the spoils reserved for the Market Shark.

Acknowledgements

In no way is a book written by a single person. While there might be the 'designated writer' in the seat banging away at the computer, there is a team behind him or her keeping them on track, feeding them copious amounts of coffee, and creating an environment in which the words can be extracted (sometimes through brute force) out of the head and onto the page.

I want to thank my wife Jacqueline for creating the environment at home where our two little noise makers were kept busy with swimming lessons, trips to the park, and other activities so I could sneak away and work on this book. Anyone who has tried to write anything (a book, a story, an email) while having one kid searching your office for a missing SpiderMan head and another wanting you to look for the missing 'Letter J' from a puzzle set, will realise what a gift these quiet moments can be.

I'd like to thank Brenda Bleackley, my editor, who along with her busy career, family, business, and studies, found time to guide me on this project. She knew when to push me and when to pull me back of tangents. One more than one occasion, I had to ask, "Ummmm...can you remind me where I am on this project?" and she'd bring me right back into focus and I'd be back on my way. This project would not have been possible without her input, encouragement, and management.

Finally, I'd like to thank the Ghost CEO™ team and all of our clients who have allowed me to be a part of their lives. They have been an inspiration to my work and to each other. Without them, this book would just be words. In them and through them, this book becomes a system of business development that I'm very happy to share with you.

About the author

Christopher Flett is the founder of Ghost CEO™ and the Chairman of **Flett Ventures Inc.** He has launched over 50 business models and his work has been featured in the New York Times, Entrepreneur Magazine, and the Globe & Mail. BusinessWeek magazine referred to him as the "Shock Jock of Business Management." He is a highly sought after speaker, trainer, and commentator on business development, sales, and gender in the workplace.

For an in-depth look at how men and women do business differently, check out his bestselling book, "What Men Don't Tell Women About Business – Opening up the Heavily Guarded Alpha Male Playbook." (Wiley, 2007)

To book Christopher to speak at your conference or event, please email: speaker@ghostceo.com or call 1-206-734-4950

www.GhostCEO.com

www.FlettVentures.com

14220189R00177

Made in the USA
San Bernardino, CA
19 August 2014